Hiking through History
Colorado

HELP US KEEP THIS GUIDE UP TO DATE

Every effort has been made by the author and editors to make this guide as accurate and useful as possible. However, many things can change after a guide is published—trails are rerouted, regulations change, facilities come under new management, and so forth.

We welcome your comments concerning your experiences with this guide and how you feel it could be improved and kept up to date. While we may not be able to respond to all comments and suggestions, we'll take them to heart, and we'll also make certain to share them with the author. Please send your comments and suggestions to the following address:

FalconGuides
Reader Response/Editorial Department
246 Goose Lane
Guilford, CT 06437

Or you may e-mail us at: editorial@falcon.com

Thanks for your input, and happy trails!

Hiking through History Colorado

40 Hikes from the Great Sand Dunes to Bobcat Ridge

Robert Hurst

FALCONGUIDES

GUILFORD, CONNECTICUT
HELENA, MONTANA

FALCONGUIDES®

An imprint of Rowman & Littlefield
Falcon and FalconGuides are registered trademarks and Make Adventure Your Story is a trademark of Rowman & Littlefield.

Distributed by NATIONAL BOOK NETWORK

Copyright © 2016 by Robert Hurst

All photographs by author unless otherwise noted

Maps: Alena Pearce © Rowman & Littlefield

British Library Cataloguing-in-Publication Information Available

Library of Congress Cataloging-in-Publication Data Available

ISBN 978-1-4930-2292-2 (paperback)
ISBN 978-1-4930-2293-9 (e-book)

∞™ The paper used in this publication meets the minimum requirements of American National Standard for Information Sciences—Permanence of Paper for Printed Library Materials, ANSI/NISO Z39.48-1992.

The author and Rowman & Littlefield assume no liability for accidents happening to, or injuries sustained by, readers who engage in the activities described in this book.

Contents

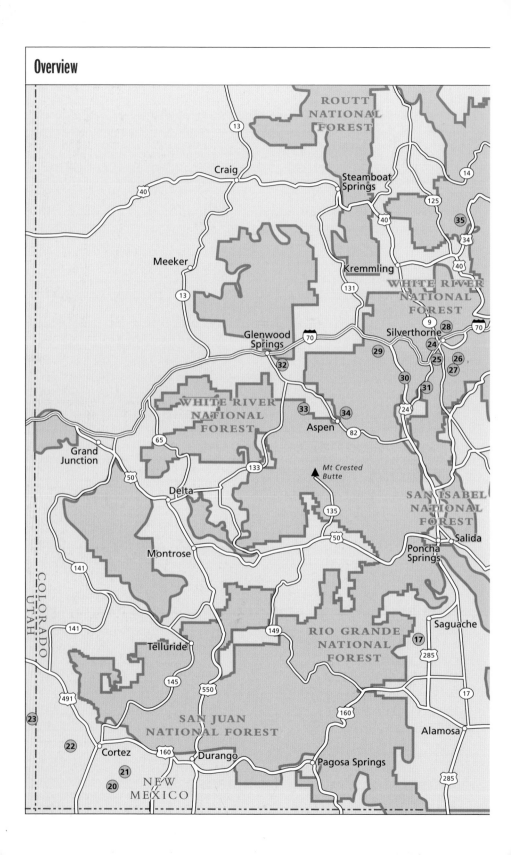

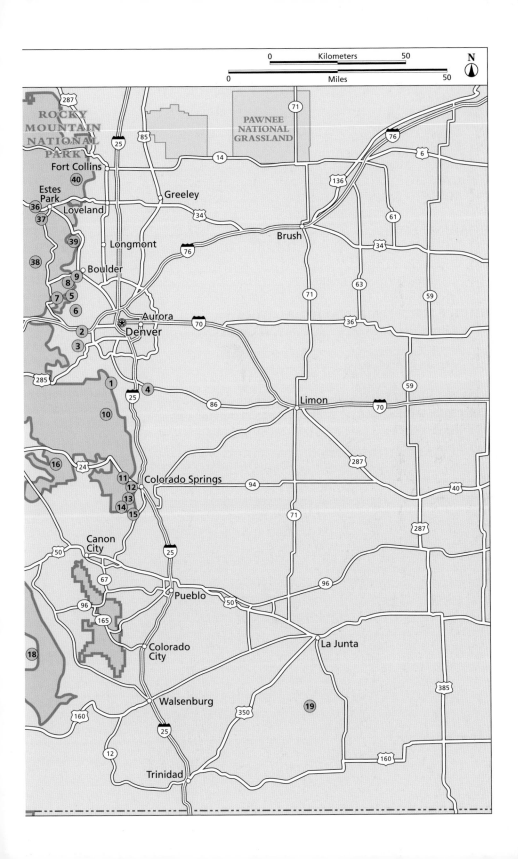

Acknowledgments

Thanks to everyone who helped make this book happen, especially my dad, who drove all over the state with me, paying for stuff and taking photos, and playing his incessant country-rock jangle music. Not only did I get to hike several of these routes with him, which was a real treat, but Christie and our iron-willed 3-year-old Bea joined me on some of the easier local hikes, after which Christie decided she never wanted to go hiking "ever again." I think she'll change her mind, eventually, after the trauma wears off.

Thanks to the Barbers of southwestern Colorado for their hospitality and historical knowledge. Thanks to Coi at the Denver Public Library for her help with historical photos, and to all the editors over at Falcon who gave me the job and picked up my slack. Finally, thanks to you, the brave reader.

Introduction

The hikes in *Hiking through History Colorado* include easy, flat strolls and rugged, strenuous marches, and everything in-between. No matter the difficulty or distance, all the hikes are tied together by a common thread. Each has historical interest attached to it, some historical twist that makes it much more than just a walk in the pretty woods.

In many cases the routes take you right past crumbling structures left over from a bygone era—old mills, mining camps, a teepee ring, or the dramatic ancient structures of the Ancestral Pueblo. Humans were around for thousands of years prior to the cliff dwellers' iconic thirteenth century, but those early residents didn't leave much for contemporary hikers to gaze upon, much less crawl through as they can at Mesa Verde.

Blown-out Castlewood Dam stands as a monument to modern failures. It failed several times over 40 years. The Devil's Head fire lookout stands as an unassailable emblem of twentieth-century American gumption, silhouetted against the stormy skies. The remnants of Camp Hale remind us of our ability to complete seemingly impossible tasks when the chips are down, and our trouble cleaning up afterward.

We'll visit the site of a massacre, but not Colorado's most infamous massacre. This one occurred on the opposite side of the state, 600 years earlier. (If that's the pattern, we've got a good 450 years before the next one.) And here's a word for you:

Castlewood Dam a modern failure

◁ *Mayflower Gulch*

Brontosaurus tracks on the Purgatoire River (hike 19)

anthropophagy. That's right: *anthro*—"man"; *phagy*—"eat." We like to think of ourselves as civilized creatures, but our ancient predecessors dined on the flesh of their vanquished enemies (according to some theories anyway). Human history has been as frightening here in Colorado as it's been elsewhere.

In almost all of the chapters, there is a story to be told that predates humanity. The geological record is plenty fascinating without mankind there to bloody it up. Usually the story of what was going on tens of millions, hundreds of millions, billions of years ago is told by rocks. Talking rocks.

As interpreted by the geologists who have learned to speak their special language, rocks tell us many things about what was going on for untold eons before humans walked the earth. They tell us that the Rockies are relatively new; that there was at least one mountain range here before, which popped up just as high and was eroded down to nothing over a few hundred million years; that the climate was tropical or warm-temperate most of the time (primarily because the continent was farther south); that the southwestern part of the state was at times covered in reddish dunes, like a Hollywood version of Mars; that huge active volcanoes dominated the state for many millions of years, spewing ash and drooling hot mud; that the area was often covered by an ocean, or shallow seas and lakes that came and went; and that for a time dinosaurs tramped all over the shorelines of these seas, making cartoonish three-toed tracks. In this book you'll find lots of those rock stories but also a story told by sand dunes and another told by massive, petrified redwood stumps. Yes, there were redwoods in Colorado. And they were spectacular.

One thing we learn on these hikes is that Colorado has existed in at least several million different iterations. The latest one is quite nice, but chances are there were better ones.

Some of the hikes are of the "outdoor museum" variety—heavily manicured routes through historic sites, with interpretive signage and other outbursts of committed curation. Iowa Hill, the placer mining exhibit spread out on a steep hillside near Breckenridge, is a classic example. Sometimes a little explanatory signage is just what you want. Other times it spoils the atmosphere. Several of the hikes exist in a more "wild" state, with landscapes unsullied by signage and historic sites left to your own interpretation.

Though the historical content varies a great deal from chapter to chapter, each of the described routes makes for a fun hike in its own way. That is, even if you hate history and don't want it to clutter your brain at all, you'll still like these hikes. There's something here for every level of hiker, from the grizzled, unfazed veteran to the wide-eyed toddler. If you're looking for a challenging most-of-the-day adventure, I recommend the Snowmass-to-Aspen Government Trail or the nearby Sunnyside/Shadyside Loop. In the mood for a short but crushing test of determination? Try climbing High Dune at the Great Sand Dunes, or up the Manitou Incline. And if you're hankering for moderate or easy hikes with some historical bling, this book is full of them. All told, there are forty mapped chapters and several dozen options and alternatives explained in the text.

Thank you for reading this! I hope you enjoy the book and that it gives you some interesting things to think about while you hike through this amazing, beautiful state.

Weather

Like few places on earth, the weather here swings from extremely hot and dry to whiteout blizzards with amazing speed. Almost all the state's outdoor lovers have experienced the weirdness of being snowed or rained on at the very same moment that the sun is shining hot and bright.

Colorado's summer storms pack a punch. The state gets zapped by more lightning strikes than almost anywhere else on earth. It's not a wet state, but our wet comes out of nowhere and hits with a lot of violence. And things are getting nuttier as the climate changes. In recent years we've seen increases in thunderstorms during morning and nighttime hours; we've seen tornadoes in the mountains and forest fires in the winter. All bets are off.

Hikers should carry warm layers and waterproof shells on every outing in the mountains. Short hikes near civilization probably don't require extra gear, but you may very well find yourself sprinting back to the car!

Several of the hikes are in the state's desert-like areas, where extreme heat and lack of water can be deadly for unprepared hikers. *Always carry enough water* (what if you get lost?). Use sunscreen, sunglasses, hats, and long-sleeve shirts.

Fauna

Hooves: You might see some majestic bighorn sheep, the state animal. Much more common are mule deer, elk, and moose. Moose were intro-doosed; they're not native, but they seem to like it here, hanging out in boggy areas of Summit County and Rocky Mountain National Park. They get surly, so don't mess with them. You'll see some antelope out on the wide-open spaces.

Fangs: The ubiquitous bears want or need your food, but, with the exception of mama bears with cubs, they are shy about humans. There are mountain lions all over the state. They prefer to eat deer, so don't act like one, and you're fine. Keep an eye on young kids. We also have lots of coyotes and foxes. Rattlesnakes are extremely common on the Front Range, so watch where you step. It's not a good idea to take your snake-sniffing dog on some Front Range hikes.

The desert hikes are a showcase for lizards and raptors. Watch for the sacred banded lizard running across the sand like a freak.

Flora

The iconic tree of the Front Range and foothills areas is the ponderosa pine, with its long needles. The gambel oak is also a foothills mainstay, a scraggly pygmy tree that provides acorns and shelter for black bears. Fluttering aspen stands (each a single organism) grow in the mountains in areas of disturbance, and if all goes well are steadily replaced by fir and spruce. In the drier areas the trees consist of much shorter piñon pines and junipers, standing among cactus, yucca, sage, and mountain mahogany. Gorgeous wildflowers can be found all over the state in almost every ecosystem. The state's favorite wildflower, the Columbine, can be seen all over the mountains, tucked into grassy meadows in dappled sunlight.

◄ *Looking south from Devil's Head, with Pikes Peak in the distance*

How to Use This Guide

Hiking through History Colorado features forty mapped and cued hikes. Here is a brief outline of the book's major components.

Each chapter opens with a very brief overview of the hike in a sentence or two. Below that you'll see hike's **Distance** and the **Approximate hiking time** required to complete it. The hike's **Difficulty** is estimated. The **Trail surface** is described in general terms (for instance, "rocky singletrack"). I give my opinion about the **Best season** to do the hike and list **Other trail users** you might encounter. **Canine compatibility** is listed, as are **Land status**, necessary **Fees and permits**, **Schedule** information, a supplemental **Maps** suggestion, **Trail contact**, and **Special considerations**. Detailed driving directions are provided under **Finding the trailhead**, with GPS coordinates.

The Hike is, of course, the hike. Here I describe the journey, the surroundings, and the historical interest. I hope you enjoy reading it and that it makes things easier and more fun. Below that are the **Miles and Directions**, mileage cues for important intersections and waypoints that will help keep you on the right track. The routes in this book are generally pretty straightforward, but if questions arise, use the book's map, the miles and directions, and the description in the main text in combination to find your way. GPS coordinates shouldn't be necessary, but I have provided coordinates for critical route-finding waypoints and points of historical interest.

Of course there is a lot more to Colorado hiking and history than what you'll find in this book. I hope it provides a platform to launch your own custom explorations into the woods and into the past.

Trail Finder

BEST HIKES FOR...

FAMILIES

1 Roxborough State Park
2 Red Rocks: Trading Post Trail
7 Tallman Ranch
10 Devil's Head
13 Palmer Trail–Section 16
14 Captain Jack's
15 Cheyenne Mountain State Park
16 Florissant Fossil Beds
18 Great Sand Dunes
21 Soda Canyon Overlooks
23 Hovenweep
25 Iowa Hill
31 Mayflower Gulch
37 Sprague Lake
38 Caribou Ranch

DOGS

3 Mount Falcon (watch for bikes)
4 Castlewood Canyon
5 Mount Galbraith (trail has a sizable descent on a steep set of rock stairs that could be too much for some dogs)
12 Red Rock Canyon (watch for bikes)
17 Penitente Canyon
19 Picketwire Canyon
24 Mount Royal
26 French Gulch (watch for bikes)
28 Buffalo Cabins
31 Mayflower Gulch

GREAT VIEWS

1 Roxborough State Park
3 Mount Falcon
5 Mount Galbraith
8 Rattlesnake Gulch
9 Mallory Cave
10 Devil's Head

11 Manitou Incline
12 Red Rock Canyon
13 Palmer Trail–Section 16
14 Captain Jack's
18 Great Sand Dunes
20 Petroglyph Point Trail
24 Mount Royal
29 Meadow Mountain
30 Camp Hale
31 Mayflower Gulch
33 Government Trail
34 Sunnyside/Shadyside Loop

LAKES AND STREAMS

4 Castlewood Canyon
7 Tallman Ranch
15 Cheyenne Mountain State Park
18 Great Sand Dunes
19 Picketwire Canyon (must cross stream to see dinosaur tracks; otherwise very dry)
28 Buffalo Cabins
35 Holzwarth Ranch
36 Moraine Park
37 Sprague Lake

HARD CLIMBING

3 Mount Falcon
5 Mount Galbraith
6 Lookout Mountain
8 Rattlesnake Gulch
9 Mallory Cave
10 Devil's Head
11 Manitou Incline
18 Great Sand Dunes
24 Mount Royal
27 Barney Ford Trail
28 Buffalo Cabins
29 Meadow Mountain
32 Doc Holliday Trail
34 Sunnyside/Shadyside Loop

Crossing Medano Creek puts an interesting spin on a Great Sand Dunes hike.

WILDFLOWERS

ANCESTRAL PUEBLO RUINS

20 Petroglyph Point Trail
22 McElmo Loop
23 Hovenweep

NINETEENTH-CENTURY MINING STRUCTURES/ARTIFACTS

24 Mount Royal
25 Iowa Hill
26 French Gulch
31 Mayflower Gulch
38 Caribou Ranch

HOMESTEADERS' CABINS AND HOMES

1 Roxborough State Park
7 Tallman Ranch
16 Florissant Fossil Beds
38 Caribou Ranch
40 Bobcat Ridge

Map Legend

Municipal

≡(84)≡ Interstate Highway

≡(202)≡ US Highway

≡(100)≡ State Road

≡[300]≡ Local/County Road

==== Unpaved Road

⊢——⊣ Railroad

— · · — State Boundary

——— Leader line

Trails

------- Featured Trail

- - - - - - Trail

——— Paved Trail/Bike path

Water Features

⬭ Body of Water

∼ River/Creek

≋ Waterfall

Land Management

▣ National Park/Forest

▢ State/County Park

Symbols

⏝ Bridge

▪ Building/Point of Interest

⛺ Campground

▲ Campsite

∩ Cave/Cavern

† Cemetery

— Dam

⌇ Gate

🅿 Parking

⏜ Pass

▲ Peak/Mountain

🛆 Picnic Area

🚻 Restroom

🔭 Scenic View/Lookout

🐎 Stables

○ Town

⑳ Trailhead

❓ Visitor/Information Center

Denver and Boulder

Mount Galbraith has one of the few hikers-only trails in the Golden area (hike 5).

1 Roxborough State Park

Walk through an area of unique beauty on a wide, gently sloped trail that is great for casual family outings. While natural history and geology hog all the attention at Roxborough State Park, the ground here is rich with artifacts that betray almost 10,000 years of human occupation.

Start: Roxborough State Park Visitor Center
Distance: 2.6-mile lariat loop
Approximate hiking time: 1 to 2 hours
Difficulty: Moderate
Trail surface: Fairly smooth paths with occasional puddles and ruts; terrain is flat on the west side of the loop and hilly on the east.
Best seasons: Spring and fall
Other trail users: Humans; no bikes, dogs, or horses
Canine compatibility: No pets allowed!
Land status: State park
Fees and permits: Entering Roxborough State Park requires the purchase of a temporary park pass.

Schedule: Park hours vary from month to month. In general, it is open from sunrise to sunset.
Map: Colorado Parks and Wildlife map of Roxborough State Park
Trail contact: Roxborough State Park, 4751 E. Roxborough Dr., Roxborough, CO 80125; (303) 973-3959; http://cpw.state.co.us/placestogo/parks/roxborough
Special considerations: There's not much shade on this route, and the sun is often intense. Hats and sunscreen, hike in early morning or late afternoon; you know the drill. Please stay on the trails at Roxborough State Park. No rock climbing or scrambling is allowed. If you go up the Fountain Valley Overlook side trail, it will add about 0.2 mile to your overall mileage.

Finding the trailhead: This hike starts from the Roxborough State Park Visitor Center, which is located at the end of the park's only road. From Denver get to CO 470 and Wadsworth Boulevard (from the north side use the 6th Avenue Freeway or I-70 to get out west, and then take CO 470 south to Wadsworth; from the south side use I-25 or Santa Fe Boulevard to get to CO 470, and then go west on CO 470 to Wadsworth). Go south on Wadsworth; then turn left onto Waterton Road. Turn right onto North Rampart Range Road, left onto Roxborough Park Road (not the housing development), and then right onto Roxborough Drive. The parking area is at the end of the road. GPS: N39 25.78' / W105 04.18'

The Hike

Roxborough State Park seems impressively wild. Among the famous angled sandstone formations are expanses of tall grasses and mobs of gambel oak where deer wallow and birds sing happily as hawks cruise just over the treetops. About six dozen different butterfly species can be found fluttering in the grass.

The classification of Roxborough as a state park, National Natural Landmark, and state archaeological area has kept it relatively human-free, restricting foot traffic to a few trails, keeping people and hell-raising dogs off the rocks and out of the lush

The west side of the Fountain Valley Loop

lagoons of grass, and removing the voracious livestock that had stomped the meadows into submission for most of the twentieth century. After several decades of being left almost entirely alone—the last cattle or sheep were ushered off by 1977—the place is really expressing itself. It's not a perfect scene. The housing development to the west comes into prominent view at times and reminds us that humans of Colorado take real estate profits as seriously as they take nature and conservation.

This little lariat loop is great for quiet hikers who like to listen and look closely at nature but who don't want to (or can't) walk difficult terrain. It will get your blood pumping with a few notable inclines, but the route, culminating at an old stone ranch house, is entirely composed of a wide gravel path that maintains fairly mellow slopes, even on the east side, where it goes up and over a big hill.

The east side is also quite drab compared to the west side, which is among the rocks. On the east side you can't even see any of the rocks at all, believe it or not, unless you hike up to the Lyons Overlook (a top-notch viewing platform). At the far end of the loop, no matter which way you go, is the Persse homestead, the quaint and inviting little house still standing. Looking west past the house, notice the rock that looks like George Washington's face looking straight up at the sky. This rock once gave this place the name Washington Park.

Most of the red rocks that make Roxborough famous are made of deposits created when the ancestral Rockies were washed away and ground down to nothing

Fountain fins and a sea of green

between 300 million and 150 million years ago. When the Lyons and Fountain Formations were laid, dinosaurs did not yet exist. The fossil record does betray the existence of dog-sized dragonflies, huge centipede-like creatures, and various types of
smaller lizards living among trees that had scales instead of bark.

In its dead-flat phase, lasting 100 million years or so, Colorado was covered in
desert sands, then shallow seas and tidal areas, then deep water. The light-colored
rock that tops the long Front Range hogback to the east is Dakota sandstone, an
extra-resistant layer packed with tiny marine creatures. In this layer we often find
comically obvious evidence of dinosaurs that walked along the shorelines of these
seas, and Roxborough is no exception. There are dinosaur tracks here, although their
exact location is not well publicized. (Ask the folks at the visitor center about taking
a guided tour if you're really interested.)

About 69 million years ago the mountains—the mountains we see today—began
to form. Plate movement thrust the old granite that lay under all those sedimentary layers upward through the overlying sandstone, forcing the sandstone layers into
obscene angles in the process. Incredibly dramatic, but at a rate of a smidge per year,
the uplift that created our Rockies and stacked our sandstone all akimbo would not
have been noticeable on a human scale. We are now in another long phase wherein
these mountains, and the accompanying sandstone, are again being ground down to
nothing.

The first humans appeared on the scene long after all these processes had been completed: in geological terms, about 20 seconds ago. But it wasn't quite the same world we know today. Glaciers extended far down the mountain valleys. Nomadic people spear-hunted giant mastodons to extinction.

The huge angled rocks of Roxborough seemed to attract mysterious ancient people to live among them. Some may have been attracted to the protection from the elements provided by the natural lean-tos, or the rocks' usefulness for hunting or defensive purposes. Archaeologists have found plenty of evidence of both human use and habitation around Roxborough going back about 7,000 years. That's relatively old for artifacts on the North American continent.

This blows the mind a little bit. Some of the artifacts that have been found at Roxborough are about seven times farther removed from the Early Ceramic people—the "Cliff Dwellers" whose leftovers have been collected and documented so frequently—than we postmodern humans are from those Early Ceramic people. And it must be said that we barely know those Early Ceramic people at all. They are still a great mystery.

A Cultural Resources Inventory of Roxborough Park, conducted in the 1970s, turned up forty separate archaeological sites on the park's original acreage (its size has quintupled since then). A few of the sites were freakishly large campsites—town sites might be a more accurate term—covering tens of thousands of square feet. Here researchers found the typical mix of lithic scatter, projectile points, pottery sherds, grinders and grinding stones, and the crude tools used to make these things. Unlike many prehistoric sites along the Front Range that contain evidence of very short use, perhaps even one-time use, the findings at Roxborough indicate that the park was inhabited for thousands of years, that it was one of the "prime, long-term habitation localities that served as winter residential localities from which to carry out logistically organized resource procurement," according to one scientific description. In simpler terms, it was home.

One of the important archaeological sites near Roxborough is known to researchers as "Tenth Fairway," because it's located substantially under the tenth fairway of the Arrowhead golf course. Unfortunately, when this site was first excavated in the 1950s, its artifacts weren't documented very well, or were documented using some kind of code that today's researchers don't understand. Then the construction of the fairway destroyed the site. (The hike does not go directly past this site.)

Archaeologists today are engaged in the traditional activity of searching for artifacts in the ground, but they are also tasked with rediscovering and documenting the piles of stuff that were taken from the field and stashed away in the 1950s and 1960s. According to Colorado archaeologist Kevin Gilmore, "The collections from many important archaeological sites excavated during the last 70 years in Colorado have never been adequately analyzed and/or published . . . and for the most part lie forgotten in various repositories, laboratories, and closets throughout the state."

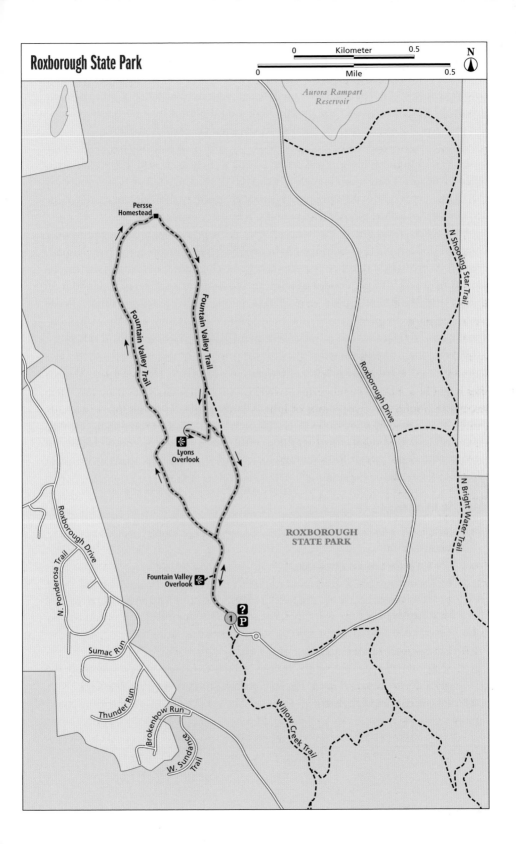

For hundreds of years the Utes would pass through Roxborough, although they didn't leave much evidence of their having been here. This was long after the Ceramic period people had disappeared—or the Utes might have descended from these same people. Nobody knows for sure exactly how long the Utes have been around here, but the Utes always claimed that Colorado was their ancestral homeland.

Archaeologists and anthropologists look for fire rings and teepee rings, stone lookouts and hunting blinds, rock art and trails to help reconstruct the Utes' existence in an area. There wasn't much of that type of evidence left at Roxborough by the 1970s, but we know the Utes were nearby because they show up constantly in the accounts of Spanish explorers, traders, and US military expeditions.

Henry Persse was one of the last people to live here. The Irishman acquired a big chunk of land among the sandstone fins in the 1880s, planning to develop the visually spectacular area with a golf course, big hotel and clubhouse, and homes and streets around the rocks. (To get an idea of what he had in mind, visit Perry Park about 20 miles south, where similar plans were realized among similar rock formations.) Persse hosted guests at his understated home, built in 1903, and, if they were the rich, influential types, lobbied them to invest or otherwise support his development scheme.

Roxborough (Persse named it after his historic family estate in Ireland, not as a cutesy play on words) was just too special for all that. Even Denver mayor Robert Speer, an unlikely poster child for a conservation movement, told Persse that Roxborough should be left untouched and open to the public. Through the decades the right people managed to resist the wholesale development of Roxborough, although fancy green-lawned subdivisions ate much of the most strikingly beautiful land and the Arrowhead golf course took some of the rest. In 1975 the state made its first purchase here and created Roxborough State Park.

Miles and Directions

0.0 Start from the Roxborough State Park Visitor Center and begin walking up the Fountain Valley Trail.

0.3 Veer left at the fork to start the loop.

1.2 Reach the Persse house. Continue the clockwise loop. (**Option:** Turn around here and retrace your steps back to the start to enjoy a slightly easier, perhaps prettier, but more repetitive route.)

1.6 Turn right and head up to the Lyons Overlook, then back down to the trail.

2.0 Turn right, back onto the main trail.

2.3 At the end of the loop, veer left. Pay attention to this seemingly carefree waypoint. Many people get turned around and go right here, accidentally embarking on another loop!

2.6 Arrive back at the visitor center.

2 Red Rocks: Trading Post Trail

Great for families and social outings, the Trading Post Trail in Red Rocks Park meanders among the massive sandstone formations that define this unique and stunning location. The loop is short but plenty vertical, requiring moderate exertion and dexterity.

Start: Red Rocks Park Trading Post
Distance: 1.5-mile loop
Approximate hiking time: 1 hour
Difficulty: Moderate
Trail surface: Rugged and rocky sections alternate with flat, smooth gravel paths; lots of steps/stairs
Best seasons: Spring and fall
Other trail users: Many, including people of all ages and sizes, and dogs. No bikes are allowed.
Canine compatibility: Leashed dogs permitted

Land status: Denver Mountain Park
Fees and permits: None
Schedule: Sunrise to sunset
Map: Red Rocks Park Map, Denver Mountain Parks. http://redrocksonline.com/images/files/RedRocks_ParkMap.pdf
Trail contact: Denver Mountain Parks; (720) 865-0900
Special considerations: There's not much shade around here, and the sun is often intense. Hats and sunscreen, hike in early morning or late afternoon; you know the drill.

Finding the trailhead: There are many ways to reach Red Rocks and the Trading Post. Most straightforward is to drive to Morrison via CO 470. Go west through Morrison on CO 74; then turn right into Red Rocks Park, onto Red Rocks Park Road. Drive up Red Rocks Park Road past a few intersections, and then turn left onto Trading Post Road. Drive up the hill to the Trading Post and park. (**Note:** If parking isn't available here, try the big dirt lot below.) GPS: N39 39.83' / W105 12.15'

The Hike

This tasty little loop starts directly from the Trading Post parking lot and descends the first of many sets of stone stairs as it drops into a draw, gulley, *arroyo*, or wash, depending on your favored vernacular. Below the steps the trail is moderately rocky and trickily off-camber all the way down to the bottom of the descent, and occasionally flirts with the warning track of a short but sheer drop to the scrubby creek.

The terrain is not exactly easy, but it wasn't too much for our 3-year-old, nor did it seem to overwhelm a number of other toddlers and very dainty elderly folk we encountered. It's a good family hike. That's not to say our little girl walked the whole loop. She did not. Most toddlers will require a good long carry to make it all the way around, and one of those toddler-carrying backpacks comes in handy for that. Grade-schoolers should be able to make it around, with a little whining, of course.

Among the many notable features of this immediate area is its aridity. Very desert-like. Trails like this tend to be hot and potentially unpleasant in midsummer, and delightfully warm and dry for much of the off-season. We could hear plenty of water in the creek after one of the rainiest Mays in Front Range history, but in typical years

Christie and Bea amble where rock stars have vomited, probably.

the creek is bone-dry. Keep this hike and the rest of the trails in the area in mind when you're seeking a bit of sun in the middle of winter. However, the west side of this loop passes through some surprisingly dark and shady groves, where you can expect muddy slop to persist for several days after any heavy precipitation.

Red Rocks is not considered a top-notch wildlife viewing area due to the concentration of humans, roads, and cars. We don't hear many reports of rattlesnake encounters or large-animal sightings in Red Rocks Park, for instance. Too many boots on the ground. But the bird watching is plenty good, judging by the satisfied coos emitted from the guided tour groups. Many types of feathered creatures live in the nooks and crannies of the cliffs.

Much of the history at Red Rocks is locked in those rocks. The fantastic spires and arches are the solidified remnants of the land hundreds of millions of years ago. At one point this area was covered with red dunes. The dunes became the smooth red sandstone known as the Lyons Formation. Later the ancestral Rockies (not the mountains you see today) eroded away, in the process creating a layer of mud-red sediment, the Fountain Formation.

Both the Fountain and Lyons Formations sat there for millions of years, flat, while they were steadily buried below thousands of feet of subsequent layers. Out on the plains these sandstone layers remain completely flat and buried. Along the Front Range of the new Rockies, the Lyons, Fountain, Dakota, and other sandstone and limestone layers were brought to the surface and shoved into a near-vertical position by the Precambrian bedrock's colossal skyward thrust. If you could speed up the last hundred million years and put it into a single YouTube video, you would see the earth's core rocks dramatically bust through the overlying crust—shazam!—and then begin to melt away.

The making of the Rockies, and the jagged sandstone shards and hogbacks, was dramatic on a geological scale. On a human scale nobody would have been able to notice the change occurring at its glacial pace of a centimeter per year or so. But no humans were around while the Rockies were being formed anyway, not by a long shot. The first humans appeared on the scene here maybe 13,000 years ago, when all those geological processes were long completed and the landscape looked very much as it does today, despite the ice bridge across the Bering Strait.

The dinosaurs made their mark on these rocks—just across the road on the hogback, where the light-colored limestone Dakota Formation pops out. It's no wonder this bit of hogback is known as Dinosaur Ridge. There are two famous sites on the sides of the ridge where exposed slabs of limestone contain rows of dinosaur tracks. Each of the sites is obvious, behind rails and interpretive signs. There is one on each side of the hogback, on Alameda Parkway, the road that crosses it (now closed to motor traffic). The dinosaur tracks are not located along this route but are worth a look.

The exploitation of this place as a tourist destination began in earnest in the early 1900s, a project of John B. Walker, one of the more ambitious characters in the state's history. Walker purchased Red Rocks and the cross-valley Mount Falcon after trading his wildly successful *Cosmopolitan* magazine for a chunk of William Randolph Hearst's fortune. Walker had big plans for the whole area—a summer White House on Mount Falcon, a funicular railroad up Mount Morrison, and a casino at Red Rocks, which he called "Park of the Titans." The idea was to create "a second Colorado Springs," a resort within easy striking distance of Denver's leisure class. Walker's development ambition crashed and (literally) burned, but the goal was adopted and transformed and, we must say, achieved in ways he probably couldn't imagine.

As Walker's empire crumbled, his land was devoured by speculators and much of it eventually became public. The spectacular (but to a rancher, useless) parcel that would be known as Red Rocks Park was acquired by the City of Denver for around $50,000 in 1928.

Though Walker gets the credit for staging the first concerts among the rocks, the idea for the formal venue is credited to George Cranmer. He is said to have visualized the amphitheater during a high school field trip to the park. The budding engineer held the idea inside for years until he was appointed Manager of Parks and Improvements by Denver mayor Ben Stapleton, then applied full steam promoting it to local and federal purse-string holders. His effort was successful despite the mayor's well-known hatred for theater.

The construction of the Red Rocks Theater began in 1936, a Civilian Conservation Corps project. Working for a dollar a day, about 200 men dynamited and removed a small sea of boulders to make room for the seating area, which they then created along with a huge stage and orchestra pit.

In its first few decades, the rock-walled amphitheater earned a worldwide reputation for its acoustics and unique setting, hosting classical music concerts, ballets, religious festivals, and the like. In the 1950s and early 1960s, great jazz and R&B artists like Ray Charles, Nat King Cole, Louis Armstrong, and Ella Fitzgerald expanded horizons at Red Rocks. The Beatles played here in August 1964, ushering in the new rock-and-roll era at the venue. Jimi Hendrix, in September 1968, sealed the deal. Imagine Hendrix at Red Rocks!

When Jethro Tull came to Red Rocks in 1971, concertgoers fought over unassigned seating. The minor riot had far-reaching effects—no hard rock shows took place at Red Rocks for several years.

Bruce Springsteen played here in 1978, a big year for the venue. Also playing that summer were Cheap Trick, the Kinks, Willie Nelson, and Barry Manilow, among many others. Hard rock came back in September, with AC/DC and Blue Oyster Cult. The hills were thumping with drum and bass.

In July 1978 the Grateful Dead played two consecutive shows, the first of their many legendary Red Rocks appearances. In August the Dead and the pungent carnival of crunchy superfans who followed the band all over the country ("Deadheads") came back for two more shows—and then they came back for multiple appearances every summer for the next 9 years, helping to define the band and the venue. When

What Hendrix Said about Playing at Red Rocks

After his show at Red Rocks in 1968, Hendrix went back to his hotel room at the Cosmopolitan in Denver (demolished in 1984 and replaced by a parking lot) and wrote the liner notes for *Electric Ladyland* and this bit in his journal:

> We played out there at Red Rocks and I had a lot of fun. People are on top of you there. At least they can hear something. It's very hard sometimes if you know those people out there are not going to hear anything. That's how it should be, natural theater-type things, outside where a hundred thousand people can get together. The Grand Canyon or Central Park. I'd like for us to play outside more because the air does something to the sounds. [*Jimi Hendrix, Starting at Zero: His Own Story* (A & C Black, 2013), p. 153.]

Rock among the rocks

Jerry Garcia died and the Dead ceased to exist, the impulse for epic hippie jams among the towering rocks continued with bands like Phish and Widespread Panic, and the traveling circus started following those guys instead. Widespread Panic has played Red Rocks at least forty-nine times, an astonishing tally.

The Clash show, in 1982, was a clear sign that alternative rock had invaded the mainstream. In 1983 U2 rocked through the pouring rain, giving what could be the best-known concert to take place here. As a teenaged Larry Mullen Jr. pounded out an unmistakable beat and giant torches blazed on top of the rocks, Bono proclaimed, "This is not a rebel song . . . This is Sunday Bloody Sunday!" The spectacle was recorded in the movie *Under a Blood Red Sky* and the album of the same name.

If you're an old Colorado kid like me, no doubt you have some Red Rocks memories of your own. After all the concerts I've seen here, I think what I remember most is the smell. Not rancid, not unbearable, but certainly strong. Concerts at Red Rocks during the 1980s were accompanied by a unique stench, produced by the combination of sweat, sunscreen, beer, piss, weed, hard liquor concoctions, and vomit.

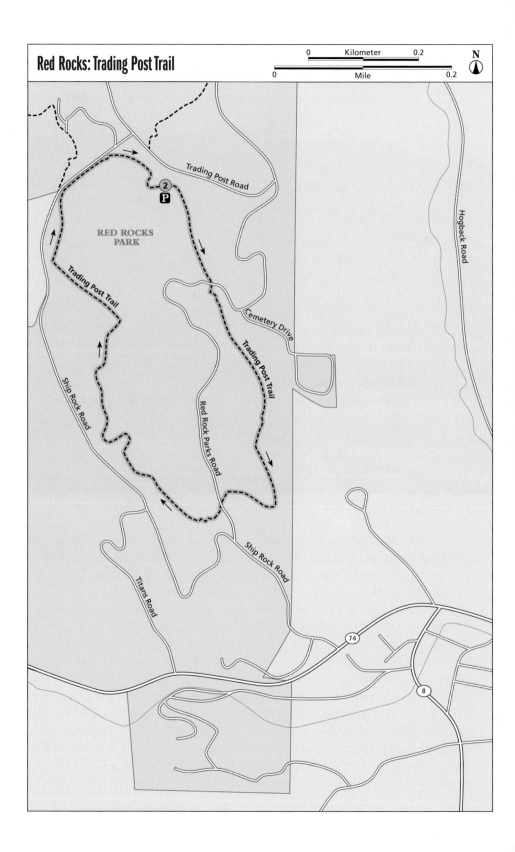

Red Rocks: Trading Post Trail

Trading Post Road

Hogback Road

② P

RED ROCKS PARK

Trading Post Trail

Cemetery Drive

Trading Post Trail

Ship Rock Road

Red Rock Parks Road

Ship Rock Road

Titans Road

74

8

N

0   Kilometer   0.2

0   Mile   0.2

It hasn't been all loud music and smells and debauchery, though. The sunrise service on Easter Sunday draws a huge crowd every year, and the amphitheater is in regular use by fitness freaks engaged in quad-building dashes and leaps from bottom to top. For many reasons this is a treasured place. In 2015 Red Rocks was designated a National Historic Landmark.

The hallowed stage is not far from the Trading Post and the top of this loop. The amphitheater is worth a look if you've never seen it before. It's a bit of a grunt to get to the seating area, as you can guess from the concrete walkways that ramp up to the arena overhead (if you want, you can drive to the top). Red Rocks is the most vertical of the four main Front Range rock gardens, and concertgoers experience that verticality firsthand.

It's quite possible that you will see an armada of tour buses parked near the Trading Post or hear the roadies tuning up the guitars for the night's gig. Who's playing tonight?

Miles and Directions

0.0 From the Trading Post start descending the Trading Post Trail.
0.2 Cross Red Rocks Park Road.
0.7 Cross Red Rocks Park Road again.
1.4 The trail comes up to Ship Rock Road and becomes, essentially, a sidewalk for a bit.
1.5 The Trading Post Trail ends at the Trading Post.

3 Mount Falcon

Tackle a tough climb on an angry, rocky trail. Tour the burned-out aerie of John Brisben Walker while gazing over a spectacular and unique landscape from the heights of Mount Falcon.

Start: Mount Falcon east trailhead (there is another trailhead on the west side of the parcel)

Distance: 6.8 miles out and back

Approximate hiking time: 3 hours

Difficulty: Strenuous

Trail surface: About half the trail is trickily rocky, and the rest is fairly smooth and easy to deal with; tough climbs

Best seasons: Spring and fall

Other trail users: Hikers, runners, and dogs. Bikes are not allowed on the Turkey Trot Trail, but they are allowed on the upper portion of the route (Castle Trail).

Canine compatibility: Leashed dogs permitted

Land status: Jefferson County Open Space

Fees and permits: None

Schedule: 1 hour before sunrise to 1 hour after sunset

Map: Mount Falcon Park map, Jefferson County Open Space

Trail contact: Jefferson County Open Space, 700 Jefferson County Pkwy., #100, Golden, CO 80401; (303) 271-5925; http://jeffco.us/open-space/parks/

Special considerations: This is a strenuous, hot hike, particularly on summer afternoons. Bring lots of water and use sunscreen. There is an easier way to reach the burnt ruins of Walker's castle. From the western trailhead of Mount Falcon Park, the walk to the ruins is much shorter, and much easier. To reach the western trailhead, take US 285 west to Parmalee Gulch Road. Drive up to the old development called Indian Hills and watch for signs pointing the way up and to the right toward Mount Falcon Park.

Finding the trailhead: From Denver go west on the 6th Avenue Freeway; exit onto I-70 west as you approach Golden. Take an immediate exit off I-70 onto CO 470 southbound. Take CO 470 to the Morrison exit and go west toward Morrison. Drive slowly through Morrison; then turn left onto CO 8 at the stoplight. Take CO 8 up the hill, and near the top turn right onto Forest Avenue. (Watch for signs directing you toward Mount Falcon.) Drive a few blocks up the hill and turn right onto Vine Street, which leads past a few houses and down to the parking area of Mount Falcon's eastern trailhead. GPS: N39 38.81' / W105 11.79'

The Hike

This hike is a strenuous but scenic outing right in Denver's back yard. The out-and-back route reaches to the dramatic burned-out ruins of John Brisben Walker's mountain chateau, a unique waypoint to be sure.

The hike's first phase, on the Turkey Trot Trail, is at times unmistakably steep. The ascent becomes delightful as the trail makes its way around the north side of the mountain. The incline eases and the trail enters the shade of the pines, where you can look down into Clear Creek Canyon or across the hilltops to Red Rocks and the

Better to burn out than fade away

jagged line of hogbacks angling across the horizon, and to little downtown Denver spiking up in the background.

The Turkey Trot Trail, a hikers-only trail, soon rises to the saddle and rejoins the Castle Trail. The Castle Trail is the remnant of an old road built or improved by Walker, now doing duty as a popular mountain bike trail. Much rockier than Turkey Trot, it's the kind of trail that makes you think about almost every step. Much of the toughest part is also exposed to the hot sun, which is likely to be on the oppressive side during summer months.

The route enters a third phase beyond the gazebo at the top of the hill (not the real top of the hill, mind you, but a false summit). Here the Castle Trail looks more like the old road that it was in its youth, as it stair-steps up onto the shoulder of the mountain, continuing to gain altitude. The ruins of Walker's big house are just around the corner from here. (**Note:** The site is much closer and easier to reach from the western trailhead of Mount Falcon Park, for history buffs who aren't looking for a challenging hike.)

John Brisben Walker was born in 1847 in Pennsylvania, not far from Pittsburgh. Walker's early adulthood is deliciously mysterious. He attended West Point but retired from the Academy and went to China. Some say he traveled with the US minister; others say he joined the Chinese military, took part in battles, and became a general at a very young age.

Walker returned from China and went into iron production and the real estate development business in West Virginia, building a huge fortune on the real estate side. His fortune was all but wiped out in the Depression of 1873. Walker's fortunes are like the ancient mountain ranges of Colorado on a human scale, pushing up to the sky and then wearing down to nothing, over and over.

Walker saw Colorado for the first time as a government surveyor in the 1870s. Somehow, perhaps through speculation or as part of some kind of government partnership (young Walker was always adept at securing other people's money for his big ideas), he was able to acquire 1,600 acres just northwest of Denver, the area that would eventually be known as Berkeley. Walker expertly irrigated and grew winning crops of alfalfa on the land. As another fortune grew, he acquired 500 acres just west of downtown Denver on the Platte River. There he built a horse racing track and various amusements, including the vast and somewhat bizarre "Castle of Commerce," which stood until it was destroyed by fire in 1951. River Front Park was a great success and an important cultural institution. Walker sold off the Berkeley land in 1888 and River Front Park just prior to the Panic of 1893.

A Socialist Tycoon?

Much of John B. Walker's writing in *The Cosmopolitan* was paradoxically anticapitalist. For example, in a 1901 article called "The City of the Future—a Prophecy," Walker compares capitalism and "the other" system. "One represents human effort disastrously expended under individual guidance in the competitive system which takes no thought of neighbor. The other represents organization intended for the best enjoyment of all. One stands as the remnant of a barbarism handed down through the centuries. The other stands for the aspirations of the human mind under the unfolding intelligence of an advancing civilization." He channels Marx as well as Plato in this line about real estate development, from the same article: "When commerce ceases to be war, when the world ceases to educate its best brains for the destruction which is meant by competition, when human talent shall be converted to its highest sphere of usefulness, then we shall have the sites of cities selected by commissions having the highest good of the proposed community at heart, instead of by cornerers and peddlers of real estate." Interesting thoughts from a cornerer and peddler of real estate! And quite a turnaround for the guy who built the Castle of Commerce in River Front Park to glorify capitalism for Denver's schoolchildren.

Walker's short-lived kingdom: Bear Creek Canyon below and Red Rocks in the distance.

Walker was just getting started. His next obsession was *The Cosmopolitan* magazine, which he acquired in 1889. Not only did Walker grow the magazine and shape it into an influential publication concerned with big issues—not at all like the *Cosmo* we know today—he wrote for the magazine too, on a wide variety of topics.

We can see from Walker's writings that he spent quite a bit of time wondering about Big Things, like the survival of the Republic, for instance. He became very concerned about the distribution of wealth and was distressed by the extreme level of inequality in the country, though he was among the very rich.

In 1895 *The Cosmopolitan* promoted what was possibly the world's first automobile race. As the first commercial ventures to make and sell horseless carriages were taking off that year, Walker mused on personal transportation and correctly predicted that the popularization of the automobile would lead to the development of suburbs and business parks on the outskirts of cities: "The day will undoubtedly arrive when great establishments employing many clerks and workmen will ask themselves whether it is worth while to put up with narrow quarters, high rentals, insufficient light, and bad air, while the advantages of sunlight, health, and economical conditions are within such easy reach elsewhere," he wrote. Like almost everybody else at that time, Walker didn't yet foresee pollution from automobile engines infringing on the healthiness or attractiveness of the countryside.

Walker urged the development of rail transit systems, owned by the public, for transporting people and freight, but eventually he would invest heavily in the private auto. In 1899 he purchased the patents of the Stanley Brothers' steam-powered auto and their factory and machinery for the almost absurd sum of $250,000, with a partner, A. L. Barber.

Walker and Barber soon parted ways, with Barber creating the Locomobile Company and Walker the Mobile Company of America. It was a losing bet, at least for Walker. Barber and Walker had a tough enough time competing with each other and the growing number of manufacturers of electric- and gasoline-powered cars; then the Stanley Brothers themselves got back into the steam-powered game (armed with over $200,000 in profit from their deal with Walker) in 1902 and started making improved steam cars under their own name.

In the summer of 1900, Walker attempted to drive one of his steamers up Pikes Peak on the barely passable wagon road that existed at the time. The publicity stunt failed at about 11,000 feet, when the steamer's water ran out; retrieving more water was a major ordeal. When the fuel oil ran out a second time, the jig was up. Walker's chastened auto chugged back down to Colorado Springs, a fine metaphor for his foray into the transportation business. In the papers Walker described the aborted venture as a fine success—after all, the car and its passengers made it back; nobody drove off a cliff. It might have been quite a jolt to Walker's psyche when one of Barber's Locomobiles steamed all the way to the top of the Peak in August 1901.

Ultimately, Walker's investment was a bust. He was right that the auto was the next big thing, but wrong about what type of machine would come out on top. Though the Locomobile Company switched to making gasoline-powered vehicles within a few years and thus stayed viable, Walker didn't make the leap. In 1903 his Mobile Company of America ceased production.

In 1905, perhaps reeling from losses in the auto biz, Walker sold *The Cosmopolitan* to William Randolph Hearst for a huge sum. Not long after, Walker could be found again in Colorado, buying up land around Morrison. He had a very large stone house built on top of Mount Falcon for himself and his family, and set about transforming the Morrison and Red Rocks area into a tourist attraction. He built a funicular railway up Mount Morrison, a casino, and auto roads, and started holding concerts in the natural amphitheater at Red Rocks (the place would be made into the world-famous concert venue we know today in the 1930s by Civilian Conservation Corps crews). Walker called Red Rocks "Park of the Titans"—with this moniker and other eerily familiar features he hoped to recreate the success of the resort to the south, to make "a second Colorado Springs."

Walker then embarked on his last great scheme. He wanted to build a summer White House for US presidents high on the slopes of Mount Falcon. Publicly he argued that the summer White House would be good for presidents who used it and

Mount Falcon

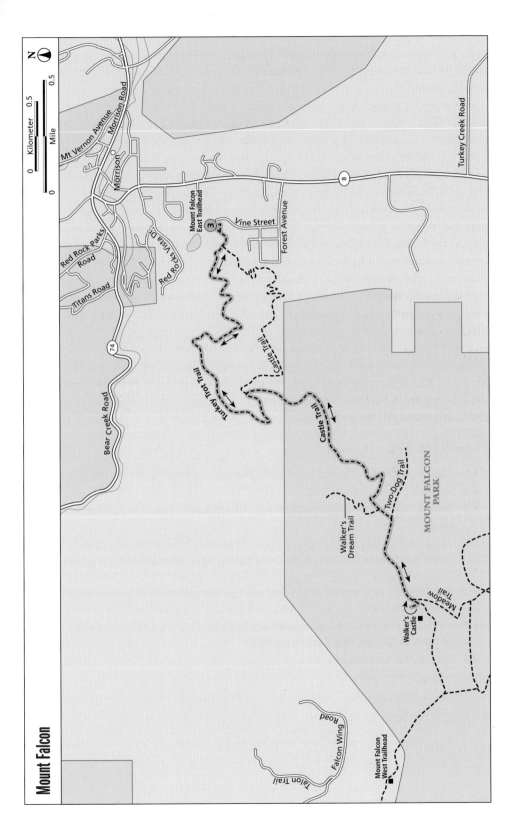

good for the country. Privately he probably figured that building such a thing here would be fantastic publicity for his resort, as he no longer had his magazine to provide free advertising.

The site he chose for the summer White House is accessible from the route described here, at the end of the trail called Walker's Dream. There isn't much other than the old cornerstone to see up there. Walker couldn't procure funds to build the place, and the arrival of World War I put the idea on the back burner for good.

For a time it seemed like Walker's vast real estate holdings around Morrison would end up in the hands of the "corners and peddlers" he decried. After his wife Ethel died in 1916, and the family's huge stone house burned in 1918 (cause undetermined), leaving the spectacular ruins you see today, Walker was busted and unable to pay the taxes on his land. It was foreclosed and condemned, or picked up for a song by speculators. But thanks to the example that Walker set and his infectious vision of a mountain playground—and the fact that you can't raise cattle on rocks—much of the land would eventually become publicly owned open space. So, even though he left Colorado broke and went to Brooklyn to live out his days, he gave the people of Colorado a tremendous gift.

Historian Sally White sums up the far-reaching consequences of Walker's boosterism: "His efforts to promote the foothills led to the establishment of the Denver Mountain Park system; ultimately the vision of foothills parks he pioneered guided the acquisitions of Jefferson County Open Space as well . . . he is rightly known as the 'Father of the Mountain Parks.'"

Miles and Directions

0.0 Start from the east trailhead at Mount Falcon Park and begin walking up the Castle Trail.

0.1 Turn right onto the Turkey Trot Trail.

1.7 Turn right, rejoining the Castle Trail. Note that the Castle Trail is shared with mountain bikers.

2.9 As the climb tops out for a moment at a gazebo, pass the intersection with the Walker's Dream Trail, then the Two-Dog Trail. The Castle Trail has taken on the personality of an old road.

3.3 Pass the intersection with the Meadow Trail and turn right onto the trail that leads shortly to Walker's castle.

3.4 Arrive at the burned-out Walker house (GPS: N39 38.12' / W105 13.62'). After poking around a bit, turn around and retrace your steps.

6.8 Arrive back at the trailhead.

4 Castlewood Canyon

This is a moderately challenging loop with a special historic site and unique scenery southeast of Denver.

Start: Falls Trailhead in the northwest quadrant of Castlewood Canyon State Park
Distance: 3.7-mile loop
Approximate hiking time: 2 hours
Difficulty: Moderate
Trail surface: Some steep sections of rocky steps
Best seasons: Spring and fall
Other trail users: Hikers, runners, and dogs; bikes not allowed
Canine compatibility: Leashed dogs permitted
Land status: State park

Fees and permits: Per-vehicle fee to enter Castlewood Canyon State Park
Schedule: 8 a.m. to 8 p.m.
Map: Castlewood Canyon State Park trail map, Colorado Parks and Wildlife
Trail contact: Castlewood Canyon State Park, 2989 S. State Hwy. 83, Franktown, CO 80116; (303) 688-5242; http://cpw.state.co.us/placestogo/parks/CastlewoodCanyon
Special considerations: Note the trailhead for this hike is reached via CO 86 and Castlewood Canyon Road, and the west entry, not CO 83 and the main park entry.

Finding the trailhead: From anywhere on the Front Range, take I-25 to Castle Rock. Take the Founders Parkway exit and go east on Founders Parkway/CO 86. With Franktown and CO 83 in sight, turn right onto Castlewood Canyon Road and continue to the Falls Trailhead, the last available parking on this road. GPS: N39 20.92' / W104 45.85'

The Hike

The Castlewood Dam may have been cursed from the beginning. During its initial construction in late 1890, many of the men working on it came down with typhoid fever. Almost immediately after it was finished, creating a corporate-owned reservoir, the dam's structural integrity was questioned—it seemed to be leaking quite rapidly. Wild rumors started flying in Denver that the dam was going to fail and leave the city under water.

"Having so many inquries [*sic*] about the Castlewood reservoir we drove around there last Friday to see what could be found out about it, and came back but little wiser than we started," began an article in the *Castle Rock Journal*, June 24, 1891. "The water has all been let out but at present on account of the heavy rains above, a small quantity has collected again. Expert engineers are examining the dam and figuring on strengthening it so that it will not only hold water but be absolutely safe beyond a possibility of doubt and thus forever silence the howls of those who for reasons of their own have tried to obstruct the progress of this gigantic enterprise . . . The efforts of those who are opposed to it, to crush the enterprise, will result in retarding its success but will not cause its defeat."

Castlewood Dam, 1890–1933

The dam and its apparent engineering issues had already become politicized. Castlewood was controversial. But it wasn't a public project. The dam and the water behind it were owned by a development company, Denver Land and Water. The company, a project of venture capitalists from Ohio and Pennsylvania, intended to provide water only to those who lived on land owned by the company.

On September 16, 1891, the *Journal* reported: "A large force of men"—another large force—"has been set to work on the dam at Castlewood and it will be but [*sic*] in a perfectly safe condition." November 25, 1891: "According to reports work is soon to commence again on the Castlewood dam." The fixes seemed to do the trick for several years.

Things were very quiet at the reservoir until May 1897, when the dam sprung a colossal leak. "The break in the Castlewood dam on last Friday caused great anxiety among the residents along the creek below it," reported the *Journal* on May 14, "yet we are glad to say that we think the danger point is passed, except that a heavy rain or water spout should come in above. Our state engineer will be out soon to look after and condemn the dam if it is not safe."

The state engineer decided the dam was not safe at all, that it was likely to bust wide open and ruin several ranches downstream, if not Denver itself. Area kids went to Castlewood to gawk at the leaking structure during the summer of 1897. In August tensions rose along with the water as violent storms pounded the Palmer Divide, overfilling the reservoir and causing visible damage to the dam. The *Castle Rock Journal* had switched from reflexively attacking the dam's critics to openly calling for its removal.

On August 11, 1897, a large party from the city of Denver, including the mayor and several city engineers, came down to inspect Castlewood for themselves. They declared the dam a hazard to the city. The dam's owners assured the Denver officials that it would be sufficiently repaired and reinforced.

Then the dam's architect, A. M. Wells, visited the site to prepare his own report. With all these reports being prepared, it's a wonder nobody figured out how to plug the dam with reports. Not surprisingly Wells found his dam to be the greatest thing ever and predicted that nothing could destroy it, except perhaps the force of its own awesomeness.

In reality, yet another small army of contractors, teams, and laborers had to be assembled for another attempt at reconstructing the barricade. Strangely, the *Castle Rock Journal* was back on the bandwagon by June 10, 1898: "When completed the dam will not only be a credit to this section of the country but will be a great source of profit to its owners and a work of mechanical engineering that will be the pride of every citizen." Hope springs eternal! Unfortunately, so did the Castlewood Dam.

In the spring of 1899, snowmelt filled the reservoir to new heights, and of course rumors of the dam's imminent failure began to fly again. In mid-April water was overflowing the spillways. Confounding the dark expectations of many, the dam survived the summer. Various city and state engineers declared their confidence in the new dam. In late September the state fish warden had the reservoir stocked with 8,000 trout, according to the *West Creek Mining News*.

The spring of 1900 brought even more snowmelt, intense storms, and renewed sense of emergency. In April the city engineer traveled to Castlewood to—guess what—investigate and prepare another report on the dam's condition. But the road from Castle Rock was impassable, covered with huge amounts of snow. He returned to Denver and vowed to try again as soon as possible. Meanwhile the ranches along the creek below the dam emptied as families and stock moved to higher ground, just in case.

Then, on May 2, the news hit Denver like a storm. The dam had finally burst, and the wall of water was on its way! The truth was slightly less sensational: A massive crack had opened, and water was pouring out of the back side of the dam. At that rate total failure seemed probable, but no wall of water was yet hurtling toward Denver. "Everyone at the city hall was excited," wrote one reporter in the *Aspen Daily Times* the next day, "one moment being on the lookout for the waters coming down, and the next assuring their friends that the dam was safe and nothing could happen."

Over in the Platte River Canyon, on the other side of the first line of foothills, the Owl Creek Dam put an unexpected exclamation point on the whole situation when it suddenly ruptured and sent a flood washing through the canyon. The water subsided to manageable levels before it reached the city but took out bridges, roads, and miles of track on the way.

The injured Castlewood Dam stubbornly stood up, but all the water in the reservoir leaked through and it was again a useless pile of rock. As a rep from the Denver Land and Water Company headed east to grub for yet another line of credit to rebuild the thing one more time, the trustee for the original bond holders fore-closed, forcing the company into receivership. The entire venture was coming apart along with the dam.

By August the reservoir was missing. "The vast expanse which was under such a great depth of water in May, is now a great field of sunflowers and weeds," lamented the *Castle Rock Journal*. "The company has no caretaker at the dam now, and the receiver, J. W. Alsop, is off on a hunting expedition in the western part of the state." The locals had come to enjoy having a sizable lake in this semiarid area. Now they feared the dam would be abandoned forever almost as much as they feared it would fail catastrophically.

At this time you might be wondering, is Castlewood Dam the worst dam of all time? Oh, you ain't seen nothin' yet.

In May 1901 the land, dam, and empty ditches of the Denver Land and Water were auctioned. A certain Seth Butler from Connecticut picked up the whole bit for $8,000, a tiny portion of Denver Land and Water's overall debt. (In the end, creditors recouped less than one cent on the dollar.) The company had spent over $200,000 on the dam. The estimated cost of repairing it again was over $40,000.

Still, amazingly, some looked at Castlewood Canyon with dollar signs in their eyes. On February 14, 1902, the *Castle Rock Journal* reported: "The Denver Sugar, Land and Irrigation company, which was incorporated Wednesday, proposes to rebuild Castle-wood dam and use it for watering an immense area in Cherry Creek valley, which will be converted into sugar beet farms." The company announced plans to build a huge sugar factory near Franktown, in addition to an electric railroad between Franktown and the dam, and a summer resort on the reservoir. Locals were excited by the plans and barely noticed that the company planned to spend only $25,000 on improving the dam.

In May the state engineer signed off on a scheme to strengthen the existing dam and place an earthen embankment in front of it. The contract for the work was awarded to J. A. Osner, who had been the contractor presiding over earlier failures. Red flags were again popping up all over the place.

By the fall of 1902, the work on the dam was finished and the reservoir was filling up. But Denver Sugar, Land and Irrigation was struggling with its land racket. It was having much difficulty convincing would-be farmers to move here to grow discount beets for the Man. Two years later, in August 1904, the company's sugar factory was still in the conceptual stage, the start of construction having been falsely announced several times. The plant was never built. And the dam . . . the dam was under repair again early in 1905. In early 1907 there was another crew at the dam performing "extensive improvements." In late 1907 still more work was needed. Apparently these repairs were effective, because the dam didn't crumble or crack for 5 years.

A massive rainstorm and flood along Cherry Creek brought death and destruction to Denver in July 1912. Castlewood Dam didn't look good. Water was sloshing over the top. The old fears and rumors came back momentarily. The newspapers were more tight-lipped than ever about it, however, showing little curiosity about the dam's condition. There was no talk of inspections or reports. The dam held on.

A decade passed, and all was quiet over at Castlewood. The reservoir had become the favorite picnic spot for locals and, in the auto age, a popular destination for Denverites as well.

By 1923 the massive sugar beet scheme had dried up, and once again the dam and the land in question went into receivership. In July 1923 another epic downpour overflowed the reservoir and started to eat the dam alive. Ranchers along Cherry Creek again moved their families to higher ground rather than try to sleep under threat of a catastrophic breach. The dam survived the storm, more or less, but after the collapse of its corporate ownership, would anyone pay for the repairs this time?

We can't really say that it occurred without warning. But when the dam finally burst, in grand fashion, after a decade of uneventful service, it was a surprise.

August 3, 1933, was an exciting day in Denver. At around 2:30 in the morning, the call came in, after the dam caretaker's midnight ride to the nearest telephone operator in Parker. At 3 a.m. police cars were speeding up and down streets along Cherry Creek with sirens blaring to give warning. "This ain't no joke!" they cried. While some Denverites scrambled to evacuate the flood zone, others piled into cars and, out of sheer curiosity, rushed over to Speer Boulevard and the Cherry Creek flood channel that flowed down the middle of the Boulevard.

After its remarkably slow 30-mile journey, the flood arrived at the edge of town as a frothing, violent wave filled with broken farmhouses and screaming livestock. The wave blasted away the Colorado Avenue bridge at 5:40 a.m. and then hurtled through the Speer Boulevard channel, turning it into a roaring river. Twenty-five-foot waves lapped over the 12-foot walls, filling the streets with water.

Finally the flood arrived in lower downtown, spilling out of the channel and covering the streets in several feet of water. The *Rocky Mountain News* reported, "Union Station was inundated, warehouses were filled with evil-smelling water which backed its debris into the streets, scores of families were driven from their flooded homes and telephone communication and all forms of traffic were hindered or brought to a dead stop for a time." The Castlewood flood was, after the 1965 Plum Creek/Platte event, the second-most-damaging flood in the 155-year history of Denver. Officials estimated the cost of the disaster at [Dr. Evil voice] one million dollars. Fortunately, as such timely warning was given, only two people were killed.

Many of Denver's residents were entertained by the spectacle. According to the *Rocky Mountain News*, the drive-in disaster proved to be sort of an all-day festival: "Old men, women, and barefoot boys reaped a harvest in nickels and dimes yesterday selling ice cream, candy bars, and popcorn to the thousands of motorists who drove along Cherry Creek to see the damage caused by the flood. 'Here you are! Here you are! Buy a cone!' a gray-haired man called as he stood near Champa St. and Speer Blvd. One boy had an accident and lost a dozen or more cones when he dropped his icebox on the sidewalk. In nearly every automobile children, women, and men were

The aftermath of the flood at Union Station. DENVER PUBLIC LIBRARY, WESTERN HISTORY COLLECTION

seen eating cones, popcorn, or candy. Police officers and firemen, tired from the hard labor of cleaning up the wreckage, stood here and there, enjoying refreshments." Fun for the whole family!

Hundreds of Denver's unemployed obtained temporary work shoveling the muck out of lower downtown. Between the city and Castlewood Canyon, 30 miles of cleanup was performed by crews hired under the banner of the Civilian Conservation Corps.

The people of Douglas County wanted their dam rebuilt, despite all the nerve wreckage it had caused over the years. They wanted the reservoir back. But now they preferred the government to be responsible for the work. They got part of their wish.

As you can see, Castlewood was never rebuilt. In the late 1930s the Army Corps of Engineers started making plans for a new dam on Cherry Creek. A new dam was built many miles downstream of Castlewood, where Kennedy golf course is today.

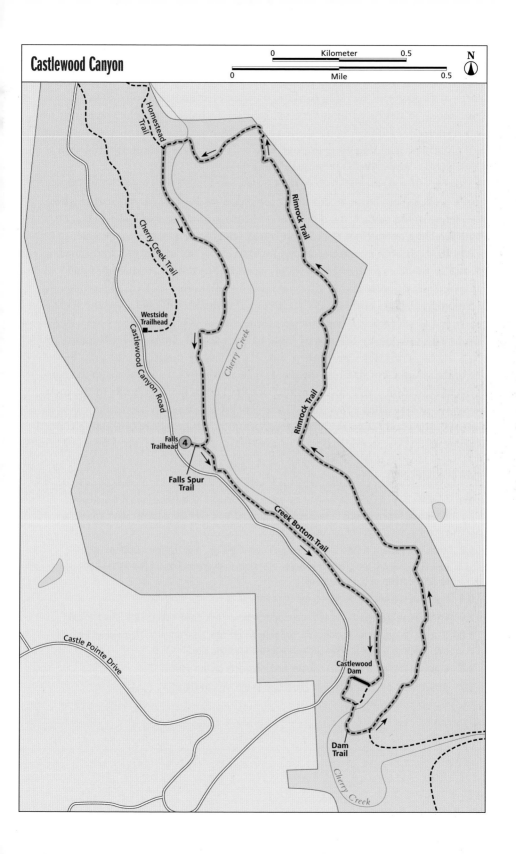

Castlewood Canyon

Homestead Trail

Cherry Creek Trail

Castlewood Canyon Road

Rimrock Trail

Cherry Creek

Westside Trailhead

Falls Trailhead **4**

Falls Spur Trail

Rimrock Trail

Creek Bottom Trail

Castle Pointe Drive

Castlewood Dam

Dam Trail

Cherry Creek

After World War II the Army Corps decided this new dam was inadequate and built another, the Cherry Creek Dam, which was completed in 1950. These days the Army Corps of Engineers is working hard to convince everybody that the Cherry Creek Dam could be destroyed by a very unlikely, yet technically possible, rainstorm of unprecedented volume. Among the many options for fixing what may or may not be a problem, depending on your point of view, is the construction of a new dam at Castlewood Canyon. We'll see what happens there.

So that's the tragicomic story of the Castlewood Dam. This canyon is much more than a broken dam, however. It's also a geological freak show. As you start the hike, descending to the sandy canyon floor, note the giant boulders that line the trail. They came tumbling down from the canyon rim at some point, perhaps a consequence of one of the big floods mentioned above. Encased in the boulders you'll find a medley of smaller boulders and rocks of widely varying provenance, including chunks of Fountain Formation sandstone (the same dark red rocks that stick up so prominently at Eldorado Canyon and Garden of the Gods), volcanic tuff, and quartzite. This is the famed Castle Rock Conglomerate, formed by heavy floodwaters—very heavy floodwaters, judging by the size of some of the encased chunks, which themselves are 2 meters across. The age of the Castle Rock Conglomerate is estimated by the age of the chunks. For instance, the pieces of Wall Mountain Tuff locked in the conglomerate are from a volcanic event that occurred 36 million years ago, so we know for sure it isn't any older than that. Castle Rock Conglomerate forms the cap rock here at Castlewood Canyon, but also tops various buttes in the area, including Castle Rock itself.

Miles and Directions

0.0   From the Falls Trailhead (south of the Westside Trailhead on Castlewood Canyon Road), begin walking southeast down the Falls Spur Trail. Turn right immediately and begin walking along the Creek Bottom Trail.

0.7   Arrive at the dam. A little huffing and puffing will get you over the top. (**Option:** Go left and down toward the creek, find a trail that goes through the broken gap in the dam, and rejoin the route at 0.9 mile below.)

0.9   Continue straight up the hill on the Dam Trail.

1.0   Continue straight past an intersection with another trail. You're now on the Rimrock Trail.

3.0   Turn left on the Creek Bottom Trail. (**Option:** A right turn here onto the Homestead Trail will take you to the cool-looking Lucas Homestead historic site.)

3.5   Continue straight and up as another trail intersects on the right.

3.7   Turn right on the Falls Spur Trail and return to the Falls Trailhead.

5 Mount Galbraith

Walk in the footsteps of ancient people on this rugged, rocky route near Golden. This is a truly fun hike with a lot of vertical and visual appeal.

Start: Mount Galbraith Open Space Trailhead
Distance: 4.1-mile lariat loop
Approximate hiking time: 2 hours
Difficulty: Moderate to strenuous
Trail surface: Lots of rock steps and some minor scrambling over rock outcroppings
Best seasons: Spring and fall; great off-season potential
Other trail users: Hikers, runners, and dogs; no bikes or horses allowed
Canine compatibility: Leashed dogs permitted. Some dogs may have difficulty on parts of the route that include lengthy sections of rock steps.

Land status: Jefferson County Open Space
Fees and permits: None
Schedule: 1 hour before sunrise to 1 hour after sunset
Map: Mount Galbraith Open Space trail map, Jefferson County Open Space
Trail contact: Jefferson County Open Space, 700 Jefferson County Pkwy., #100, Golden, CO 80401; (303) 271-5925; http://jeffco.us/open-space/parks/
Special considerations: This trail requires good dexterity as well as stamina. There is one long, steep rock staircase and several smaller ones.

Finding the trailhead: From Denver go west on the 6th Avenue Freeway; stay on the 6th Avenue Freeway as it passes by Golden and turns to the north, becoming CO 93. Turn left onto Golden Gate Canyon Road. Drive about 1.5 miles and turn left into the Mount Galbraith Open Space parking area. GPS: N39 46.42' / W105 15.25'

The Hike

When the first round of American gold-grubbers moseyed west in 1849-50, passing through Colorado on their way to California, some of them dipped into the creeks of the Front Range to see what they could find. Lewis Ralston found traces of the glittery treasure near the confluence of Clear Creek and what is now called Ralston Creek. Not enough to stop their journey to California, but enough to cause some excitement. News of the discovery percolated for years after the California rush fizzled, then helped drive the new rush to "Pikes Peak," as would-be gold-seekers called the Front Range region. Ralston Creek is now best known for its contamination, caused by an old uranium mine.

Soon after Golden City (aka Golden) was established in the initial frenzy, the town found itself consistently overshadowed by its rival Denver. Though it became seat of the territorial government in 1862, Golden City would hold on to the honor for just 5 years. "It is not saying to [*sic*] much to assert that her advantages, as to contiguity to the mines and to all the mineral wealth that goes to build up a town, immense water power, etc., are second to none in Colorado," wrote the editors of the

Golden Transcript in 1866, in the newspaper's first issue. By that time, however, it was already becoming clear to some of Golden's boosters that the mining camp would never become a shining metropolis.

While Denver was overshadowing Golden, Golden was overshadowing Golden Gate City, an upstart little town at the mouth of Golden Gate Canyon. Both Golden and Golden Gate City are said to be named for Thomas Golden, an early miner and civic leader. (Like many other southerners, Golden drifted away from Colorado at the beginning of the Civil War and was never heard from again.) Golden Gate City was banking on its toll road to the mines, the Golden Gate Canyon route. The Clear Creek Canyon toll road was preferred by travelers, and Golden Gate City quickly withered and died. I don't know about you, but I'm fine with that.

The most historically interesting aspect of Mount Galbraith Open Space is the Hall-Woodland Cave (archaeologists know it as 5JF9), one of three sites in the park known to have been occupied by prehistoric people. Archaeologists working in the 1960s found seventeen projectile points about a foot beneath the surface inside the cave, along with a load of pottery sherds, grinding stones, and bone fragments. The ceramic pieces and notch-corner projectile points found at the Hall-Woodland Cave date its habitation to the Early Ceramic stage, between 1,500 and 1,000 years ago.

The bone fragments at the site, primarily from mule deer, supply more detail to the story. The bones had been broken into small pieces, evidence of marrow extraction. Clearly the people here were trying to get every last bit of nutrition out of their deer kills, perhaps betraying a certain desperation. In addition, all the artifacts were found inside the cave, and very few were outside as would be expected.

Charles Nelson, who performed most of the original excavation, theorized that the south-facing cave was used intermittently during severely cold and harsh winter storms. "Even though these people undoubtedly were accustomed to living with nature and all her elements," he wrote, "there must have been times when it was even too much for them to bear."

The locations of Mount Galbraith's three prehistoric sites, especially the cave, are very tightly held by in-the-know archaeologists and government agencies. They don't want riffraff up there poking around, disturbing the sites, and carting off any remaining artifacts. If I knew where the cave was, I probably couldn't disclose the location in a book like this. Beyond the cave's general south-facing orientation, I can tell you what I learned from a Jefferson County Open Space document: that the cave is unfenced, unmarked, and not near any of the park's trails, all of which they hope will help keep the general public away from it.

Knowing that there is an archaeologically important cave nearby, with a secret location, makes this hike even more fun than it would be otherwise. You'll be scanning all the south-facing rock faces along the route for possible prehistoric rock shelters. As well you should, if you're interested in this sort of thing. Chances are most of the decent-sized caves and rock shelters along the Front Range were used at some point by the ancient people who lived in the region for at least 10,000 years. And if

Classic Front Range view from Mount Galbraith

you're walking up Mount Galbraith in high summer, you won't have much trouble imagining how a north-facing shelter might be much more pleasant during certain times of the year.

The hike itself is a moderately strenuous lariat loop with lots of rock steps and quasi-technical scrambling over chunky outcroppings. It's a nice reprieve for local hikers that this place is off-limits to mountain bikers. But you'll soon see why, with all the steps and ledges. I've got you walking clockwise around the upper loop. The counterclockwise loop takes on quite a different personality, mainly due to the long steep staircase on the back side, in the shade of the pines.

The views are nice all the way around, but visual wonderment ensues when the Mount Galbraith Loop pops up onto the east flank of the mountain. Suddenly almost all of Golden comes into view, and Denver as well. The smaller town is framed by the huge benches of North and South Table Mountains, the green athletic fields of the School of Mines, and of course the concrete-blocked smoke-puffing Coors facility, one of the most distinctive-looking industrial sites in America.

The famous School of Mines was established in the early years of Golden and has been a public institution since 1876. In recent decades the focus at Mines has been more on oil than minerals.

The Coors plant, now the largest single brewery complex in the world, dates to 1873, when Adolph Coors and a partner commenced operations right there on Clear Creek. Nobody but the company's marketing department could argue that it's a great beer, but Coors' historic unavailability to drinkers back east gave it some weird value in the late twentieth century. The movie *Smokey and the Bandit* (1977) was about a plan to haul an illicit shipment of "the Banquet Beer" across the southeast. Of course Bandit (played by Burt Reynolds) gets mixed up with the very agitated Sheriff Buford T. Justice (Jackie Gleason), which greatly complicates the journey. Nonstop antics. In 2005 Coors merged with Canadian beer giant Molson, forming Molson Coors.

Walk a little farther, and you'll see Lookout Mountain from a unique perspective, due south across the chasm known as Clear Creek Canyon. The road that wraps around Lookout Mountain was constructed in 1913–14. It was a tourist road for the new Denver Mountain Parks system, but also part of State Primary Road Number One, which in turn was a link in the transcontinental highway. It was known to some as the Lariat Trail. Some simply called it Lookout Mountain Road, while others called it Williams Highway, after its builder "Cement Bill" Williams.

Some Jefferson County residents were unhappy about the county's agreeing to pay 25 percent of the road's $30,000 cost (50 percent was paid by the state highway commission and another 25 percent by the City of Denver). Although today JeffCo might blow that much maintaining a single vehicle for a year, the county had to scramble to come up with that $7,500 in 1913. Representatives defended the deal in the *Colorado Transcript,* Golden's daily, noting that existing roads near the creek bottoms were plenty expensive already, getting periodically washed away. "Mountain floods confined between canyon walls obliterate with distressing frequency and completeness. The present road as laid out, should be beyond the reach of such calamities." Sure enough, the road has never been washed away.

Before the new road's existence, vehicles, primarily of the horse-drawn variety, rocked and rolled to the top of Lookout Mountain via the Chimney Gulch route, the vestiges of which form the Chimney Gulch Trail. The Chimney Gulch Trail crosses the road twice, or, more accurately, as the route was long established when the road was created, the road crosses the trail twice.

In 1919 the Denver City Council passed a strange new law, according to the *Transcript.* Anybody caught throwing tacks or nails or other pointy objects onto the roads of Denver Mountain Parks could be fined $300 or tossed in the slammer for 90 days. This law was aimed at violators along the new Lookout Mountain road, and reflects a certain public disdain for the new automobile age in general, and for this road in particular. No trace of that resentment survives today.

A little more walking, and you can look all the way into the bottom of Clear Creek Canyon and see US 6 disappearing into Tunnel 1. Though the highway is often strewn with rock wreckage from the crumbling canyon walls, and coach drivers seem to have trouble keeping their buses out of the creek, the canyon that was once known as "Toughcuss" has been tamed.

Mount Galbraith

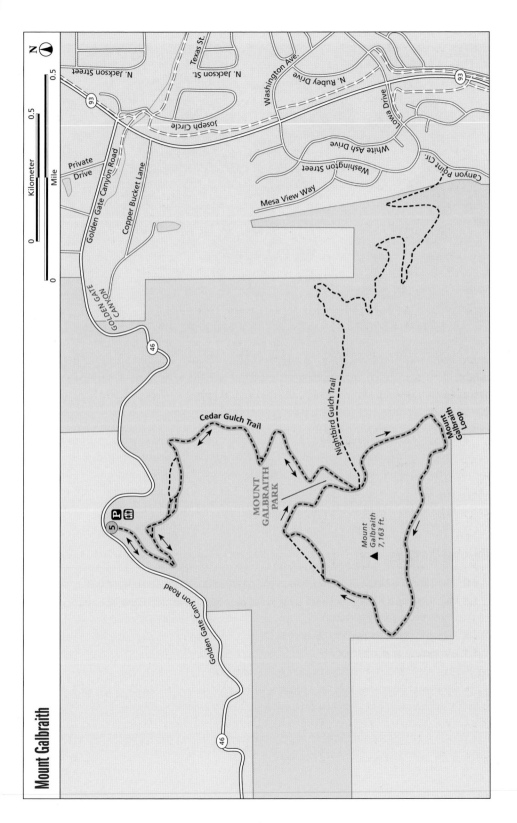

N

Kilometer
0   0.5

Mile
0   0.5

Private Drive

Golden Gate Canyon Road

Copper Bucket Lane

N. Jackson Street

Texas St.

N. Jackson St.

Joseph Circle

Washington Ave.

N. Rubey Drive

Luwna Drive

White Ash Drive

Washington Street

Mesa View Way

Canyon Point Cir.

93

93

GOLDEN GATE CANYON

46

Cedar Gulch Trail

Golden Gate Canyon Road

46

MOUNT GALBRAITH PARK

Nightbird Gulch Trail

Mount Galbraith Loop

Mount Galbraith 7,163 ft.

5

P

Wild rose

These days a huge percentage of the highway's users are heading to or from the casino towns of Blackhawk or Central City. During the early gold rush days, travel through the canyon was a notorious struggle. Native Americans and gold rushers alike preferred to climb up high onto the flanks of Mount Galbraith and walk west along the ridges instead of negotiating the narrow and overgrown canyon bottom. Look for possible evidence of old trails on the surrounding hillsides.

Miles and Directions

0.0   Start from the Mount Galbraith Trailhead and begin walking up the Cedar Gulch Trail.

1.2   Turn left onto the Mount Galbraith Loop. (Don't descend the Nightbird Gulch Trail, which drops into the neighborhood.)

2.8   Turn left, back onto the Cedar Gulch Trail.

4.1   Arrive back at the trailhead.

6 Lookout Mountain

This is a hill climber's route up Lookout Mountain, visiting the grave of Buffalo Bill Cody and an accompanying museum.

Start: Small dirt parking area on Lariat Loop Road (aka Lookout Mountain Road)
Distance: 5.6 miles out and back
Approximate hiking time: 2 to 5 hours
Difficulty: Moderate to strenuous
Trail surface: Expect a moderately rugged and rocky surface and lots of loose gravel
Best season: Fall
Other trail users: Mountain bikers, joggers, and family hikers
Canine compatibility: Leashed dogs permitted

Land status: Denver Mountain Park
Fees and permits: None for the hike; Buffalo Bill Museum requires admission fee
Schedule: Dawn to dusk
Map: Windy Saddle Park map, Jefferson County Open Space
Trail contact: Denver Mountain Parks; (720) 865-0900
Special considerations: Restroom available in gift shop of the Buffalo Bill Museum. Museum has an admission fee.

Finding the trailhead: From Denver go west on the 6th Avenue Freeway to Golden; then turn left onto 19th Street/Lariat Loop/Lookout Mountain Road. Drive up the road about 1 mile and park in an informal dirt pull-off on the left side of the road, on the inside of a curve. The Chimney Gulch Trail crosses the road here. GPS: N39 44.56' / W105 14.09'

The Hike

In 1917 Buffalo Bill Cody—the former trapper, Pony Express rider, army scout, and buffalo meat supplier to railroad crews, who parlayed his nationwide celebrity as a frontiersman into worldwide celebrity with his Wild West Show—found himself not only dead but trapped on Lookout Mountain.

Buffalo Bill had expressed a wish, in writing no less, to be buried above his namesake town, Cody, Wyoming, so it's a Colorado mystery how he ended up here. Revenge of the buffalo? According to one theory, his widow subverted his final wish because she was bitter about Bill's infidelities. But that may be a bit of a smokescreen to cover what really happened.

Five years before Cody's death, he was broke and beholden to a financier named Harry Tammen, who auctioned off Buffalo Bill's remaining possessions. Cody was made to perform in Tammen's own circus-like production. When Cody died in 1917, it was Tammen who had him interred on Lookout Mountain. Rumor has it that he paid Cody's widow to claim that her husband had changed his mind about his final resting place. You lay where you fell, Bill.

This is an abbreviated route that uses the upper portion of the Chimney Gulch Trail. It starts where the trail crosses the road for the first time (the first of two crossings). (**Option:** To start the hike from the bottom of the Chimney Gulch Trail, park at

Chimney Gulch Trail is the remnant of the old wagon road to the top of Lookout Mountain.

Lions Park in Golden or at the Golden rec center and access the start of the Chimney Gulch Trail from the concrete bike/pedestrian path just south of Clear Creek and east of 6th Avenue Freeway. The trail goes through a tunnel under the highway. That's a longer, more difficult route, of course. Another option is to shorten the route considerably by starting at the Windy Saddle Trailhead/parking area—the trail's second/upper crossing of Lookout Mountain Road—located about two thirds of the way up Lookout.)

No matter which version you choose, the hike is essentially uphill all the way. The grade eases to near flat before the second bridge, but not for long. Above Windy Saddle the trail surface chunks up quite a bit. You'll find a few tenths of a mile that are severely rocky, turning much of the final stretch between Windy Saddle and Bill's grave into an ankle-biting challenge, uphill and downhill. The terrain and trail surface both chill out before the summit.

A fork in the trail a half mile from the top provides an opportunity to visit the Lookout Mountain Nature Center and Boettcher Mansion on top of the hill. It's a fairly strenuous hike to get there, but not far. Built about the same time as Buffalo Bill's shrine, Charles Boettcher's summer home was just the latest of the palatial part-time residences built for Colorado's self-made sugar beet and cement magnate. There are public trails that peruse the grounds and nature center, and the mansion itself has been open on Saturdays.

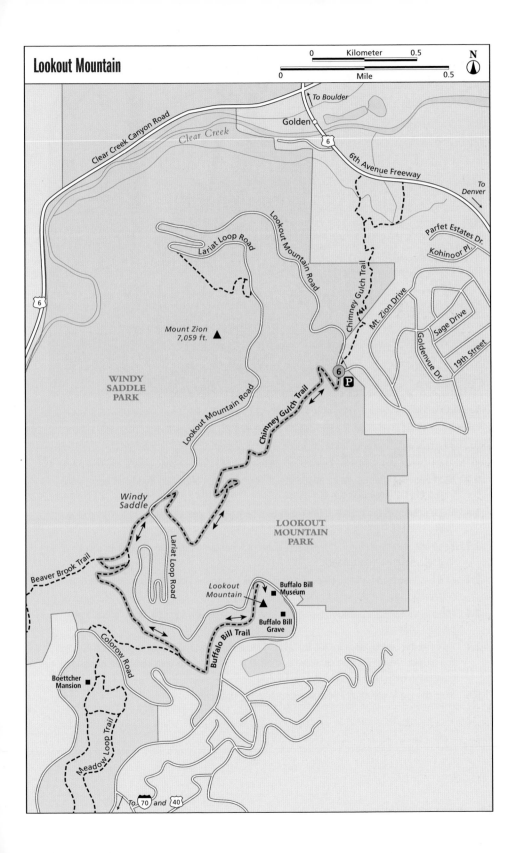

Near Buffalo Bill's grave

Miles and Directions

0.0   Start from the informal trailhead about a mile up Lookout Mountain Road and begin walking up the Chimney Gulch Trail.

1.4   The trail crosses the road and the Windy Saddle parking area. Continue on the Windy Pass Trail.

1.7   Keep left, staying on the Windy Saddle/Lookout Mountain Trail where the Beaver Brook Trail intersects at a switchback.

2.2   At a T-intersection turn left. (The right branch goes up to the Boettcher Mansion and Colorow Road.)

2.4   The trail crosses the picnicking area and kind of loses its way for a bit. Look for trail markers and continue.

2.7   Arrive at the parking area for the Buffalo Bill Museum and Grave. Enjoy the concessions as you please. (**Note:** Bill's actual grave is another 0.1 mile up the path above the museum; no charge. GPS: N39 43.96' / W105 14.30')

5.6   From the grave site retrace your steps back to the trailhead.

7 Tallman Ranch

Hike through Golden Gate Canyon State Park to reach a bucolic homestead site.

Start: Bridge Creek Trailhead in Golden Gate Canyon State Park
Distance: 3.4-mile lariat loop
Approximate hiking time: 2 hours
Difficulty: Moderate
Trail surface: Moderately rugged singletrack and a semi-overgrown dirt road
Best seasons: Summer and fall
Other trail users: Hikers, dogs, and bikers
Canine compatibility: Leashed dogs permitted
Land Status: Golden Gate Canyon State Park

Fees and permits: Daily pass required
Schedule: Daylight only without camping permit
Map: Golden Gate Canyon State Park trail map, Colorado Parks and Wildlife
Trail contact: Golden Gate Canyon State Park, 92 Crawford Gulch Rd., Golden, CO 80403; (303) 582-3707; http://cpw.state.co.us/placestogo/parks/GoldenGateCanyon

Finding the trailhead: From Golden or Boulder take CO 93 to Golden Gate Canyon Road (just north of Golden), drive about 13 miles, and turn right into the turn-off to pay your fee at the station. Then turn right, entering Golden Gate Canyon State Park on Crawford Gulch Road. Drive another 2-plus miles until the road becomes Ralston Creek, then Drew Hill Road, and park on the left side of the road at Bridge Creek. There is a parking area. GPS: N39 50.79' / W105 22.68'. (**Caution:** A warning from Colorado Parks and Wildlife, "Most GPS will instruct you to take the Crawford Gulch turn 5 miles up the canyon. This is a windy dirt road that will take longer. For the most direct route to the park, please stay on Golden Gate Canyon Road.")

The Hike

This somewhat gravity-tinged but otherwise easygoing hike takes you back into Forgotten Valley at Golden Gate Canyon State Park. A promising name for a valley, no doubt.

Unfortunately, Forgotten Valley isn't quite as forgotten as the name would suggest. It gets its fair share of visitors these days, as word has gotten around about this moderate family-friendly hike to a cool old house perched above a nice little fishing pond. Imagine it during the beast-and-wagon days, however. Back then it would take almost all day to reach the nearest town from here, and Forgotten Valley was much easier to forget.

In this version of the Forgotten Valley hike, you'll hike to the Tallmans' homestead, and then go a little beyond, completing a tidy loop around the head of the valley before retracing your steps to the trailhead.

The Tallmans were Swedish immigrants. They embarked with their three children for the New World in 1869. By the time they arrived, Mrs. Tallman had perished.

Forgotten Valley: A long wagon ride from the nearest town.

There were many Swedes in Colorado in the nineteenth century, but they gathered in this area in particular. Swedish immigrants managed to escape the aggressive xenophobic vitriol, and violence, that was directed at Colorado's Asian, Italian, and Mexican immigrants (not to mention, of course, the subjugation of African-Americans and Native Americans).

Consider this bit from May 1860, one of the many race-obsessed asides from the early days of William Byers's *Rocky Mountain News*: "It is stated that twenty thousand Swedes and Norwegians are preparing to embark early in the coming summer for the United States. They will bring much wealth with them, but what is better, being a sober, moral and industrious race, they will bring with them habits of industry and morality, which will render them most valuable citizens." [*Rocky Mountain News*, May 30, 1860, p. 1.] Byers was one of Colorado's all-time most effective "boosters," but he really was a J-hole.

I can't speak for their morality, but the Tallmans did bring their industrious habits and ingenuity to the mountains here, building a nice little dairy operation. The house is an old schoolhouse—why build a new house when you can commandeer a perfectly good old building? The family kept the place until 1955.

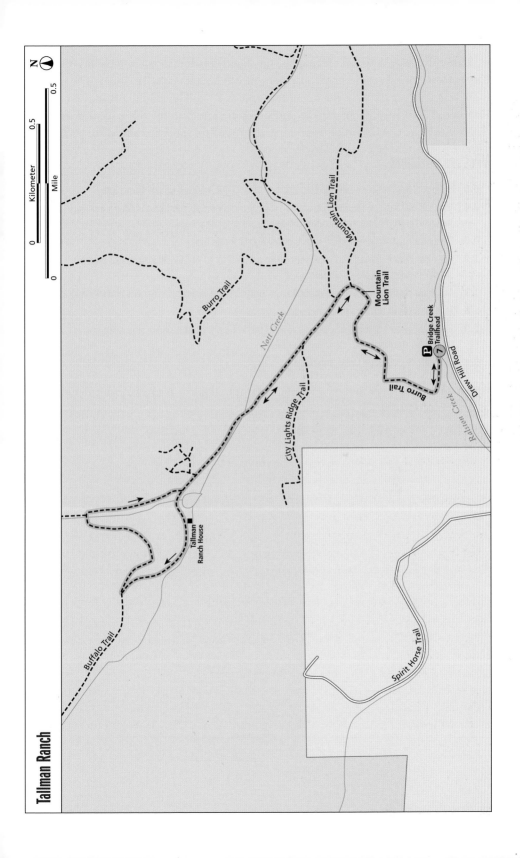

Tallman Ranch

If this hike has a downside, it could be the slightly ho-hum scenery—Golden Gate Canyon State Park keeps its vistas on a low boil. Not that it's ugly. Far from it. The trail is nice enough, especially at the homestead and above it. The gurgling Bridge Creek section is special as well. The middle portion of the route, on the other hand, doesn't do itself any favors when it joins an old, straight road for quite a while. Blah.

Miles and Directions

0.0 From the Bridge Creek Trailhead and picnic area, begin walking up the Burro Trail.

0.4 Turn left, joining the Mountain Lion Trail; shortly thereafter stay left on the Mountain Lion Trail as the Burro Trail heads off to the right.

0.6 Continue past an intersection with the City Lights Ridge Trail.

1.2 After the house comes into view, veer down and left to go for a visit. I hope you brought some biscuits or a pie or something.

1.3 Continue past the house and outbuildings, and climb, now embarking on a clockwise loop.

1.6 Turn right at an obvious trail junction.

1.9 Turn right again, headed back down toward the house. Pass the house and keep on truckin' to the trailhead, retracing your steps.

3.4 Arrive back at Bridge Creek Trailhead.

Accommodations: Backcountry camping sites near Tallman Ranch. Permit required (in addition to park pass).

8 Rattlesnake Gulch

A moderately strenuous and rocky trail leads out of strikingly beautiful Eldorado Canyon to the site of a burned-out hotel.

Start: Rattlesnake Gulch Trailhead, Eldorado Canyon

Distance: 2.4 miles out and back

Approximate hiking time: 1 hour

Difficulty: Moderate to strenuous

Trail surface: Some rugged and rocky sections; maintains consistent moderate uphill grade

Best season: Summer

Other trail users: Hikers, runners, and dogs. Bikes are allowed but not likely.

Canine compatibility: Leashed dogs permitted

Land status: State park

Fees and permits: Per-person or per-vehicle fee; annual Colorado State Parks pass may also be purchased

Schedule: Sunrise to sunset

Map: Eldorado Canyon State Park map, Colorado Parks and Wildlife

Trail contact: Eldorado Canyon State Park, 9 Kneale Road, Eldorado Springs, CO 80025; (303) 494-3943; http://cpw.state.co.us/placestogo/parks/eldoradocanyon

Special considerations: Upper loop may be closed under certain circumstances to protect wildlife.

Finding the trailhead: From Denver go west on the 6th Avenue Freeway; stay on the 6th Avenue Freeway as it passes by Golden and turns to the north, becoming CO 93. Drive north on CO 93 for about 10 miles and turn left onto Highway 170/Eldorado Springs Drive. From Boulder go south on Broadway/CO 93 and turn right onto Eldorado Springs Drive. From CO 93 drive about 3 miles on Eldorado Canyon Drive. Drive (slowly) through town and pay your fee at the guard shack. The Fowler Trailhead parking is on the left a few tenths of a mile up from the guard shack. (**Note:** You might be able to save a few bucks by parking below the guard shack and walking into the state park instead of driving.) GPS: N39 55.77' / W105 17.41'

The Hike

What killed the Crags Hotel above Eldorado Springs?

Well, fire killed the hotel. But who, or what, started the fire that killed the Crags Hotel?

Some say it was lightning. Others suspect arson. Personally, I'm going with arson.

The Crags Hotel was built on a hilltop (lightning bait) about 800 feet above Eldorado Springs in 1908, when the resort below was truly hoppin'. By one estimate, 40,000 people were visiting Eldorado Springs each day, by car and via a new electric rail line connecting to nearby Marshall.

Eldorado Springs is a fun but very relaxed place now. There was a carnival-like atmosphere at the turn of the century. Among other things, visitors could count on seeing Ivy Baldwin walk a wire hundreds of feet overhead, all the way across the canyon. Baldwin was well known around Denver after many years as a balloonist and

The Crags Hotel as seen from the stop on the Moffat Road. DENVER PUBLIC LIBRARY, WESTERN HISTORY DEPARTMENT

aerial acrobat. In the 1890s he performed regularly at the old Elitch's amusement park. At Eldorado Springs, Baldwin walked the wire with apparent joy until he was into his 80s.

There are still aerial acrobatics going on at "Eldo." Look up on the rocks. Eldorado Canyon is one of the best-loved rock climbing venues in the world. Climbers of all abilities flock to famous routes like Naked Edge and Bastille Crack.

The Crags Hotel was accessible by incline railway from the resort below; or by the Moffat Railroad, which passed above the hotel (and still does); or by the same trail you're walking, which used to be a road. The hotel burned in October 1913—not 1912 as reported on various plaques and pamphlets—after just 5 years in existence. The fire occurred when the hotel was closed for the season, in October, not a huge month for lightning strikes. Reportedly there was no insurance. The following summer Joe Mills, brother of conservationist Enos Mills, the American naturalist who helped create Rocky Mountain National Park, opened a different Crags Hotel near Estes Park, and that establishment remains in business today.

There's not much left of the old Crags Hotel. Poke around on the hilltop to find the remains of the fountain, almost completely intact, as well as the hotel's fireplace and some very sweet retaining walls. Near the site two different trails set off; these are the ends of the upper loop. When we were up here, much of the upper loop was

This place had a lot of hearth.

closed in order to give some space to the golden eagles nesting in the vicinity. About 0.4 mile up the right-hand branch of the upper loop, there's a spur leading out to a cool overlook.

The hike from the narrow canyon floor is plenty strenuous and moderately rough as well, but the modest distance (about 1.2 miles each way) keeps it doable for hikers of varying abilities. The hike starts on the Fowler Trail, the remains of a railroad bed dating to the 1880s. The bed was never actually used for a railroad, but it makes a nice trail. After a short walk on the Fowler Trail, turn right and up on the rocky Rattlesnake Gulch Trail.

Along the way you'll come to a massive concrete bunker-like structure with steel doors, like something that might have been stormed by Allied troops in 1944. This is a concrete aqueduct, created in the 1930s to siphon water from South Boulder Creek. The aqueduct becomes a canal and drains into Ralston Reservoir, where it may or may not become contaminated by the leakage from an old uranium mine. The trail continues to the right, across the bridge.

At about this point you might start to hear some strange noises coming from up on the mountain somewhere. Definitely an unnatural, industrial-type noise, but not immediately recognizable—*ch-ch-k-ch-ch-k-ch-ch*—is that some kind of bulldozer working up there? Soon the source of the noise should become apparent as you glance up and see a train rolling across the mountainside high above. That's the Moffat

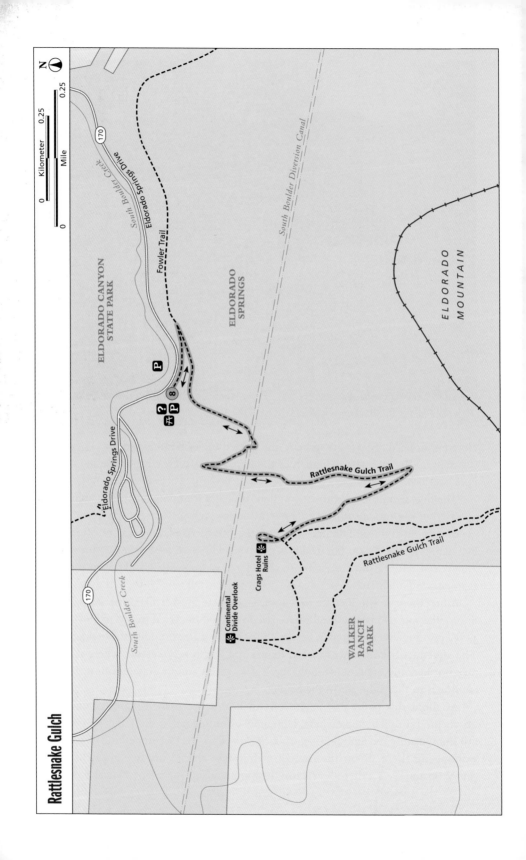

Rattlesnake Gulch

Eldorado Canyon

Road, as it was informally known, built in 1904 to connect Denver and Salt Lake City. The line didn't make it all the way to SLC, construction having terminated abruptly at Craig, Colorado, after David Moffat's death.

Today the tracks are owned by Union Pacific, and trains can be seen and heard passing between tunnels every half hour or so. The trains go through twenty-eight tunnels between Rollins Pass and Denver, and about half of the tunnels are clustered right here on Eldorado Mountain. This part of the line is known as the "Tunnel District."

Miles and Directions

0.0 Start hiking from the Fowler Trailhead in Eldorado Canyon State Park.

0.1 Take a sharp right onto the Rattlesnake Gulch Trail.

1.2 Arrive at the Crags Hotel burnout. Peruse the site; then turn around or walk the 1.4-mile upper loop, if open.

2.4 Arrive back at the bottom of the canyon.

9 Mallory Cave

A short but sharp little climb takes you to an unusual location among the Flatirons. Start at the National Center for Atmospheric Research (NCAR) campus and end at the bats' own Mallory Cave, about 700 feet above.

Start: NCAR, South Boulder
Distance: 2.3 miles out and back
Approximate hiking time: 1 hour
Difficulty: Moderate
Trail surface: Tricky, rocky, and vertical
Best season: Summer
Other trail users: Hikers, climbers, runners, and dogs; bikes not allowed
Canine compatibility: Leashed dogs permitted
Land status: City of Boulder Open Space and Mountain Parks
Fees and permits: None
Schedule: Parking lot closed from 11 p.m. to 5 a.m.
Map: NCAR Trailhead map, City of Boulder Open Space and Mountain Parks
Trail contact: City of Boulder Open Space and Mountain Parks, 66 S. Cherryvale Rd., Boulder,

CO 80303; (303) 441-3440; https://boulder colorado.gov/osmp/national-center-for -atmospheric-research-trailhead
Special considerations: Near the cave, at the top of this route, the trail heads straight up a rock face. The face isn't exposed, but getting up it does require some fairly serious scrambling. The cave itself has been closed to the public. In recent years hikers have been able to approach quite close to the cave, which was protected by an iron gate. Lately, however, even the final approach has been off-limits. The barricade is in place to protect the bat colony that lives in the cave. Wildlife officials hope that keeping humans away will save the Mallory Cave bats from "white nose syndrome," a mysterious fungus that has devastated bat colonies around Colorado.

Finding the trailhead: From Boulder head south on Broadway to Table Mesa Drive. Go west on Table Mesa. The road exits the suburban zone and becomes the approach road to the National Center for Atmospheric Research (NCAR) on top of the mesa. Park in the expansive lot. Walk back toward the north side of the complex where the road tops out and find the trailhead. The hike begins with a short section of concrete sidewalk. GPS: N39 58.72' / W105 16.53'

The Hike

This is a fun, quick, but vertical hike that puts you right in there amongst the Flatirons.

The start/finish and the destination are both a kick in the pants. The hike starts at the National Center for Atmospheric Research, on a pretty mesa top above South Boulder. The research complex was designed by I. M. Pei. Well, sort of. The young architect's complete design was not fulfilled due to time and budget constraints. It seems likely that the imposition of capital reality drove Pei up a textured concrete wall, as he was clearly focused on the aesthetics of the Whole. Nothing in Pei's NCAR design is by accident—the angle of buildings in relation to the Flatirons, the color of the concrete, all carefully thought out. To leave the structure unfinished, after all that,

Looking south from NCAR

is kind of like cutting a few feet off Picasso's *Guernica* because it doesn't fit through the museum door.

Nature is the real architect here in South Boulder. The Flatirons, massive chunks of Fountain sandstone that have been torn out of the earth by the uplift of the Rocky Mountains, dominate the scenery. The 300-million-year-old layer of red rock was formed by the complete erosion of a previous mountain range, the so-called Ancestral Rockies. Out on the eastern plains of Colorado, the red Fountain sandstone layer is thousands of feet beneath the surface, and dead flat. Faults and orogeny (mountain building) and a whole lot of time, probably more than a human can truly conceptualize, have busted up the formation, lifted it thousands of feet, turned it on its side, and exposed it to the world. Amazing, isn't it? The Mallory Cave Trail is one of a few routes that lead right up among the massive rocks, for great views and workouts.

"Buried deep in the obscurity of Dinosaur Mountain, and hidden behind a multitude of rock buttresses is this lost cave," wrote Pat Ament of Mallory Cave in his 1967 rock climbing guide *High Over Boulder.*

I. M. Pei's NCAR complex was left unfinished.

The cave has been discovered and forgotten several times over the centuries, no doubt. In 1932 it got its name when a curious and adventurous fellow named Mallory located the discreetly hidden cavern that some lumberjacks had been talking about. Maybe the size of a small house inside, the cave has always been more interesting to bats than spelunkers. Biologists pressed for the closure of the cave, then the final approach to the cave, to protect the resident bat colony.

There are several options for great hikes from the NCAR Trailhead. The Bear Canyon and Fern Canyon Trails can be accessed easily from the Mesa Trail, which crosses this route, opening up some nice loop options or mountain-climbing out-and-backs for more advanced and/or ambitious amblers.

Miles and Directions

0.0 Start from the NCAR Trailhead and begin walking southwest along the NCAR/Walter Orr Roberts Trail.

0.1 Continue straight as another trail comes in from the left. Then continue on the main track as yet another trail intersects on the left. (From here the trail branches off into a few side trails, all of which lead to the same general place.)

0.2 Turn left at a prominent intersection and switchback briefly off the side of the mesa.

0.4 Continue past the water tank and find the trail continuing on the other side of the clearing.

0.5 Turn left at the fork.

Mallory Cave

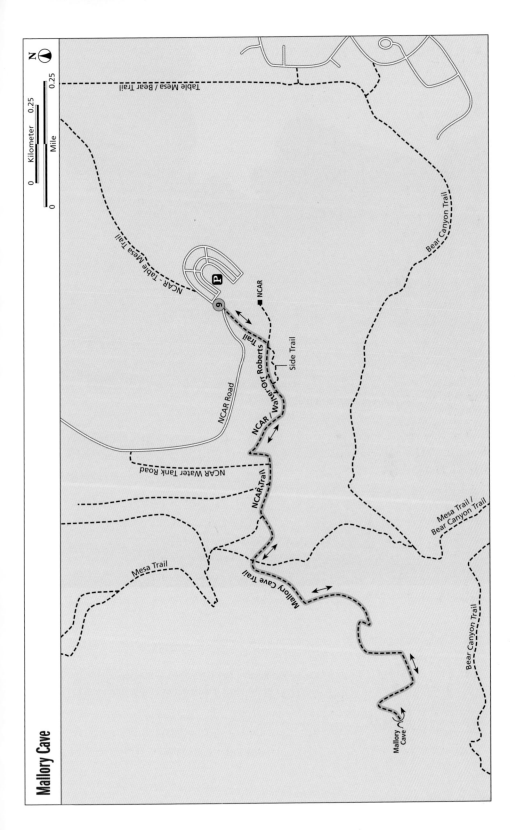

The final approach to Mallory Cave is a serious scramble—but is probably closed off anyway.

0.6 Continue straight through a prominent four-way intersection, crossing the Mesa Trail and starting up the Mallory Cave Trail.

1.1 Arrive at the base of the rock face below Mallory Cave. If it's open to the public, you can scramble up the rock to get a better look at the cave. If closed, this is your turnaround point.

2.2 Arrive back at NCAR.

Pikes Peak

Twenty thousand people climb these stairs each year (hike 10).

10 Devil's Head

Hike uphill to a spectacular location—the granite peak called Devil's Head, crowned with a well-preserved fire lookout tower. Bring the whole family on this exciting mini-adventure into the sky and into the past.

Start: Devil's Head Trailhead off Rampart Range Road
Distance: 2.7 miles out and back
Approximate hiking time: 1 to 2.5 hours
Difficulty: Moderate to strenuous
Trail surface: Wide, gravelly trail with some rocks and lots of step-ups; not steep, but never level
Best season: Fall. Note that Rampart Range Road is closed for the winter from Dec 1 through Mar.
Other trail users: Hikers, runners, dogs, and horses
Canine compatibility: Leashed dogs permitted. Don't take your dog if you want to go up to the lookout, however.
Land status: National forest

Fees and permits: None
Schedule: Sunrise to sunset
Maps: USGS Devil's Head quad; Pike National Forest map, US Forest Service
Trail contact: Pike National Forest, South Platte Ranger District, 19316 Goddard Ranch Ct., Morrison, CO 80465; (303) 275-5610; www.fs.usda.gov/detail/psicc/about-forest/districts/?cid=fsm9_032799
Special considerations: This hike culminates in a long staircase bolted to giant rocks. It's not suitable for dogs, frail individuals, or those who are afraid of heights or suffer from vertigo. Rampart Range Road closes for the winter from Dec 1 to Apr 1, possibly longer if winter conditions persist.

Finding the trailhead: From Denver go south on Santa Fe Boulevard/US 85. At Sedalia turn right onto CO 67. Drive up CO 67/Jarre Canyon Road for roughly 9 miles and turn left onto Rampart Range Road. Rampart Range Road is dirt-surfaced (although it looks like a paved road at the intersection, mind you) and features some gnarly washboard sections and potholes. It works best in a rugged vehicle, but a regular city sedan will be able to handle the journey at subdued speeds. About 8.5 miles south of CO 67, veer left onto the road leading to Devil's Head Trailhead. GPS: N39 16.17' / W105 06.31'

The Hike

This is a special hike, a highly memorable but relatively brief climb (about 1.35 miles one way) through the forest to the top of a massive hunk of Pikes Peak granite known as Devil's Head, the most prominent point on the Front Range between Denver and Colorado Springs. At the top of one of the huge granite lumps is a historic fire lookout station. The final push to the top is dramatic, on a thin stairway bolted into the rock. The views from the lookout are as incredible as the hike itself.

Before there was a lookout tower up here, Devil's Head was a popular hike with the locals. In the 1890s settlers' kids with last names like Nickson and Kinner entertained themselves by making the trip, often on horseback. Today the hike is even

I volunteer to stay here and watch over the area.

more attractive due to the fantastic novelty of the lookout station, and the local population is much, much larger. So some trail overcrowding is inevitable here, mitigated only by the somewhat remote location of the trailhead on Rampart Range Road. The Forest Service reports that almost 20,000 people hike this trail each year.

Thinking of becoming a fire lookout yourself? Sounds awesome to me too! Unfortunately, the fire lookout is a vanishing breed. The Forest Service has been steadily phasing out human lookouts in favor of digital cameras and various types of remote fire detection systems. In the meantime, rampant exurban development and the use of cell phones have made lookouts obsolete in many areas. If there's a fire deep in the mountains, the people who just moved into the subdivision nearby will call it in on their iPhones! And take some video too while they're at it.

There were once almost 10,000 lookout towers around the United States. Most of the old towers have been dismantled, removed, or destroyed. Most of those that remain are unmanned historical relics, operating primarily by remote, like this one. In Colorado—never a big fire lookout state, surprisingly—there are only fourteen stations left in operation, and fewer than half of those are manned. The Devil's Head Lookout, built in 1912, is the last of the original seven Front Range towers to remain in operation. It is now listed in the National Register of Historic Places, a legend in its time.

The climb is significant but not super oppressive—just tough enough to take the starch out of your teenager's attitude and give him or her a true sense of accomplishment. (This is an effective family bonding hike.) Although it by no means could be described as smooth, the trail remains luxuriously wide and moderately sloped, conducive to social hiking. From parking lot to lookout tower: almost 1.4 miles and almost 1,000 feet.

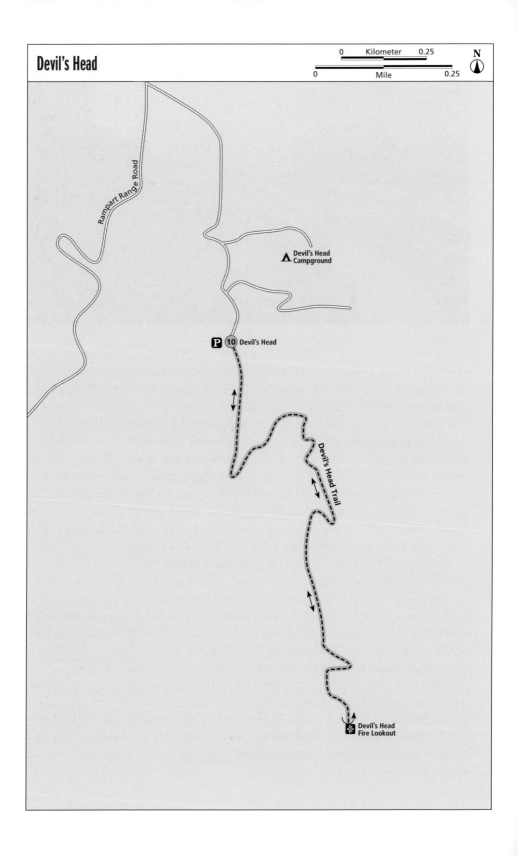

Devil's Head

0   Kilometer   0.25

0   Mile   0.25

N

Rampart Range Road

△ Devil's Head
Campground

P ⑩ Devil's Head

Devil's Head Trail

Devil's Head
Fire Lookout

The view from Devil's Head, looking west

If you get to the lookout, your time up there will be limited. Don't expect to picnic or lounge around. Personally, I could sit and stare out over the foothills for hours from this perch, but that's not really possible here. Only a few people are allowed on the lookout at a time, and there will likely be some folks waiting for you to get on with it. On weekends there is a danger of having to queue up at the bottom of the stairs.

Your biggest foe on this hike is likely to be weather-related. It's hard to imagine a worse place to be in a lightning storm than up on that staircase. Luckily, climbing the stairs doesn't take too long. But don't mess around with it if the thunder is booming. The rest of the route is under the rock towers and not terribly exposed.

Miles and Directions

0.0   Begin hiking up the Devil's Head Trail.
1.3   Reach the lookout after a very cool stair climb. Return the way you came.
2.7   Arrive back at the trailhead.

Tornadoes in the Mountains?

During the summer of 2015, something kind of freaky happened right here at Devil's Head. A tornado touched down and tore up the forest. Colorado is no stranger to this meteorological phenomenon, but our twisters typically have confined themselves to the plains. As the climate changes, we've been seeing mountain tornadoes, which puts an interesting twist on our already intense weather.

11 Manitou Incline

This hike heads directly up a historic incline railway in Manitou Springs—a route so ridiculous that it has become world-famous.

Start: Manitou Incline Trailhead, Ruxton Avenue, Manitou Springs
Distance: 3.6-mile loop
Approximate hiking time: 1.5 to 4 hours
Difficulty: Difficult
Trail surface: Railroad ties, gravel trails
Best season: Year-round
Other trail users: Pedestrians
Canine compatibility: Nope! No pets allowed.
Land status: Pike National Forest, City of Manitou Springs
Fees and permits: None

Schedule: Dawn to dusk
Map: City of Manitou Springs, Mount Manitou Incline vicinity map
Trail contact: City of Manitou Springs; www .manitouspringsgov.com/government/projects/ incline
Special considerations: The traffic and parking situation around the trailhead has been absolutely horrible. It's best to ride a bike to the trailhead or use Manitou's shuttle system. *Note:* The Incline may be closed to the public during the weekend of the Pikes Peak Marathon.

Finding the trailhead: From Colorado Springs go west on US 24 to Manitou Springs and exit onto Manitou Avenue, continuing westbound. Go almost all the way through Manitou Springs; then turn left onto Ruxton Avenue at a traffic circle. Take Ruxton past the Pikes Peak Cog Railway station; then turn right onto Hydro Street. Drive 1 block on Hydro Street and park in the Barr Trailhead parking lot (fee). Alternately, park in the Cog Railway parking lot (if available) or in the parking lot below the Iron Springs Chateau. These lots will also cost some money. Better still, ride a bike or park in Manitou and use Manitou's free shuttle system, which sends short buses up Ruxton Avenue on a regular basis. GPS: N38 51.41' / W104 55.93'

The Hike

I didn't know that there was a zoo in Manitou Springs! Holy mackerel.

To say this is a busy hike doesn't really do it justice. More like a communal hike. As if there was some kind of extravagantly hatted holy man with a healing touch or free smoothie coupons waiting at the top of the mountain.

There were easily hundreds of other people struggling with me on the Incline (and struggling with me to find parking beforehand). Of course, I had to try it for the first time on Labor Day, maybe the busiest day of the year. I'm sure it's not so packed most days.

Anyway, I was shocked at how many people were up here, Labor Day or not. For an old west-side townie like myself, who remembers when the Barr Trailhead parking lot seemed annoyingly busy with five or six cars in it, the crowding was difficult to process. Is this the geometric progression of global population that my eleventh-grade biology teacher warned us about? I was listening, Mr. Heckle!

You might literally run into someone you know on this unique hike.

As insanely busy as it was, the procession . . . proceeded. From the crawl of cars looking for parking spots to the lines of pilgrims trudging up the massive railroad-tie staircase, no major clogs were evident. Movement up the Incline was restricted only by our physical limitations.

On the way down, however, I did find the Barr Trail becoming clogged to a certain degree, which was a totally foreign experience to me. I noticed lots of runners and hikers, including myself, getting bottled up behind others, and some long lines were formed—generally not what we look for in a hike. People filed off the top of the mountain like concertgoers leaving a stadium. My wife tells me this is what it's like to attempt hiking in Japan.

That kind of crowding is exactly what the nineteenth-century developers of Manitou and Colorado Springs dreamed of. Interestingly, the promoters' strategies for attracting big numbers to their resorts always focused on transportation. Stage lines and railroads, then auto roads, were seen as key to any tourist attraction. They spent more energy developing easy access to the resorts than they did on the resorts themselves. (In the case of General Palmer, his development of Colorado Springs was meant to benefit his railroad, rather than the railroad being built to benefit the resort.) For these nineteenth-century promoters, comfort was the name of the game. The Manitou Incline's career as a tourist hauler grew out of this tradition, a machine meant to give people the mountain experience and mountain views without mountain exertion.

Guys like William Jackson Palmer and John Brisben Walker would probably be floored to learn that tourists are seeking out such increasingly physical, non-motorized experiences. General Palmer, who had recreational trails built through the mountains above Colorado Springs, envisioned wealthy users trotting along on horseback, as he did. He'd be flabbergasted to see people running among the ponderosa pines like does. Walker built an incline railway to haul pleasure-seekers to a lodge on Mount Morrison. He'd be amazed that a similar incline railway that used to transport tourists to a mountaintop is now, in its skeletal afterlife, crawling with far more tourists than it ever saw in its funicular heyday.

It's an impressive turnaround. Very much for the better, I would argue.

The Incline was built in 1906–7 to facilitate the construction of a pipeline to a hydroelectric plant. The tourist value was obvious, and soon it was converted to a semi-famous attraction. It was never hugely popular, but the cable-pulled trams ran more or less continuously until 1990, when a mudslide compromised the railway bed enough to cause the final shutdown. The original wooden 1906 railcars were used for 72 years before they were replaced with aluminum cars in 1978.

I got to ride the Manitou Incline at least once when I was a kid. I remember the top of the mountain, where there was a concession stand and picnic area (the structure I remember was built in 1958) and lots of hungry little chipmunks darting around. But I most remember the downhill trip. As the cars approached the steepest portion of the descent, it looked like the little train was going over a cliff. All I could see was air, and Colorado Springs far below. "Don't worry," the train operator/tour guide said over his loudspeaker, "if the cable breaks, there are two giant springs at the bottom that will slow us down . . . Manitou Springs and Colorado Springs." I'm sure they used that on every trip.

Hikers and runners—"fitness nuts"—started using the Incline soon after the shutdown. As the challenge became more popular, conflict arose with the Cog Railway people down on Ruxton Avenue. Parking-related conflict, primarily. For a long time Incline users were trespassers. At times nobody seemed to care, and other times there were crackdowns on illicit use. But in recent years everybody seems to have come together in the name of public space and recreation—as they are known to do, somewhat paradoxically, in this government-phobic locale—and the Incline challenge is now a legal, officially sanctioned, funded, and promoted rite of passage. Some private parties are making bank on the parking crunch, and the Incline has even been shored up and repaired for the expected throngs, using public funds.

Manitou Incline

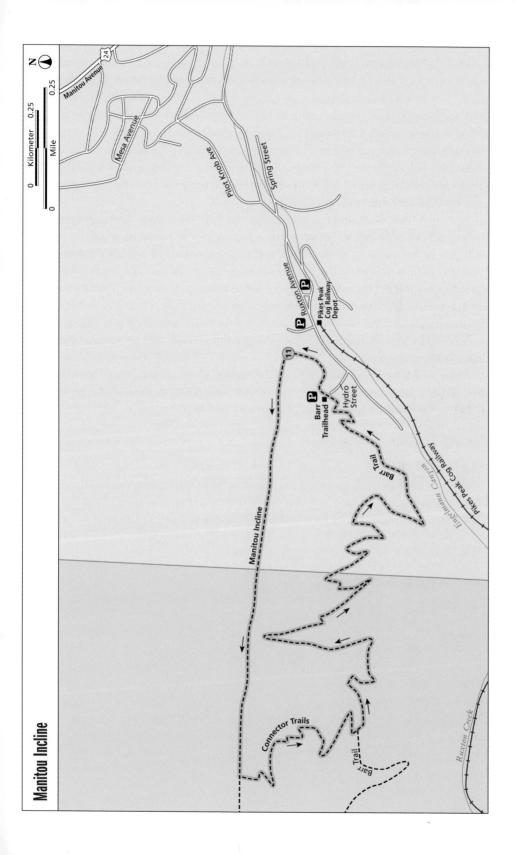

How hard is hiking up the Incline? Well, it's kind of ridiculous, then it gets nuts, then it eases back to ridiculous briefly, then it gets nuts again, and then you're at the top. It's a relatively intense battle with gravity. It will get your heart beating like a punk rock song and make your legs feel like lead zeppelins. It will make you sweat ... so much. But it doesn't last all day. Those in really good shape can probably power up the thing in 30 minutes. The rest of us should probably allot a full hour for the ascent. Some folks will battle for a few hours up there, gasping for breath at each platform, searching deep inside for a little more strength to continue the journey, one step at a time. And the downhill isn't necessarily restful.

Note that there is a bailout connection to the Barr Trail about three-quarters of the way up. But once you've come that far, you may as well just finish it out.

Many people come up here in their trail running shoes, but one does not really "run" the Incline. Certainly there is a wide range of speeds and abilities on display, but the steps are really too tall and steep for actual running. At its steepest the Incline's ties may even require some use of the hands, a bit of scrambling. Having long legs can be a big advantage here. The runners stomp up the ties as best they can, then glide down the gravelly trail, putting their shoes to good use—until they get caught behind slower hikers anyway.

If you have a hankerin' to walk down the Incline, it's an option. People have been doing it for a long time. Hikers are discouraged from doing so these days—because it's hard—but there are no actual rules against it.

Miles and Directions

0.0 Start from the bottom of the Incline, and, well, you know what to do.

0.8 Top of the Incline! Take a sharp left and head down the trail that leads to Barr Trail. (There may or may not be a sign.) It's all downhill from here.

3.4 Reach the bottom, popping out at the Barr Trailhead. Not quite home yet; continue through the parking lot and find the trail leading toward the bottom of the Incline.

3.6 Arrive back at the bottom of the Incline. One more time?

12 Red Rock Canyon

Tour the "Secret Garden of the Gods" on this loop around Red Rock Canyon Park, just west of Colorado Springs. The centerpiece of the hike is a historic quarry. The trail goes right through it, then past the site of a very unusual home as it winds through this rugged and unique parcel of public land.

Start: East parking lot, Red Rock Canyon Open Space (on 31st Street)
Distance: 5.1-mile lariat loop
Approximate hiking time: 2 to 3 hours
Difficulty: Moderate
Trail surface: Varies from wide dirt road–like trails to tight, winding singletrack; lots of up and down
Best seasons: Spring and fall
Other trail users: Hikers, runners, bikers, and dogs
Canine compatibility: Leashed dogs permitted
Land status: City of Colorado Springs Open Space
Fees and permits: None

Schedule: 5 a.m. to 11 p.m. May through Oct; 5 a.m. to 9 p.m. Nov through Apr
Map: Red Rock Canyon Open Space trail map, City of Colorado Springs
Trail contacts: Friends of Red Rock Canyon Open Space; redrockcanyonopenspace.org. City of Colorado Springs, Parks, Recreation, & Cultural Services; https://parks.colorado springs.gov/explore-play/explore/open -spaces/red-rock-canyon-open-space.
Special considerations: The route through the quarry has some steep steps. Route-finding can be annoyingly confusing in the park. Watch for rattlesnakes.

Finding the trailhead: From central Colorado Springs drive west on US 24/Cimarron Expressway to 31st Street. Take a left (south) on 31st Street. (**Note:** The main trailhead/parking for Red Rock Canyon Park is on the north side of the park, off US 24.) GPS: N38 50.88' / W104 52.40'

The Hike

Since the gold rush days, Red Rock Canyon and the land around it was continuously held by private owners. Few knew what it was like beyond the KEEP OUT signs, although we could guess it was interesting.

Of course, out-of-state developers with bottomless pockets had their eyes on the prize—same old story. They wanted to put wide suburban roads, estate homes, hotels, and a golf course in Red Rock Canyon. The developers' plans were positively humble compared to the futuristic city that the owners, shotgun-toting John Bock Jr. and his brother Richard, envisioned. The Bocks had never displayed much preference for preserving natural beauty over paving it, according to Ruth Obee, author of the definitive history of Red Rock Canyon. It was plain to see that Bock had sought to use his land in any way possible, including leasing a substantial portion of it to be used as a trash dump.

The out-of-state developers declined their option to buy, maybe after reconsidering the unknowable liability contained in the landfill, or simply because of the growing grassroots opposition to their plans. Meanwhile the hardheaded John Bock Jr. died in 2002. The community coalitions that had been sparked into existence by the prospect of mega-development, and their allied government agencies, moved to pounce on the loose ball. Crucially, the people of Colorado Springs—the notoriously stingy and conservative people of Colorado Springs, mind you—voted just in time to extend a tax to fund open spaces, parks, and trails. Thus Red Rock Canyon was saved from further development, at least for the time being.

When the 789-acre Red Rock Canyon Open Space was finally opened to the public in 2003, it wasn't exciting just for the local hikers and mountain bikers. Geologists, archaeologists, and historians had also been itching to get in there.

A geological survey of the "Secret Garden of the Gods" confirmed that the city's new property contained one of the most impressive records of the earth's history to be found anywhere. Two hundred and thirty million years worth of unfaulted stratification is on display here, much of it thrusting dramatically out of the ground, in what geologists call "fins," after the whole layer cake was turned 70 to 90 degrees on its side as a result of the uplift of the Rocky Mountains. In a more orderly world, we would never see these layers. They would have remained flat and buried far beneath the surface.

From east to west the twisted and exposed layers are arrayed from youngest to oldest. The oldest rocks within the boundaries of the original Red Rock Canyon Open Space are outcroppings of the Fountain Formation, probably the most enthusiastically exhibitionist of the Front Range sandstones. (Since the area of Red Rock Canyon Open Space was doubled by subsequent acquisitions after 2009, technically the oldest rocks in the park today are Pikes Peak granite.) The Fountain Formation, deposited about 300 million years ago by streams that eroded the ancestral Rockies flat, is about 700 meters thick on the west side of the park, busting out in some impressive mud-red fins.

"Due to the high energy streams at the time of deposition, fossils are rare in the upper 700 m of the Fountain formation in RRCOS," notes geologist Sharon Milito. Next to the Fountain is the younger Lyons sandstone, consisting of wind-blown dunes. The Lyons sandstone of Red Rock Canyon, forming the most prominent ridge in the park, was even more devoid of fossils than the neighboring Fountain Formation.

The east side of the open space, however, proved to be a hot zone for fossils. In the Morrison Formation dinosaur bones were found. Farther east, in the Dakota sandstone, were dinosaur tracks, as well as leaf and tree impressions and ripple marks. In the Benton Shale, shark teeth, ammonites, and pelecypods (clams). The precise locations of the fossils, especially the dinosaur tracks, have been kept deliberately unpublished for obvious reasons.

No archaeological survey in this area would be fruitless, but a survey of Red Rock Canyon Open Space may have been a little disappointing. Considering the proven archaeological richness of the surrounding area, with evidence of prehistoric people

The view from the top: Pikes Peak, the Manitou Incline, and old cuts in the sandstone.

all over the Front Range and Pikes Peak region, the survey team was doubtless hoping for more. But archaeologists have just scratched the surface here so far, and we could very well hear of blockbuster finds in the future.

There was only one prehistoric site identified in the initial survey at Red Rock Canyon, a "lithic scatter" on the Dakota sandstone ridge overlooking the landfill—a smattering of flakes and tools suggesting a prehistoric campsite. Ruth Obee, in *History in Stone: The Story of Red Rock Canyon*, tells us exactly what was found there: "The scatter . . . includes a tan ortho-quartzite core with one piece of angular debris and one flake. The site also revealed one broken, salmon-colored chert biface (which is defined by Snyder [the author of the survey report] as being 'a flaked stone artifact exhibiting evidence of facial thinning on both dorsal and ventral faces'), one chert-tested cobble (a rounded rock with percussive marks testing it for chert), and one Black Forest petrified wood flake."

In addition to this telling debris, the archaeologists also documented previous finds of projectile points that seemed to be very old. And after the survey was completed, the vestiges of a possible prehistoric stone structure were found not far from the lithic scatter. The many prehistoric sites at nearby Garden of the Gods also strongly suggest that prehistoric people were present in Red Rock Canyon as well.

The evidence of Ute habitation here was clearer. It was long documented that there were apparent stone battlements (round mini forts and walls) built by the Utes on top of the Dakota hogback within the open space. The exact purpose of these structures was unknown. Perhaps the simplest explanation is correct, that these were defensive structures guarding the Ute camps among the rocks from attack by their historic enemies, the Arapaho and Cheyenne. From the hogback a sentry would be able to communicate ample warning in case war parties were approaching. Maybe the structures protected the sacred springs at Manitou or the trail up Ute Pass. Others think these were "drift fences" and hunting blinds—prey would be herded along the wall, on the other side of which the hunter crouched, waiting for an easy kill. Still others, Ute descendants among them, suggest the round "forts" may have actually been eagle traps (!).

The archaeological survey also revealed metates and a mano on the busy Dakota ridge, also thought to be of Ute origin. Some of the metates, stones shaped with bowl- or trough-like impressions in which to grind corn or other materials, were portable, while others were carved right into the Dakota outcropping, as if the users were standing there grinding and serving as lookouts at the same time.

As usual, the precise locations of these finds have not been publicized. But obviously a lot of this stuff is located on the prominent light-colored Dakota sandstone hogback toward the east end of the open space. The route described in this chapter doesn't go up there, but it's easy to find social trails that do. If you freelance up that direction, don't touch anything; pretend it's a big outdoor museum.

This hike starts in a not-so-promising fashion. Rising from a somewhat bland-looking trailhead tucked away in one of the least glamorous corners of the city (the east trailhead instead of the main trailhead on the north side), the route follows a dirt road up and over a rocky hogback scarred by human enterprise.

Slowly and steadily the wonders of the place start to reveal themselves. Within a mile or so, hikers will be gazing across a shallow canyon—Red Rock Canyon—to a huge gorgeous ridge of red rock, very much like the rocks that made Garden of the Gods famous. This is that nice hunk of Lyons sandstone, the particular focus of quarry operations in the vicinity during the time when red stone was a popular building material. This beautiful red hunk of rock, the hardened remains of a 250-million-year-old windblown dune tipped up on its side, was especially uniform, and especially valuable.

Go around another corner, and a dramatic-looking quarry cut comes into view. We'll be right in there before too long, but first, the Dump.

Our route takes us directly across the grassy cover of a not-so-old landfill. From 1970 to 1986 a great deal of Colorado Springs' trash ended up here. In addition to commercial waste management companies using the landfill, Springs residents would haul their discarded appliances and weed killers and anything else they didn't want to put in their regular trash to this gorgeous valley hidden behind the hogback. John Bock Jr. hoped to fill up the valley with garbage so a golf course could be built on top of it. Ironically, the presence of the dump is probably what torpedoed his plans to cash in on developing the property.

In 1986 the dump was "decommissioned" and topped with clay. Today there is little other than a big green grassy scar and some methane vents to suggest that anything funky was going on here. Time heals all wounds, and covers all smells.

After crossing the Dump, take a left and continue up the valley to the Roundup Trail, a delightful singletrack twisting among the rocks, gambel oak, and ponderosa pine. Emerging on the other end of the Roundup Trail, you see trails going this way and that. It's certainly not the easiest route to follow, unfortunately. The confusion is compounded by the fact that someone has written false directions with a sharpie marker on the signposts here. You might see the abbreviation *qry* with an arrow below it. In 2015 these arrows were pointed the wrong direction, so beware.

The correct route continues north and begins angling to the east. Don't start walking down the hikers-only Contemplative Trail, as inviting as it may be (a great walk for another day). You want the trail labeled "quarry pass trail." This trail climbs ruggedly out of a draw and then enters the quarry cut itself. It's a fun little section.

There were actually several quarries here. In the 1860s, the early days of large-scale Euro-American exploitation of the area, small outfits worked sections of the hogbacks with simple tools to extract sandstone and limestone. Scars from these early operations are still visible here and there. Later on, in the 1880s, much more industrialized efforts came on line, using small armies of men, steam power, explosives, funicular trams, and cranes ("derricks") to swing huge blocks onto wagons and rail cars. The Midland Railway ran a spur up the canyon. The Kenmuir Quarry, the centerpiece of this hike, was the biggest and most successful operation, but there were two other serious sandstone quarries in Red Rock Canyon.

The Kenmuir Quarry chugged along from the mid-1880s until it died out before World War I, at which point building trends had moved on from cut stone to more economical brick construction. The proudest structures produced from Kenmuir sandstone are mansions in Denver's Capitol Hill neighborhood. Many were destroyed to make way for modern buildings, but there are still a few up there—the Croke-Patterson Mansion, for instance.

It's not clear why the Greenlee brothers, who owned the quarry and the land around it, called their quarry Kenmuir. Kenmuir is a place in England, apparently, so it seems most likely that the name was an homage to somebody's old home. It was also the name of a character in a novel published in 1872. The character named Kenmuir was a thinly veiled John Muir. It is admittedly unlikely, but perhaps the Greenlees were channeling some environmentalist energy when they chose the name. Maybe they felt somewhat guilty about creating this huge notch in the rock in such a beautiful place. Okay, that's a stretch.

Kenmuir Quarry

Climbing down from the quarry on the other side, the tour continues down Red Rock Canyon itself. Soon you arrive at the site of John Bock's house, now featuring an open-air pavilion. The remarkable stone structure (Lyons sandstone from Red Rock Canyon, of course) and surrounding rock spires were mirrored in a gorgeous little lake that Bock created for aesthetic purposes.

Continue toward the main parking area; then cut to the right up the hill to continue the loop. As you wind down the hike, watch for the foundations of buildings that used to be part of a big gold mill, actually two separate mills that joined into one. The Standard Mill at the base of the hogback, and any other gold mill in the area, went bust when the bigger and more modern Golden Cycle Mill opened east of here, not far from the Midland roundhouse (another structure made out of rock quarried here). The Golden Cycle Mill's cyanide reduction operation produced a massive tailings pile. Toxic though it was, and remains, the artificial hill is being developed like crazy.

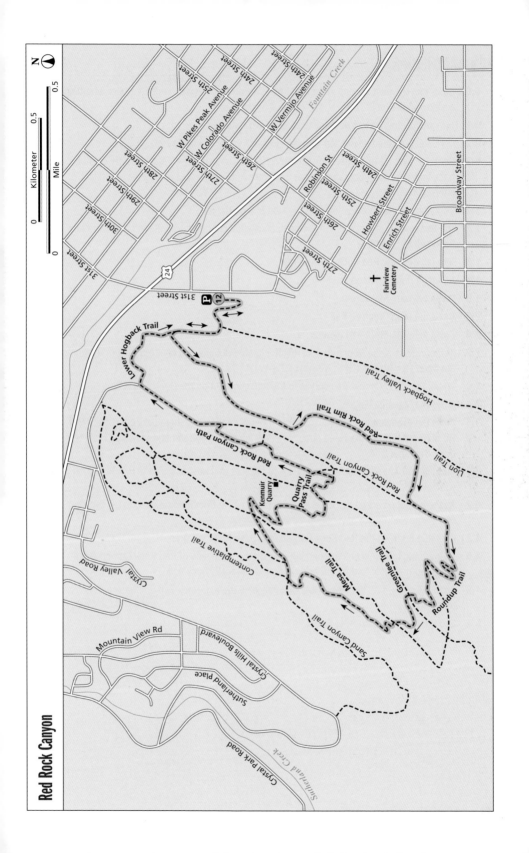

Red Rock Canyon

Miles and Directions

0.0 Start from the east parking lot of Red Rock Canyon Open Space, on 31st Street, and begin walking up the trail.

0.1 Turn sharply to the right as the trail joins an old road.

0.2 Continue past the intersection with the Hogback Valley Trail on the left.

0.3 Continue past a trail intersection on the right (the Lower Hogback Trail—we'll be coming back that way later). Continue on the Red Rock Rim Trail past several faded, unofficial intersections.

1.1 Continue past an intersection with the Lion Trail on the left.

1.3 The Red Rock Rim Trail dives to the right, across the old landfill, as the old access road heads off to the left.

1.5 Turn left onto the Red Rock Canyon Trail.

1.6 Turn right onto the Roundup Trail.

1.9 Cross the wide Mesa Trail.

2.2 Cross the wide Greenlee Trail.

2.4 Cross the wide Mesa Trail again.

2.9 At the bottom of the Roundup Trail, reach a jumble of trails and connectors. Turn right onto the Sand Canyon Trail (GPS: N38 50.72' / W104 53.32').

3.0 Where the Sand Canyon Trail curves to the left, stay right on the Quarry Pass Trail.

3.1 Cross the Mesa Trail again.

3.6 Cross the Greenlee Trail again. From here the trail heads up to the quarry cut (GPS: N38 50.65' / W104 53.00'). Head straight across the quarry cut and find the steps leading down the other side.

3.7 Turn left onto the Red Rock Canyon Path (a skinnier trail west of the wide Red Rock Canyon Trail).

4.2 As the trail approaches the water and the place where Bock's home used to be, zag right over to the Red Rock Canyon Trail.

4.2 Continue north on the Red Rock Canyon Trail, past the picnic area.

4.5 As the path/road reaches the parking area on the north side of Red Rock Canyon Open Space, turn sharply to the right and up on the Lower Hogback Trail.

4.8 Continue straight as the Lower Hogback Trail joins the Red Rock Rim Trail back to the trailhead.

5.1 End the hike on South 31st Street.

13 Palmer Trail-Section 16

This route includes a pleasant cruise on a trail that was constructed as a present from William Palmer to his wife, Queen, so she would have a nice place to ride her horses.

Start: Bear Creek Canyon, at the bottom of the High Drive
Distance: 5.4-mile loop
Approximate hiking time: 2 to 4 hours
Difficulty: Moderate to difficult
Trail surface: Palmer Trail is gravelly and loose but gently sloped on the way up; the back side of the loop (Section 16) is rugged, rocky, and steep.
Best seasons: Spring and fall
Other trail users: Hikers, runners, bikers, and dogs
Canine compatibility: Dogs allowed; must be on leash at all times

Land Status: City of Colorado Springs, Pike National Forest
Fees and permits: None
Schedule: None
Map: *Pikes Peak Atlas*
Trail contact: City of Colorado Springs
Special considerations: This route includes a long, rugged, and steep walk-down on the Palmer-Red Rock Trail through Section 16. Many hikers prefer the counterclockwise version of this loop. Others prefer to avoid the steep section altogether by doing an out-and-back on the Palmer Trail.

Finding the trailhead: From central Colorado Springs drive west on US 24/Cimarron Expressway to 21st Street. Take a left (south) on 21st Street to the top of the hill and turn right (west) on Lower Gold Camp Road. Turn left (south) onto Bear Creek Road. Drive up Bear Creek Road to the very end, where the High Drive emerges. Park in the small lot by the caretaker's house or in one of the small lots next to Bear Creek Road. Begin the hike by walking up the High Drive, closed to motor vehicles. GPS: N38 49.19' / W104 53.54'

The Hike

No history of Colorado's Great White Men would be complete without a chapter on General William Jackson Palmer. Unfortunately for him and us, his very compelling wife, Queen, did not stick around long enough to steal the show.

General Palmer started his post–Civil War career as treasurer of the Kansas Pacific Railroad, which completed a line to Denver in 1870 but failed to secure funding to build the road west along the southern route that Palmer recommended. Palmer left the Kansas Pacific to start his own railroad, hoping to sweep up what he believed was a prime opportunity that had been left on the table.

Palmer envisioned a north-south railroad between Denver and El Paso, with multiple spurs to serve the mines, quarries, sawmills, and agricultural centers. Because the spurs would traverse very rugged terrain to reach the mining communities, the road would be narrow-gauge, 3 feet between rails.

The shadowy figure in this photo is actually just two trees. That's what I tell myself.

With the Plains tribes decimated and the Utes being pushed out of the way, mineral and petroleum extraction opportunities seemed to be expanding at an exponential rate. The planets were aligned for people like Palmer. "A population engaged in mining is by far the most profitable of any to a railway," Palmer wrote to his would-be investors. "A hundred miners, from their wandering habits and many wants"—fuel, lumber, food, equipment, transport for workers, as well as ore—"are better customers than four times that number otherwise employed."

But Palmer would go far beyond just servicing the mines. Part and parcel of Palmer's scheme was the development of Colorado Springs. In 1870 the land east of Colorado City (the original Euro-American settlement that was established along Fountain Creek around 1860, during the Pikes Peak gold rush) was a barren, treeless plain. Palmer envisioned a sort of "Newport in the Rockies" with wide avenues and giant mansions near a grand depot for his Denver & Rio Grande.

General Palmer persuaded his wealthy and influential Colorado friends A. C. Hunt, Irving Howbert, and F. Z. Salomon to go in on the deal. (Hunt was the former territorial governor of Colorado, not a bad connection.) The first order of business was to create a dummy railroad, in order to keep the land—and the idea itself—tied up until Palmer could finalize his plan. They also bought up as much of the valuable land along the Front Range as they could, acquiring big blocks as quietly and quickly as possible. A measure of secrecy was critical to their business plan. The less people knew about the impending railroad, the easier and cheaper the land would be to acquire. This would give the railroad control of the resources it needed to operate, and give the new landowners huge profits if the land were ever liquidated. This was especially true for the land that would become Colorado Springs, which Palmer and friends acquired for 80 cents per acre.

Palmer sought investors back East and in Europe and found takers with deep pockets. The Denver & Rio Grande was capitalized with $2.5 million in October 1870. The federal government granted the railroad a 200-foot right-of-way along its entire proposed length, and 20-acre blocks every 10 miles for depots, quite a cherry on top.

As the D & RG was coming into its existence with a silver spoon in its mouth, Palmer married Queen Mellen. Not a real queen, but a cool name nonetheless, actually a nickname given to her at a young age by her father. Mary Lincoln Mellen was her real name.

Queen was the 19-year-old daughter of a key Palmer associate, William Mellen, one of the railroad's most important financiers. William Mellen was also on the railroad's board of directors. It was a very cozy enterprise all around.

In 1871 General Palmer's new railroad was laying track at a feverish rate south from Denver. The tracks reached Colorado Springs—or the place that would soon be Colorado Springs—in October of that year. The Colorado Springs Company's promotional literature was a huge success, and the people started to stream in. The spiel really hit the mark in England, and soon the burgeoning settlement of mini-mansions was known as "Little London."

All was going swimmingly with the D & RG until it began to move south of Colorado Springs. For months the directors refused to disclose any specific plans. The railroad demanded a high price from the people in Pueblo and Cañon City to bring the tracks to their towns, and in the resulting deals the communities felt strongly that they had been had by Palmer and associates. "Duplicitous" was a word commonly used to describe the railroad's dealings at the time.

"One thing I feel certain of," Palmer had written to his soon-to-be bride Queen, "that amidst all the hot competition of this American business life there is a great temptation to be a little unscrupulous." Or a lot unscrupulous.

Not surprisingly, among the people of Colorado Springs, the city that he founded, and the recipient of many large and valuable tracts that he had acquired, Palmer's legacy was and still is presented in a much more positive light.

Queen Palmer opened the first public school in Colorado Springs in 1871 and showed every sign of becoming the real queen of the city in those early days, a true

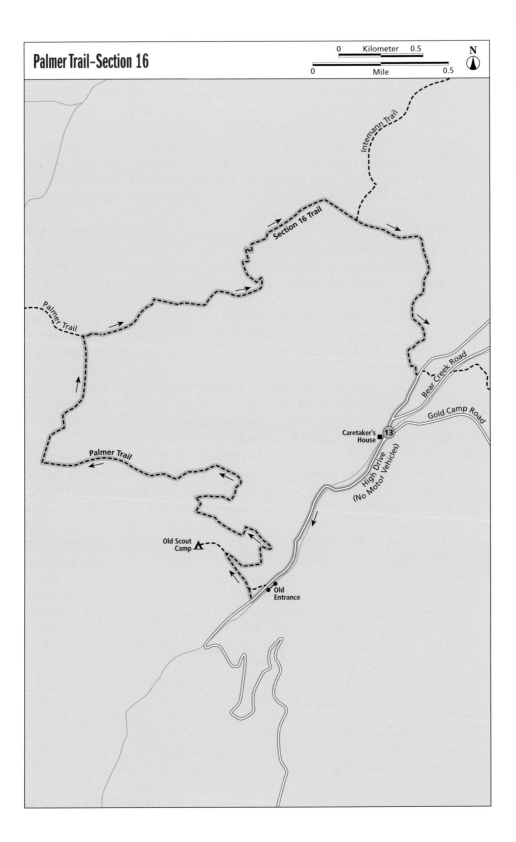

Palmer Trail-Section 16

0   Kilometer   0.5

0   Mile   0.5

N

Intemann Trail

Section 16 Trail

Palmer Trail

Palmer Trail

Bear Creek Road

Gold Camp Road

Caretaker's House

13

High Drive (No Motor Vehicles)

Old Scout Camp

Old Entrance

QUEEN PALMER

Queen Palmer, we wish you could have stayed longer WIKIMEDIA

beacon of enlightened civic leadership. Unfortunately, her stay in the Springs was limited to 9 years. She had serious heart issues, and her doctor recommended that she live at sea level to prolong her life. Queen had her first heart attack at 30, in Colorado, and died from her heart condition in 1894, at age 44, while living in England.

Palmer built a large manor house for his Queen, north of Garden of the Gods, at a place she called Glen Eyrie. But it wasn't enough to keep her around, and she hardly stepped foot in it. Later he replaced the house with a 60-plus-room stone castle. It's an amazing bachelor pad, currently owned and operated as a conference center by the neo-Christian group the Navigators. (There's a great trail behind Glen Eyrie, in Queen's Canyon, but it's closed to the public.)

Now for some Real Talk. The out-and-back to this spot is arguably a better hike than the Section 16 loop described here. Well, it's a toss-up. So if you're not feelin' the upcoming ragged descent, turn around and cruise back in contouring luxury, like Queen Palmer on her finest mount, as imagined by her husband. Another option that some like better than what I describe is a counterclockwise loop, beginning with the Section 16 slog and ending with the gentle descent on Palmer Trail to the High Drive. It's a privilege just to be up here, no matter which way you go.

Miles and Directions

0.0   Start hiking up High Drive from the bottom.

0.7   Turn right onto the Palmer Trail (GPS: N38 48.73' / W104 54.04').

0.9   Stay on the Palmer Trail as it turns 180 degrees to the right. (**Option:** Straight ahead on the half trail are the ruins of an old Boy Scout camp.)

2.9   Keep right as the Palmer Trail heads off toward Crystal Park.

3.5   Section 16 Trail dives down the mountain, a real blister-maker.

4.1   Stay on the main trail here and until you reach the trailhead.

4.2   Pass the intersection with the Intemann Trail (GPS: N38 49.80' / W104 53.63').

5.0   Pop out on Lower Gold Camp Road. Turn right and walk down the road briefly toward the bottom of High Drive.

5.4   Arrive back where you started.

14 Captain Jack's

Crunch through Pikes Peak gravel on this pleasant but crowded old route above Colorado Springs, and visit the former domain of an eccentric woman with a confusing name.

Start: Gold Camp Trailhead at the top of North Cheyenne Canyon
Distance: 3.7-mile loop
Approximate hiking time: 1.5 to 3 hours
Difficulty: Moderate
Trail surface: Gravelly singletrack trail and moderately rutted dirt roads; a few steep sections
Best season: Fall
Other trail users: Bikers, runners, and dogs; motorcycles possible on the Buckhorn Trail and High Drive
Canine compatibility: Leashed dogs permitted. Beware of speeding mountain bikers coming around blind curves.

Land Status: Pike National Forest, North Cheyenne Cañon Park
Fees and permits: None
Schedule: None
Map: North Cheyenne Cañon and Stratton Open Space map, City of Colorado Springs, Parks, Recreation, & Cultural Services
Trail contact: Starsmore Discovery Center, 2120 S. Cheyenne Cañon Rd., Colorado Springs, CO 80906; (719) 385-6086; https://parks.coloradosprings.gov/starsmore

Finding the trailhead: From Colorado Springs go west on Cheyenne Mountain Boulevard and up North Cheyenne Canyon to the very top. Park in the large dirt parking area at the intersection of High Drive, North Cheyenne Canyon Road, and Gold Camp Road. GPS: N38 47.44' / W104 54.24'

The Hike

Wow, you wonder, as you arrive at the parking area to start this hike, is there a new Walmart up here?

Sure, it's a disturbingly large and busy parking lot, which has grown like a fatty tumor. But here we are, doing our part to make it even busier. I recommend hitting this area on weekdays if possible. The same goes for all Front Range hikes.

The first portion of this route, on old Gold Camp Road, follows the abandoned railroad route that once connected Colorado Springs mills and Cripple Creek mines. Our loop leaves Gold Camp before the road (closed to automobiles) crosses Cheyenne Creek at the turn of the canyon, but if you're a railroad buff or fascinated by crumbling infrastructure, keep walking up Gold Camp to see the abandoned and collapsing Tunnel #3. A trail crosses over the top of the old tunnel and connects to the Saint Mary's Falls Trail. Hikers and bikers can continue on the Gold Camp rail route all the way to Old Stage Road, passing through other spooky old tunnels along the way.

Views get better and better as you climb Buckhorn Cutoff, a trail sometimes called Captain Jack's or Palmer Trail. The best viewpoint of the whole route is near

Near the top of Mount Buckhorn

mile 2.1, where the Buckhorn Trail hits an outcropping below the top of Mount Buckhorn. A good yodeling platform. I don't yodel, personally, but for those who do, this would be prime yodeling right here.

Then the trail descends smartly off the back down to High Drive, the historic wagon road. It was here, where the trail hits the road, that Ellen Elliot Jack, aka Captain Jack, set up a few cabins on her land. (**Note:** The Cap'n Jack Trail, as it is listed on some maps, continues from here, contouring around Mays Peak and then dropping onto Gold Camp Road near Tunnel #1. It's a nice stretch of trail to hike, but leaves you on the road. There is no easy way to loop it from there via trail. There is a new connector to the Columbine Trail beginning right across Gold Camp Road from the bottom of Captain Jack's, which is great, but the Columbine Trail deposits you on North Cheyenne Canyon Road well below the trailhead, meaning you have to walk on the side of the road or finagle your way through the woods on unsanctioned old tracks to get back to the start.)

Ellen Elliot was born in England in 1842. On a steamship returning from a trip to the United States, the ship's first mate fell in love with her. A certain Mr. Jack. She married him and returned with him to the States, settling on the East Coast.

The fairy-tale family soon descended into despair. In addition to enduring the death of her husband, Captain Jack, Ellen lost three of her four children to unnamed illnesses. Each of the deceased channeled some previously dead loved ones before their deaths, and each spoke to her from the great beyond after they were dead, according to her memoir *The Fate of a Fairy*, a nicely written, fascinating, and very strange memoir, full of death and supernatural omens. Taken at face value, her story is deeply sad and full of amazing adventures, as well as spiritual encounters. While it does seem quite far-fetched at times, the account is also detailed enough to exude authenticity.

When her husband died, Ellen opened a hotel in Brooklyn. She put many tens of thousands of dollars into the hotel, and it was popular and successful. But one day the

Escape from the Bon Ton Hotel: Did This Really Happen?

Ellen Jack, from her memoir *Fate of a Fairy*:

Coming back, driving through the park, I saw a big fire and thought it was the car stables. I met a park policeman and asked him where the fire was, when he told me it was the Bon Ton. That was the name of my hotel.

I whipped my horses, and they, being spirited animals, went full speed. When I got there I asked for my children and was told they were in the burning building and that the firemen could not find the room they were in. There was a second-story balcony. I asked a tall man to help me to get up on the balcony. He gave me a hoist. I got on his shoulder and made a jump, catching the railing, and pulled myself up and got into the hall. The smoke drove me back. I tore off a piece of my dress and tied it over my face, so that the fire would not burn my face, and crept on my hands and knees along the hall, counting the door jams as I would feel them with my hands, until I came to their room, which was locked. I braced my feet against the other side of the hall and with a desperate push with my shoulders I burst open the door. I then rushed to the window and found that I could not open it. I put my foot through it and broke the sash. Then I went back to the bed and got hold of the nurse girl. She would not move. I took her out of bed, dragged her through the window and threw her over the balcony. She was caught below. I went back and got my two children and took them out on the balcony, and by this time the people had got a cloth for me to drop them in. I dropped Jenny first and then Daisy, and they were caught without injury. Instead of dropping, I got on top of the railing and jumped. I got on top of the railing and jumped into the air. I had become excited as the people were hollering for me to jump; that the roof was going. I broke two ribs and my ankle. I did not jump too soon, for as I made the leap the roof went in with a crash, and they barely saved me from the flames.

hotel caught fire while she was running some errands and was destroyed. Her story of saving her kids from the flames is amazing, if not unbelievable (see sidebar).

She didn't get anything out of the insurance company, despite taking her case all the way to the state supreme court. Nearly broke, she dropped off her remaining child with a relative and went west. At some point she started thinking of herself as "Captain Jack," assuming the name—and rank—of her dead husband.

Captain Jack established herself near Gunnison, opening a busy roadhouse for teamsters and miners. Like many who joined her in the area, she spent a great deal of time looking for gold in the surrounding hills. When she located a paying claim, she had to defend it with deadeye gunfire to chase off nefarious con men, the likes of which were always hovering over her accounts and property. Captain Jack was frequently having to shoot guns or other objects out of people's hands with her trusty .44.

At one point she witnessed some "jack punchers" (mule drivers) abusing their mules, so she reported them to the Humane Society. After a judge fined the men and ordered them not to work the abused mules, Captain Jack heard about some predictable threats the men were making toward her.

> I jumped up and took my gun and went up to where there was a gang of punchers and tin-horn gamblers cursing, and I went in front of the man who had been fined and I said: 'You wanted to see me. I am here. Pull your gun, you cur,' and at the same time I shot his hat off of his head. Such a scattering! Some men ran one way and some the other, and the man ran to the hospital, for he thought he was shot, but I only shot his hat off his head. That was all that they wanted of me, for I heard no more threats and knew that they would not dare to try to harm me, for they were a set of cowards to be such brutes to the poor animals that were making a living for them.

If half her stories of armed confrontations are true, it's miraculous that she was never shot. Not that she escaped physical injury.

Captain Jack describes a horrific event that occurred during her Gunnison days, when a group of Ute Indians, along with some French malcontents, attacked the town and descended on her roadhouse, Jack's Cabin. As she frantically tried to stamp out another fire, one of the Utes struck her in the head with a poison-tipped tomahawk. The blow broke her skull and was nearly fatal. The story sounds like a cartoonish Hollywood script, but there is strong evidence supporting her version: Photographs taken later show the scar from a nice diagonal gash right between Captain Jack's eyes.

In 1900 Captain Jack took a claim at the top of the High Drive and continued to search for treasure in the hills. As she had in Gunnison, she set up a small operation to make some money from those passing through.

Ellen Elliot Jack died in 1921. That year the new generation of Colorado Springs boosters worked to complete an extensive system of hiking and horseback riding trails around North Cheyenne Canyon, including the trails on this route.

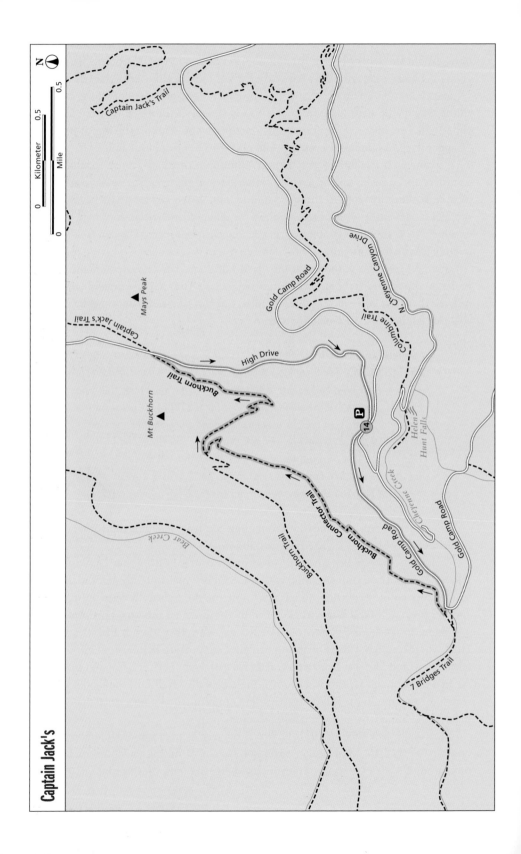

Captain Jack's

The High Drive at the turn of the century. DENVER PUBLIC LIBRARY, WESTERN HISTORY COLLECTION

After her death there were plans to expand Captain Jack's little rest stop. Thankfully they never panned out. There's very little left up here of Mrs. Jack's cabins. In the auto age the High Drive received a New Deal makeover but remained a rustic dirt road, closed much of the year. Finally it was closed to motor vehicles entirely, much to the benefit of mountain bikers and hikers.

Researching Captain Jack is greatly complicated by the presence in the state of multiple Captain Jacks during the same period. But up here in the saddle between Mays Peak and Mount Buckhorn, there was only one, and she was unmistakable.

Miles and Directions

0.0 Start from the large trailhead at the intersection of Gold Camp Road and High Drive and North Cheyenne Canyon Road and walk northwest on Upper Gold Camp Road, now closed to motor vehicles.

0.6 Turn right onto the Buckhorn Cutoff Trail as Gold Camp Road approaches the turn of the canyon. (Don't panic if you go too far and see the beginning of the 7 Bridges Trail. Go up the trail and take the first right to get on the Buckhorn Cutoff Trail.)

0.7 Turn right again (the left fork goes over to the 7 Bridges Trail).

1.9 Turn right at a T-intersection, now on the Buckhorn Trail.

2.7 The trail spills out onto High Drive. Turn right here and walk down High Drive to the trailhead.

3.7 Arrive back at the parking lot.

15 Cheyenne Mountain State Park

Take a walk at the base of Cheyenne Mountain, on some of the newer trails in the state. The route is quite close to the entrance to a very unusual military installation that is hidden inside the mountain.

Start: Limekiln parking area, Cheyenne Mountain State Park
Distance: 4.8-mile lariat loop
Approximate hiking time: 2 to 3 hours
Difficulty: Moderate
Trail surface: Varies from wide and easy to thin and rugged; rocks, mud, and lots of small creek crossings
Best seasons: Spring and fall
Other trail users: Hikers and bikers; dogs not allowed
Canine compatibility: No dogs allowed!
Land status: State park

Fees and permits: Day pass required
Schedule: Sunrise to sunset
Map: Cheyenne Mountain State Park trail map, Colorado Parks and Wildlife
Trail contact: Cheyenne Mountain State Park, 410 JL Ranch Heights, Colorado Springs, CO 80926; (719) 576-2016; http://cpw.state .co.us/placestogo/Parks/cheyennemountain
Special considerations: Cheyenne Mountain State Park is a fee area. This is just one of several possible hiking routes in Cheyenne Mountain State Park. All trails in the park are open to hikers and bikes.

Finding the trailhead: From Colorado Springs drive southwest on US 115 (for approximately 6 miles from Nevada Avenue); then turn right onto JL Ranch Heights Road and enter Cheyenne Mountain State Park. (There is a stoplight here, and a Fort Carson entrance on the other side of the highway.) Beyond the guard shack/fee station, turn left and park in the large parking lot. GPS: N38 43.88' / W104 49.28'

The Hike

Cheyenne Mountain was really the Utes' mountain, not the Cheyennes'. Although very few if any prehistoric artifacts have been found here, there is much to suggest that the land was well known to the Utes for centuries. The mountains here around present-day Colorado Springs are central in the Utes' creation myths.

According to a complicated Ute legend, Cheyenne Mountain is a dragon named Thirst. Thirst was created by the gods to drink up a huge flood, which had been precipitated by the aforementioned gods to clear the earth of bad humans. The flood-waters covered all but the high mountains. The gods sent Thirst on his epic drinking mission so the surviving people could descend from their refuge and start a new civilization. Ol' Thirst was so full of water after drinking the flood that his wings couldn't keep his waterlogged self in the air, and he crash-landed fatally, spilling his liquidy contents out of wounds in his sides. Thirst the Dragon, not a typical lifeless corpse, continued to leak water that sustained the tribe.

Water. The Utes who lived for hundreds of years or longer around these semiarid slopes never took it for granted. It was, to them, a cosmic gift.

Cheyenne Mountain does look like a giant dragon in eternal repose, from the right angle. The haunches are on the north. The Devil's Horns (for which the Utes have a separate explanation) are roughly at the dragon's knee. The tail is curled into Cheyenne Canyon. And not only does the mountain do a decent dragon impression, but the last time I walked it, after the wettest spring in memory, it did seem to leak plenty of water. The Park's few mappable creeks were gurgling loudly and the trails slogged through several mud bogs. The flora was responding mightily to the moisture. Some of the trails were overgrown by shrubs, grasses, and wildflowers. In dry years the scene is a bit different.

When Cheyenne Mountain State Park came into existence, hydrologists observed it to be a quite arid piece of land in the transition zone between mountain and plain. Limekiln Creek was a sandy arroyo; it was difficult to find a bubbling spring. This wasn't at all like the picture painted by the legend of Thirst, but, as the 2013 Park Management Plan notes, "Historically, the surface and groundwater hydrology was likely quite different." More on that in a bit.

Geologists have an explanation for Cheyenne Mountain that is very different than the Ute legend. It is not a dragon corpse, they say, but a huge hunk of Pikes Peak granite, 1 billion to 1.7 billion years old. There is a fault running along the base of the mountain on the east side. Here the Precambrian granite was pushed up skyward and exposed to form the majestic cliff faces that guard the mountain's flanks. This abrupt fortress of bedrock caught the eyes of nature lovers as well as those interested in creating a one-of-a-kind, virtually impenetrable defensive bunker.

As the Cold War sizzled in the 1950s and the development of intercontinental ballistic missiles was galloping along scarily, US and Canadian military officials decided they'd better create a Ballistic Missile Early Warning System and house it behind massive nuke-proof blast doors and a very thick shell of granite armor. Early versions of the North American Aerospace Defense Command (NORAD) were housed at Ent Air Force Base, then in the fortified Chidlaw Building in east Colorado Springs, while the famous bunker inside Cheyenne Mountain was being constructed. In 1964 NORAD started moving into the mountain.

In 1966 the Cheyenne Mountain Complex became fully operational, designed to withstand a multi-megaton nuclear strike as well as chemical and biological attacks. The mission: "monitor, process, and interpret air, missile, and space events that could threaten North America or have operational effects on U.S. forces or capabilities, using air, ground, and space-based sensors that link to the complex's computer systems located more than 2,000 feet under ground." In 2007 about 1,200 people were working inside Cheyenne Mountain, including about 500 contractors, according to a Government Accountability Office document.

Forty years after the station opened, the decision was made to move much of NORAD out of Cheyenne Mountain to a facility at Peterson Air Force Base.

Some spiffy trail work on Cheyenne Mountain

Officials cited cost savings and a lowered threat of nuclear war to justify the so-called Cheyenne Mountain Realignment, but claims of short-term savings were unfounded. Without a decision about what kind of protection level would be needed at the new facility, long-term costs were also up in the air. But the project moved forward.

Few could dispute that the threat of nuclear war had abated. In its existence the only warnings provided by the system seemed to be false alarms. People had to wonder: Are we going to get nuked due to some human error or electronic glitch? The movie *War Games*, about a kid hacking into NORAD's computers, didn't seem all that far-fetched. NORAD appeared, to the uninformed public, to spend more energy pretending to track Santa Claus than anything else, so the move was not hugely controversial.

Not an empty shell, the Cheyenne Mountain Complex is on "warm standby." Officially, computers there are used for training, and the mega-bunker serves as an alternate command center—if the Peterson AFB site is blasted away, the old NORAD will be waiting. In reality, it's difficult to say exactly how the military is using this complex in an era of intensifying conflict. Things have been heating up at NORAD as they have been heating up around the world.

Interestingly, while NORAD had been semi-open to the public via guided tours for decades, the tours have been discontinued. We are reduced to gazing at the entrance ports from afar. On this hike you can see the access road and from that locate the main entrance, but that's about it.

We can imagine what it must look like inside, as the layout of the facility is an open secret. The first thing you see as you enter the tunnel is the 25-ton high-tech door, and another behind it, both swung open to allow your entry. How else is your shuttle bus going to get in? The bus will drive into the entry tunnel and then turn around using a special alcove blasted out of the rock for that purpose alone. From the "blast tunnel" more huge doors lead to the main access tunnel. The main tunnel splits into several side tunnels, each segment leading to a different multistory building. There are fifteen buildings inside the mountain, arrayed in a rectangular grid. Each building sits on hundreds of huge springs that will keep it steady in case of blast or quake.

At the core of the complex is that iconic control room—everybody intently watching their monitors and the big screens on the wall, just like the movies. If you're a bigwig, there's a suite waiting for you in one of the buildings, with fresh water from four long, rectangular reservoirs tucked inside Cheyenne Mountain with you. If you're not a bigwig, there's a cot with your name on it. You'll also find, if you know where to look, a cafeteria and a fitness center and all the mundane facilities necessary for daily life. The air is fresh and clean, filtered like no other air in the world. Presumably engineers have provided an uninterruptible power source as well.

Sounds like paradise! Let us in! [pounds on door]

Securing fresh water for the inhabitants of NORAD in those big underground reservoirs may have had a profound effect on the local environment above ground. Again, from the Cheyenne Mountain State Park Management Plan, prepared in 2013 by the Colorado Department of Parks and Wildlife: "The construction of NORAD . . . in the early 1960s created a significant change in the local groundwater regime. Development of large sub-surface water storage facilities at NORAD is thought to have removed the primary source for surface water on the adjacent property, including the park area."

According to the son of the rancher who owned this land for much of the twentieth century, Lloyd Jones, "When they built NORAD it screwed up all the springs on the ranch. They just dried up." The Joneses moved their operation to Montana, but not before suing the government and winning, award unknown. The difficulty of raising cattle on the springless land, possibly caused by NORAD, led to its new status as public property. The suburbs are creeping southward, however. It's likely that a big

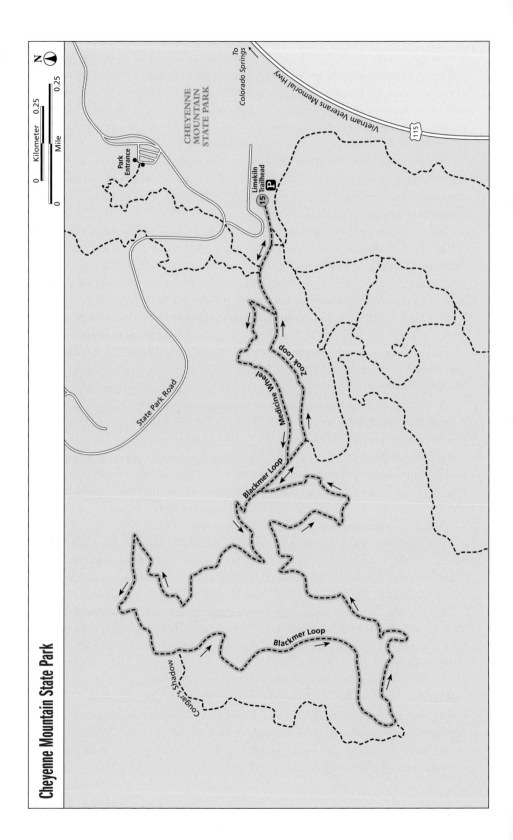

Cheyenne Mountain State Park

hunk of land adjacent to Cheyenne Mountain State Park on the north will become a development with hundreds of residences in the near future. The new suburb will be sustained with water not from Cheyenne Mountain but from some unknown mountain drainage at great expense. The legend of Thirst the Dragon takes some interesting twists and turns.

This hike begins down low and makes its way to the upper end of the park, using the Zook Loop Trail, Medicine Wheel Trail, and Blackmer Loop Trail. The Medicine Wheel Trail is a thin, rocky singletrack that was made by a local mountain bike club; it makes for difficult riding and engaged hiking. The loop features several easy (relatively) creek crossings. This is a lovely route through the park, but there are several other trails here (eighteen named trails so far), and this is just one of a few different route possibilities. You could augment this hike with the serene Cougar's Shadow Trail, higher on the mountain, or try something completely different and walk around another group of trails. There are three or four separate clusters of trails that can be reached from the same parking lot.

If you're looking for something much more intense, consider a strenuous hike to the top of Cheyenne Mountain on a new trail. So new, in fact, that it wasn't yet completed when this book went to press.

Miles and Directions

0.0 Start from the lower parking lot and begin walking up the path. At the first junction turn right onto the Zook Loop Trail.

0.1 Continue past the intersection with the Coyote Run Loop on the right.

0.2 Turn right onto the Medicine Wheel Trail, for a little extra pizzazz. (**Option:** Continue on the Zook Loop and rejoin at mile 0.7 below.)

0.7 Turn right onto the Blackmer Loop Trail.

0.8 Continue straight as the other branch of the Blackmer Loop Trail intersects on the left. You'll be coming down that way later.

1.9 Continue on the Blackmer Loop Trail as the Cougar's Shadow Trail intersects on the right. (**Option:** Turn right onto the Cougar's Shadow Trail and rejoin at mile 2.6 below.)

2.6 Continue on the Blackmer Loop Trail as the Cougar's Shadow Trail intersects on the right (again).

4.0 Turn right after completing the loop, now retracing your steps back to the trailhead. **Note:** You turn right here, after completing Blackmer Loop, onto a trail that is still called Blackmer Loop, which can be confusing.

4.1 Continue past the intersection with the Medicine Wheel Trail. (**Option:** Give it another spin and rejoin at mile 4.5 below.)

4.2 Turn left, back on Zook Loop and headed for home.

4.5 Pass the other entrance to Medicine Wheel Trail.

4.8 Arrive back at the parking lot.

16 Florissant Fossil Beds

This is an easy loop through a historically unique and fascinating area. The petrified redwood stumps of Florissant Fossil Beds make mind-blowing and unique trailside scenery.

Start: Florissant Fossil Beds National Monument Visitor Center
Distance: 1.0-mile loop (with options for much more)
Approximate hiking time: 0.5 to 1 hour (with options for much longer hikes)
Difficulty: Easy
Trail surface: Very mellow, wide dirt path
Best seasons: Spring, summer, and fall
Other trail users: Pedestrians
Canine compatibility: Dogs are not allowed on the dirt-surfaced trails within Florissant Fossil Beds National Monument.
Land status: National park
Fees and permits: Adults must purchase passes, which are good for 7 days. Children under 16 are admitted free.
Schedule: Summer hours: 8 a.m. to 6 p.m.; spring, fall, and winter hours: 9 a.m. to 5 p.m. (**Note:** The park gate closes at this time, meaning you have to be finished before closing time or your car will get locked in the lot. Park at Hornbek Homestead to hike after the park's business hours.) Closed Thanksgiving, Christmas, and New Year's Day.
Map: Florissant Fossil Beds hiking trail map, National Park Service
Trail contact: Florissant Fossil Beds National Monument, 15807 Teller County Rd. 1, Florissant, CO 80816; (719) 748-3253; www.nps .gov/flfo
Special considerations: This is just one option for hikes within the park, and one of the easiest. There are many other trails that offer longer options, for instance, the Hornbek Wildlife Loop and Boulder Creek Trail.

Finding the trailhead: From Colorado Springs go west on US 24 about 35 miles to Florissant; then turn left (south) on Teller County Road 1. Continue on CR 1 for approximately 2 miles and then turn right into the visitor center parking lot. GPS: N38 54.81' / W105 17.10'

The Hike

The giant redwood stumps were the only fossils they couldn't take. Not that they didn't try to take those too.

In the late nineteenth century and well into the twentieth, Florissant was a favorite destination for tourists who paid for the privilege of hunting for fossils, which they would take home as souvenirs. They scoured the place pretty thoroughly. A small percentage of what used to be here ended up in the hands of scientists and museums.

The famous fossil beds and redwood stumps of Florissant were divided between two private landowners for several decades, both of whom did their best to capitalize on the resource. There was fierce competition between the two outfits. At one point bullets flew (how maliciously aimed is not known) after somebody associated with

Big Stump is the fossilized remnant of a 300-foot redwood.

one of the proprietors sprinkled tacks on the access road of the other. War of the Stumps, I call it. This episode is telling for a few reasons. It illustrates the auto's take-over and transformation of Colorado's tourist industry in the 1920s, and it reminds us there was a time when automobile tires could be slain by tacks.

To say Florissant is special would be a massive understatement. A bizarre alignment of circumstances led to the perfect preservation of an entire ecosystem—plants and animals that existed here 34 million years ago—in layers of shale and volcanic ash. Frozen in time. This amazing fossil record (what's left of it) yielded over 1,700 different species of plants and animals. Included in the inventory were tsetse flies and other creatures and plants that were adapted to a warm climate. Temperature-wise, imagine Charlotte, North Carolina.

During the Eocene epoch the area was dominated by a huge volcano, or group of them, just 15 miles southwest of Florissant. The activity of this volcano repeatedly spewed ash over the region, and in nearby Florissant the ground was inundated by periodic mudflows. Volcanoes have a tendency to combine ash and mud and water and send it all flowing at high speeds down their slopes. A volcanic mudflow, aka *lahar*, picks up huge amounts of debris, trees, and boulders and pretty much destroys everything in its path before grinding to a halt on the valley floor. It was one of these lahars that encased and preserved the bottoms of the huge redwoods at Florissant. About the same time, another lahar dammed up a stream and made Lake Florissant, and the perfect conditions for preserving all those plant and insect fossils in the lake bed.

There are a half dozen or so giant petrified redwood stumps that remain excavated at Florissant Fossil Beds. There are some additional stumps that have been discovered, or are known about, but remain underground—to protect them from the unwashed hordes. Beyond that there must be some petrified stumps that have escaped discovery entirely.

Even with the excavated stumps to ponder and inspect, it is difficult to grasp just how big these Colorado redwoods really were—especially if you are, like me, a native Coloradan who hasn't ever seen a living redwood or sequoia. The Colorado giants were approaching 300 feet in height and were around 750 years old when the Guffey volcano slathered the stumps with mud. Those nicely preserved tree rings don't lie.

The trees here were petrified by a process called permineralization. Over many thousands of years, mineral-infused water invaded the buried stumps and left behind mineral deposits, primarily silica from the volcanic ash in the mudflow, in the trees' cells. To reach completion the process requires three ingredients: water, minerals, and a whole lot of time. All three were provided when the stumps were buried in the lahar.

When complete, the fossil created through permineralization contains very little of the original organic material of the tree. Although it took trees to make these fossils, these fossils are not trees.

The Petrified Forest Loop is only a mile long, but provides the best opportunity within Florissant Fossil Beds to cozy up to some petrified redwood stumps. There are several of them next to this trail, including the famed "Big Stump," which used to be hidden behind its own gift shop/tourist roach motel when the land was privately owned. Big Stump is quite a specimen, having captured at least two saw blades from greedy Victorian-age numbskulls. You can see the rusty trophies poinking out near the top of the stump.

The fence is there to keep you from hugging the stump.

Those craving more of a hike can find it within Florissant Fossil Beds. I recommend the almost 4-mile Hornbek Wildlife Loop, which ventures out to the old homestead that sits by CR 1, then crosses the road and peruses that nicely lonely section of the landscape east of the road before crossing back and joining the Petrified Forest Loop. Add the Petrified Forest Loop to gawk at the stumps and make a satisfying 5-miler. And if that's still not enough, try 2.5 miles more of walking on the Boulder Creek Trail, winding through the more heavily forested section south of the visitor center. There are also two separate trails that connect to the Hornbek Loop at its easternmost point, on the other side of CR 1, and lead out to the eastern park boundary.

Word to the wise: It costs a bit to get into Florissant Fossil Beds through the main entrance and visitor center. If you plan on doing the longer Hornbek Wildlife Loop (3.8 miles), you can park in and start from a parking lot at Hornbek Homestead right on CR 1. There is also more remote access on Lower Twin Rock Road, with a trail that leads 1.6 miles across the feds' land and connects with the Hornbek Wildlife Loop up in the woods east of CR 1. From these remote trailheads you can hike through the national monument free of charge, as long as you stay out of the visitor center. However, the exhibits in the visitor center are very well done and hugely informative, so if you're at all interested in the science and history of the Fossil Beds, just pay the Stumpmaster.

Florissant, 1875: The Marksbery Incident

In 1875 an incident occurred near Florissant that had lasting effects on the settlers' relations with the Utes. A rancher who had homesteaded near Tarryall very early during the Pikes Peak gold rush, in 1859, was passing through Florissant and visiting the local trading post when his pony was stolen, or so he thought, by some members of Shavano's band of Utes. In fact, one of the Utes recognized that the pony had recently been stolen from another member of the tribe and decided to take it back. He rode away on it, leaving the rancher's saddle and bridle on the ground.

The rancher, Pleasant Marksbery, had purchased the animal from a third party and felt it was rightfully his. When his pleas to the local Indian agent didn't produce the desired pony, Marksbery went after it. Immediately after confiscating the pony from the Ute's camp near Florissant, Marksbery was picked off with a rifle shot.

To the white settlers it looked like a murder. "Great excitement has been caused among the settlers in that part of the country, and it is feared that there will be considerable trouble," reported the *Colorado Springs Gazette* in January 1875, "unless prompt measures are taken by the authorities to have justice executed . . . Indian Agent Thompson has received telegraphic orders from the Commissioner of Indian Affairs at Washington to proceed at once to Florissant and arrest the murderer of Marksbery. Mr. Thompson will proceed to execute the order as soon as he can get a deputy marshal to accompany him."

After the killing several fired-up ranchers had gathered at Judge Castello's, the spatial and figurative center of the Florissant community. They agitated for a war party against the Utes, but eventually cooler heads prevailed and they decided to wait for the authorities to do their work. "They would have been wiped out in a few minutes," noted Agent Thompson in his memoir. There were more than 600 Utes in the camp.

The contrast between the private ownership period and the Park Service's stewardship is interesting. The Park Service is ostensibly on a mission to preserve the resource, for scientific and edutainment purposes, whereas the private owners may or may not have felt the same responsibility. In either case visitors pay a fee to the Keeper of the Stumps for the privilege of viewing these 34-million-year-old beauties.

Indian Agent Thompson expected resistance and delegated the task to his deputy. But there was no fight. Chief Ouray willingly surrendered the man, Tabweah (aka Tabernash, Johnny Tab-Biscuit, or Johnny Hot-Biscuit), who had fired the fatal shot. The Utes also offered quite a different story about what had happened. They said Marksbery came into their camp and brandished a paper that he claimed was from Agent Thompson, allowing him to take the horse. (The paper was a fake.) They said Marksbery and his teenage son took the horse and then threatened Tabweah with his rifle, and that Marksbery was shot in self-defense. All they asked for was a fair trial. Tabweah was taken back to Denver to await trial.

No real evidence was presented against Tabweah, and he was acquitted, sort of. Despite his being cleared in court, he remained in custody for a few months until the commissioner of Indian affairs ordered his release.

Tabweah (Tabernash) proved to be the type of guy who was first into that sort of confrontation. In 1878, three increasingly sour years after the Marksbery incident, he was with another group of Utes in Middle Park. After repeated deceptions by treaty-makers, this group was in an aggrieved mood. As the long-friendly Utes sometimes did when in that state, they let their horses graze in a rancher's hayfield, hacked out a racetrack, and set up camp nearby. They were doing to the rancher what they felt the rancher had already done to them.

A party was assembled to chase the surly Utes away. Among the group was Frank Byers, son of *Rocky Mountain News* editor William Byers, and a prospector named "Big Frank" Addison. The posse arrived at the Ute camp while the men were at their racetrack. Roughly the men tore through the camp collecting the Utes' rifles as the Ute women hollered in protest. The Ute men returned to camp while this was going on; when Tabweah jumped off his horse and grabbed a rifle off the pile, Big Frank shot him dead.

Though the Utes were persuaded to leave the area, the killing of Tabweah seemed to spark a flare-up of deadly violence in Middle Park. Later on, the railroad town on the site of Junction Ranch, where his killing took place, was named Tabernash in his memory.

The Hornbek Homestead is worth a look by itself. Adeline Hornbek was the head of the household here. Her first husband, with whom she had three kids and moved to a ranch near Denver, died in 1864. Adeline and the kids did fine on their own, making the ranch a success. Adeline remarried and had a fourth child, but then husband number two abandoned her and the kids. Once again she prospered without

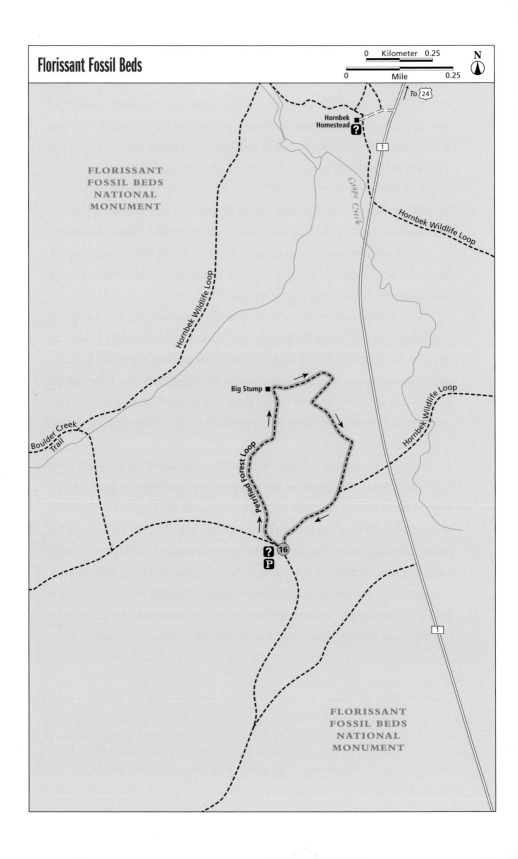

Florissant Fossil Beds

FLORISSANT
FOSSIL BEDS
NATIONAL
MONUMENT

Hornbek
Homestead

To 24

1

Grape Creek

Hornbek Wildlife Loop

Hornbek Wildlife Loop

Hornbek Wildlife Loop

Big Stump

Boulder Creek Trail

Petrified Forest Loop

16

FLORISSANT
FOSSIL BEDS
NATIONAL
MONUMENT

1

0   Kilometer 0.25

0   Mile   0.25

N

Adeline Hornbek did not need dudes on her ranch.

him, moving up to the mountains in 1878 to claim 160 well-appointed acres under the Homestead Act.

Hornbek's two-story, four-bedroom cottage was pretty slick, the finest in the area at the time. She could afford to have it crafted very nicely and filled with fancy furniture. The outbuildings were moved here from other historic ranches in the area, but are probably not too different than the actual outbuildings that sat here in the 1880s.

Miles and Directions

0.0 Emerging from the visitor center, go straight on the concrete sidewalk briefly, passing the petrified stumps under the pavilions on your left.

0.03 Turn right to begin a clockwise loop on the Petrified Forest Loop.

0.4 Reach Big Stump.

0.9 Pass an intersection with the Hornbek Wildlife Loop Trail.

1.0 Arrive back at the visitor center.

San Luis Valley

Some leftovers from the most powerful volcanic eruption in the known history of the world

17 Penitente Canyon

Tucked away on the west side of the San Luis Valley, Penitente Canyon is a unique gallery of southwestern history.

Start: Penitente Canyon Trailhead
Distance: 1.4-mile loop (with options for more)
Approximate hiking time: 1 to 2 hours
Difficulty: Moderate
Trail surface: Rocks and sand; some minor ledges and step-downs
Best seasons: Spring and fall
Other trail users: Hikers and bikers
Canine compatibility: Dogs permitted
Land Status: Bureau of Land Management
Fees and permits: None
Schedule: None

Map: Penitente Canyon Recreation Management Area mountain bike map
Trail contact: Bureau of Land Management, San Luis Valley Field Office, 46525 CO 114, Saguache, CO 81149; (719) 655-2547; www.blm.gov/co/st/en/fo/slvfo.html
Special considerations: Bring water and use sunscreen on this sunny hike. New trails have been added around Penitente Canyon at a brisk rate. The mountain bike map produced by the BLM offered the most up-to-date trail map as of summer 2015.

Finding the trailhead: From US 285 in the San Luis Valley, go west on CR G for 6 miles; then veer left at a fork onto CR 38A. Turn right onto Penitente Canyon Road. Go to the end of the dirt road and park at the trailhead. GPS: N37 50.59' / W106 17.15'

The Hike

Penitente Canyon was known as Capulin Canyon through much of the twentieth century, because of the abundant wild cherry bushes. Before that, during the nineteenth century, it was called Cañon de Rajadero, because of a nearby sawmill. A devout sect of Roman Catholic monks, commonly called Los Penitentes, started to use the secluded canyon as a retreat after 1918. The name Penitente Canyon was cemented in the public consciousness only in the mid–1980s, after some dedicated Hermanos Penitentes conspired to paint the Virgin of Guadalupe high up on the canyon wall.

Formally known as La Fraternidad Piadosa de Nuestro Padre de Nazarena (the Pious Fraternity of Our Father Jesus of Nazareth), Los Hermanos Penitentes are a religious sect of mysterious origin. Some think the Penitentes are part of a religious tradition stretching back to medieval Spain and Italy; others point out similarities to Aztec religious rituals. Michael Carroll, in his book *The Penitente Brotherhood: Patriarchy and Hispano-Catholicism in New Mexico*, has a different take. Carroll downplays the connection to the past and argues that the rituals emerged almost spontaneously in New Mexico in the early nineteenth century, "something relatively new, not the continuation of something old."

Staying on course isn't always straightforward in rocky places like this. PHOTO BY JERRY HURST

In one interpretation the religious cult's emergence was a response to the spread of American culture across the Southwest in the mid-nineteenth century. Dorothy Woodward reminds us: "American civilization was aggressive; it had changed the government, dominated civil life, and dictated religious reform, but under the shield of the *cofradia* [confraternity] the Spanish-American could continue the familiar mores that he had for generations. He clung to his religious brotherhood for, in it, he preserved his integrity as Spaniard, amidst the bewildering pressure of an alien culture."

The Penitentes are best known for their flagellation rituals—whipping themselves and each other hard and long enough to spray blood on themselves and anybody nearby. Other documented rituals that a member of the Brotherhood might subject himself to included being cut on the back with a flint, being buried up to the neck for a day or two, having cactus strapped to body parts, and being dragged over rocky ground. Each Penitente group also had its "death cart," an old-style wooden wagon with a frightening anthropomorphized figure of death riding in it. The cart was loaded with rocks, and individual Brothers were made to pull it for miles.

It's been alleged that the Penitentes performed actual crucifixions with nails, although that's probably more Anglo myth than truth. (The Penitentes certainly weren't strangers to knives and such, but the crucifixions usually involved ropes alone, painful enough without nails.) The sect's rituals have always been mostly unknown to outsiders, and given just a few sensational published eyewitness accounts over the centuries, people have been more than willing to fill in the blanks with their own overactive imaginations. Still, the reality would shock most nonmembers. The Penitentes claim that flagellation and other such "mortifications" are the only way to experience the suffering of Christ, and thus become worthy of the joys of heaven.

American newcomers to the Southwest who witnessed the bloody Penitente flagellation processions, which had been performed openly, often reacted with revulsion and hostility. The Roman Catholic Church vigorously attempted to condemn the sect and distance itself. Perceived malevolence from outsiders drove La Hermandad (the Brotherhood) to secrecy. Penitentes stopped holding rituals during the day, "unless the location was so remote as not to be witnessed by unfriendly eyes," wrote scholar Lorayne Horka-Follick (*Los Hermanos Penitentes*) in 1969. "It became customary to have the whipping processions and crucifixion held in some remote cañon known only to the Brotherhood."

The Penitentes also started to wear hoods during their ceremonies and to congregate in drab, remote "moradas." The typical morada, the Penitentes' version of a church, is styled to look like an anonymous, very uninviting, and utilitarian adobe shack. The hoods and the drab architecture of the moradas both emphasize the religious humility of the Penitentes but also provide helpful secrecy. In case some curious anthropologists showed up at the morada anyway, there would be armed guards posted to keep them out.

In 1936 a freelance journalist named Carl Taylor was living in New Mexico and working on a magazine article about Los Hermanos. Taylor entered a morada and took flash photos and bragged about it. Just days after entering the morada, Taylor was shot to death in his cabin. Most assumed that aggrieved Penitentes had committed the murder. Before long Taylor's 16-year-old houseboy confessed to killing him. Apparently the teenager's sole motive was robbery, but the narrative of bloodthirsty

Virgin of Guadalupe, courtesy of Victor, Abel and Victor

Penitentes protecting their secret cult in the wilds of New Mexico was too delicious to drop. The press favored the sensational story and repeated it in magazines and newspapers across America. The false story went viral, 1936 version.

It's no wonder that the Penitentes, actively misunderstood, hoped to shield their unique ways from the forces that were closing in around them. Penitente Canyon was another remote spot at which the Brotherhood could perform rites in secret. Their use of the canyon occurred in the early twentieth century, between the World Wars. The post–World War II years saw a big decline in Brotherhood membership as young men left the area for the cities. In recent decades, however, there has reportedly been a resurgence of Penitente membership and activity.

The canyon's blue-painted Virgin is the most photographed feature in the immediate vicinity. It was apparently painted by "Victor, Abel and Victor," signatures painted on the rock below the mural. According to what now seems like an old legend, one of Los Hermanos, perhaps one of the Victors, sat in a tire and was lowered down the cliff face by his companions. It was probably not the most frightening expression of faith Victor had engaged in as a member of Los Hermanos. Later on some huckster used the rock art for target practice and did serious damage, not only to the Virgin but also to his chances of making it past the Pearly Gates, it would seem.

The besieged blue Virgin of Guadalupe is easy to spot. There is also much older rock art still visible—not yet destroyed by the weather or shooters. Los Hermanos weren't the only ones to tag this canyon. Keep an eye out for pictographs of a big game hunt and other rock art probably made by the Utes, Jicarilla Apache, or Pueblo Indians.

Penitente Canyon is nicely tucked away on the west side of the San Luis Valley, far, far away from the nearest population center. But it's doubtful Los Hermanos use the canyon much anymore. In the past 50 years or so, it's been an increasingly popular destination for rock climbers, year-round, and that's steadily pushed out the solitude-seekers. Next to the Virgin painting is a difficult climbing route named "Virgin No More," which should give you a good indication of how things are going here.

The modest but picturesque canyons on this side of the San Luis Valley are composed of volcanic rock, legacy of the most powerful volcanic eruption in the known history of the world, about 27 million years ago. The eruption, or series of eruptions, produced 5,000 times as much ash as the Mount St. Helens eruption, blasting lava and ash all over southwestern Colorado and leaving a massive, jagged crater, La Garita Caldera. The several-hundred-foot-thick layer of volcanic rock dominates the landscape around South Fork and Wolf Creek Pass, at Spring Creek Pass and Lake City. You're just on the edge of it here.

This is a fairly short hike up the canyon and back around to the trailhead, a pretty compact loop. The terrain is rugged, but the trail maintains a civilized disposition as it picks its way through what amounts to a field of massive boulders, with interesting but easily conquered rocky sections along the way. Route-finding is fairly easy, but not a sure thing. Some very basic signage has been installed that partially counters the possibility of getting lost. There are some other trails and routes available, officially sanctioned and otherwise, that can tempt hikers into wrong turns. This little loop is probably the easiest to follow in the area—just head up Penitente Canyon and don't turn left at any junction, and you'll find yourself back at the road by the trailhead.

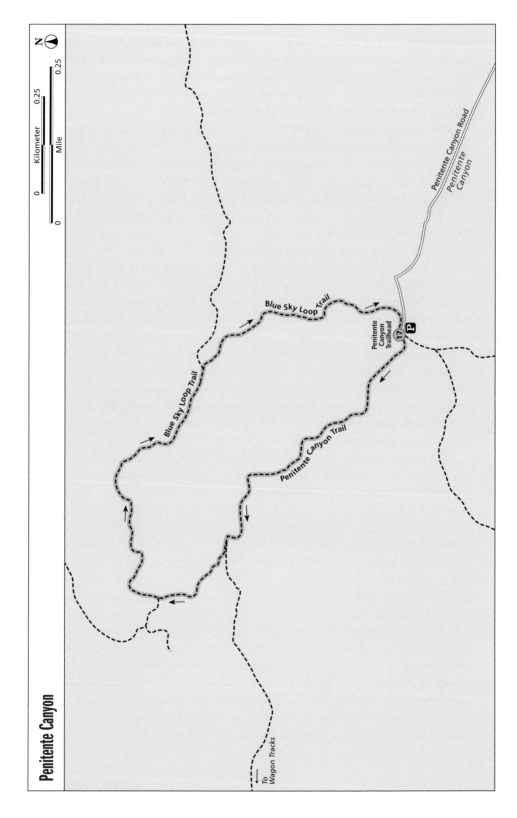

Penitente Canyon

N

Kilometer
0   0.25

Mile
0   0.25

Blue Sky Loop Trail

Blue Sky Loop Trail

Penitente Canyon Trail

Penitente Canyon Trailhead

P

Penitente Canyon Road

Penitente Canyon

To Wagon Tracks

Near the top of the loop, there is an opportunity to divert from the route and walk over to an area where old wagon wheel tracks can be seen in the bedrock. The extra distance amounts to a mile or two. The tracks are cool to see but frankly, for the non-wagon-obsessed members of the party, may not be worth the walk. The impressions appeared over many years, created by wagons hauling timber to a sawmill in the nineteenth century.

Miles and Directions

0.0 From the Penitente Canyon Trailhead, begin walking up Penitente Canyon Trail. (***Note:*** There are other trails taking off from the trailhead or very close to it, so make sure you're on the right one. There should be an obvious sign.)

0.4 Continue straight at a trail intersection.

0.7 Turn right at a junction. This is known as "Blue Sky Loop" on some maps. (It may be marked with a "b" on a small post. This is also part of Mountain Bike Loop A, so not confusing at all.)

1.1 Keep right at another junction, which you probably won't notice anyway.

1.4 Arrive back at the road, very close to the trailhead. Turn right and return to the start of the hike.

18 Great Sand Dunes

Climb a sand dune. Then another. Then three more. Keep climbing. Then tumble back down to where you started. Retrace the steps of floundering explorers in one of the most unique and fascinating places on the planet.

Start: Dunes parking area, Great Sand Dunes National Monument
Distance: 2.2 miles out and back (with options for more or less)
Approximate hiking time: 1 to 1,000 hours
Difficulty: Moderate to difficult
Trail surface: Sand dunes
Best seasons: Spring and fall
Other trail users: Hikers and sandboarders
Canine compatibility: Leashed dogs permitted (may need something to protect dog's paws from hot sand)
Land status: National park
Fees and permits: There is a fee for adults to enter Great Sand Dunes National Monument;

children 16 and under are free. **Note:** The park usually has several entrance fee–free days and weekends. Check the website for details: www .nps.gov/grsa/planyourvisit/fees.htm.
Schedule: None! (The visitor center is open during regular business hours.)
Map: Great Sand Dunes National Park map, National Park Service
Trail contact: Great Sand Dunes National Park, 11999 CO 150, Mosca, CO 81146; (719) 378-6399; www.nps.gov/grsa/index.htm
Special considerations: This is a weird hike! There is no trail, just a vast area of dunes.

Finding the trailhead: From CO 17 in the San Luis Valley, go east on CR 6; then take CO 150 north. The hike doesn't start from the visitor center, but from the parking area by Medano Creek. After passing the visitor center, turn left onto a paved access road that leads to the parking area. GPS: N37 44.38' / W105 31.06'. (**Note:** Thought I'd relate this bit from the Park Service's Great Sand Dunes National Park website. The all-caps portion is also red on their site, by the way [www .nps.gov/grsa/planyourvisit/directions.htm]: "DO NOT USE COMPUTER MAPPING PROGRAMS IN THE ROCKY MOUNTAINS FOR HIGHWAY TRAVEL. The most commonly used web and dashboard mapping programs have directed visitors to drive over hiking trails or primitive 4WD roads to reach the park. Numerous visitors have become stranded in snow or stuck at a remote trailhead trying to use GPS to reach the main park area.")

The Hike

Judging by the c. 11,000-year-old spearheads (meant to slay mammoths) that have been found in the vicinity, the massive bank of sand dunes snuggled against the Sangre de Cristo Mountains has probably been well known to people since the first humans walked over from Asia. It's obvious that modern tribes like the Utes, Jicarilla Apache, and Pueblo were intimately familiar with the dunes. The lake just west of the dunes is central to the Pueblo creation myth, for instance.

Reaching High Dune is a test of determination.

Though Spanish and French explorers no doubt were around through the seventeenth and eighteenth centuries, and Spanish colonists in New Mexico probably journeyed up here as well, not to mention the trappers and traders, there was almost nothing written about the Great Sand Dunes in that era that survived. In 1807, however, Lieutenant Zebulon Pike of the US Army crossed the Sangres—in the dead of winter!—on his misdirected search for the source of the Red River. In late January, Pike and his men crossed the range, using either Medano Pass or Mosca Pass, as we know them today, and found the sand dunes on the other side.

"28th January, Wednesday," Pike wrote in his journal, which would later be confiscated by the Spanish and held for about 100 years. "Followed down the ravine and discovered after some time that there had been a road cut out, and on many trees were various hieroglyphicks painted; after marching some miles, we discovered through the lengthy vista at a distance, another chain of mountains and nearer by at the foot of

The nation's sandbox

the White mountains [the Sangre de Cristos], which we were then descending, sandy hills. We marched on the outlet of the mountains and left the sandy desert to our right; kept down between it and the mountain . . ."

There's a lot of good stuff in that passage. A "road cut out" and markings on trees. We can infer from his description ("sandy desert to our right") that they were most likely descending along Medano Creek.

They set up camp not far from the site of the campground today, and Pike set off to climb a high dune, just like you're about to do. It's an irresistible temptation! When he got to the top (no small feat, you'll agree), he opened his spyglass and looked out over the valley. To his delight he saw a large river 40 miles distant. Finding rivers was what this expedition was all about. It was the Rio Grande, of course, but Pike, as was his custom when finding rivers, assumed it was a different river than it actually was.

"I returned to camp with the news of my discovery. The sand hills extended up and down at the foot of the White mountains, about fifteen miles, and appeared to be about five miles in width . . . Their appearance was exactly that of the sea in a storm, (except as to color) not the least sign of vegetation existing thereon. Distance 15 miles." And off they went to the wrong river.

About 40 years after Pike bagged his dune, the Fremont expedition came through; then, in 1853, John Gunnison led a mounted party across the sand dunes for the US Topographical Survey. He wrote about the difficulty the party's horses had moving through the soft sand and how it took all day to get across. By that time the information in Gunnison's reports would have been old news to a whole class of traveling gold bugs, on their way to and from California and prospecting around Colorado as they went, as well as the men housed at Fort Garland, which had been established 20 miles south of the dunes before the Gunnison expedition.

Symbolically and practically, mid-nineteenth-century explorers ushered in a new era to the San Luis Valley and Colorado: the "era of Whiteness" is one way to put it. But Whiteness, with all its industrial agriculture and extraction and real estate development, demanded something that didn't appear to exist here in large enough quantities.

In 1880 the intrepid guidebook writer George Crofutt came through on one of the new railroads and described the San Luis Valley in his book *Crofutt's Grip-Sack Guide to Colorado*:

> San Luis Park or Valley, is nearly 800 miles in length, in a general north and south direction, varying in width from 20 to 40 miles, and bordered on the west by the lofty range of the San Juan mountains. The eastern portion of this valley, north of the railroad, receives the waters of numberless springs and mountain streams, away up to the Cochetopa hills and Poncho [Poncha] pass, but they have no outlet; like the great basins in Utah and Nevada, the waters sink. . . .
>
> It is a mistaken idea that many have, that good crops can be grown only on black soil or muck. Some of the most productive farms in Colorado to-day, were once covered with sage brush and grease-wood, and this soil is composed of clay, gravel, fine sandy loam and mountain washings. At this time, millions of acres of what, with water would be the best crop-raising lands in Colorado, are called valueless, except as a range for cattle, sheep, etc. Particularly is this so in the San Luis park, and will remain so until some extensive system of canals and irrigating ditches is constructed to bring the water from the Rio Grande, or the needed supply is secured by sinking artesian wells.

Crofutt's comments were prescient. He was right that the story of the valley's development was a story of water, and he was right about the valley's swallowing almost all the water that flowed into it from the mountains, save for that which managed to mosey all the way through with the Rio Grande. While the ground looked like desolation, just below the ground there was water. And far below the ground was another aquifer, huge and pressurized. Before long the valley would be pierced and greened up by thousands of artesian wells and a maze of canals.

Towns like San Luis in the southeastern corner of the valley had been long established before the western land rush. (San Luis is the oldest Colorado town still in existence, established as a Spanish settlement in 1851.) The town's old residents owned the oldest water rights, Colorado Water Right Number 1. They dug modest ditches for modest fields, and to this day are praised for their efficient use of water. By the late 1860s people with a very different way of thinking about water—commercial ranchers and farmers, investors, real estate developers—joined them in the valley. These new arrivals wanted to exploit as much of the resource as they possibly could, flooding fields from new ditches and artesian wells.

At about the same time that Crofutt was cruising across the valley on the train, a huge canal system was completed around the new railroad town Alamosa. This system featured a main canal as wide as a modern highway and absconded with about a third of the Rio Grande's flow.

During the drought-plagued 1890s the new farmers of the San Luis Valley were diverting so much water from the Rio Grande that the river was dry by the time it reached El Paso. The farmers south of Colorado had a major problem with that, as you might imagine. This conflict led to treaties that formalized the obligation of the valley's farmers to keep a certain minimum amount of water flowing to New Mexico, Texas, and Mexico—the Rio Grande Compact.

Water use increased into the middle of the twentieth century; then a sort of mini industrial revolution took place among the valley's commercial farmers. Instead of flooding fields from ditches and wells, they started to use the giant rotating sprinklers you see operating out there today (center-pivot irrigation). Most of the sprinklers draw straight from the aquifer.

It's worth taking the time to check out some satellite photos of the San Luis Valley. The valley looks surreal with all the dark green and beige circles packed together. Main crops include potatoes, alfalfa, wheat, and barley. Contrast the pattern of circles with the tiny rectangular strips of farm fields around San Luis and similar villages in the southeast corner.

The vast increase in the use of groundwater led the regulators to step in during the 1970s. A rule was introduced, "augmentation," requiring consumers of groundwater to offset their consumption by providing water to the basin from some other source. To administer this ethereal exchange, the San Luis Valley Water Conservancy District released water from a mountain reservoir into the Rio Grande. The arrangement was meant to conserve the valley's commercial agriculture as much as its water.

In the 1980s a company obtained a huge chunk of land on the east side of the valley, on the Baca Land Grant, which had been decreed by the Spanish in the mid-nineteenth century. Just as many had feared and warned, the outsiders' scheme involved tapping the aquifer and selling the water to the Front Range. The company claimed water rights predating American possession of the valley. After a years-long battle with citizens' groups, the company's plan was blocked in court.

In the San Luis Valley, money talks. Money talks loud and says a lot of things. But the valley doesn't always listen.

In the early 2000s drought came again to the valley. The lack of precipitation, combined with the record-high levels of pumping in response to the high prices commanded for produce, put the valley's formerly self-sustaining aquifers into an apparent death spiral. A moratorium on new wells was put in place by state regulators.

By 2013 a plan was forming to save the groundwater—and thus save the valley's ag business. Farmers would tax themselves and pay each other to leave portions of their land unirrigated. Not everybody was on board. Some farmers and ranchers felt that their established prior rights to the surface water were being ignored to keep the commercial farmers' wells flowing. The new rules were locked up in court.

During spring 2015 there was a *deus ex machina*–type reprieve as heavy rains came to Colorado for a season, like a recently divorced uncle. With aquifers recharged, the people of the San Luis Valley prudently continued planning for a sustainable future. A new plan is being finalized by state and local agencies as I write this, which, it is hoped, will satisfy the Rio Grande Compact, put the aquifers on a sustainable track through the principle of augmentation, and keep all the valley's water consumers happy. Sounds about as realistic as a flying unicorn, but we'll see.

So the story of the San Luis Valley is largely a story of water, and that story is still being written. And the history of the Great Sand Dunes is also a story of water, believe it or not. Scientists currently think that a huge lake once covered most of the valley—and not that long ago in the grand scheme of things. When the lake either evaporated due to climate change or drained away to the south, about a half-million years ago, a large amount of sediment was left behind. The prevailing west-to-east winds tumbled the leftover sand up against the Sangre de Cristos. Meanwhile, occasional easterly winds piled the dunes back onto themselves, and Medano Creek took sand that had blown against the mountains and carried it back over to the other side of the dune field to begin its journey again. These unique conditions conspired to create the tallest dunes in North America, in a place where a reasonable human wouldn't expect to see any dunes at all.

The biggest dangers to the Great Sand Dunes have been man-made. After all the prime prospects and secondary prospects and long shots had been picked over by gold-seekers in the early twentieth century, mining companies and capital investors started to leer greedily at the sand dunes themselves. Maybe a large operation could suss out any gold in there and make a good profit. Of course, it would mean the complete destruction of this unique landscape, but that wouldn't stop it from happening if there was profit to be had. The looming possibility of large-scale mining of the dunes spurred many of the citizens into action, and they lobbied a new national monument into existence.

Protecting this unique corner of the world required more than turning it into a national monument (1932) or a national park (2000). Protecting the sand dunes means protecting the water that sustains them. Unfortunately, the water that sustains them was largely outside the park's boundaries, either up in the mountains or in the aquifer underneath the Baca Land Grant—owned by investors who had already tried to export the water to the Front Range for suburban development. After the groundwater speculators were stymied by the courts and bugged out, or were driven out, the Baca land was in limbo for years and then purchased by the Nature Conservancy. Meanwhile, the headwaters of Medano Creek, owned by the federal government,

The Great Sand Dunes are made from the sand left over from a lake that covered the San Luis Valley.

were set aside as a separate preserve. So—for the time being—the protection is in place and the dunes will live.

Though Crofutt ignored the dunes completely in his nineteenth-century *Grip-Sack Guide*, they became a popular destination. Most Colorado kids have memories of visiting the Great Sand Dunes as kids. It was a traditional road trip for families within striking distance of a '76 station wagon.

Most journeys to the Sand Dunes begin with a delightful crossing of Medano Creek. Very shallow, but plenty wide and very cold, Medano is taking its time shuttling sand grains back to the upwind side of the dune field. On the other side of the creek is a no-man's-land, a 200-yard dead-flat buffer before the dunes rise.

If you make it up to the highest dune visible from the parking area, called High Dune, it will give you a major sense of accomplishment even if you're a seasoned hiker. Don't get too excited, however. High Dune is only the sixth-highest dune in this mountain range made of sand. At the top you'll look out over a wavy ocean of dunes stretching off into the distance. About a mile to the west is Star Dune, the highest in the dune field, at 755 feet.

The Park Service used to measure the highest dunes every year with traditional survey equipment. Lately they've been using LiDAR mapping (light detection and ranging), which involves scanning the topography with a laser from an airplane to pin down exact elevations for every dune in the park. It's also interesting that the elevations don't change. It's obvious when you're up there that the dunes are an ever-changing thing—stop in your tracks, and it seems like you're still moving; then you realize the ground is moving. But the action of the competing winds from the west

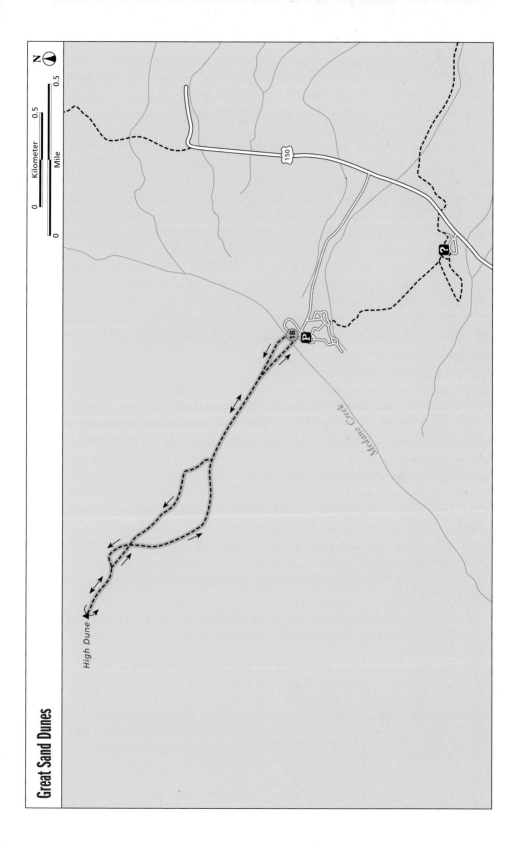

Great Sand Dunes

and east piling the dunes back on top of themselves apparently keeps their heights constant. Also, the sand below the surface is moist and relatively solid, so the core structure of the big dunes is unaffected by wind. A photo of the dunes from the 1870s has been compared to a photo from 130 years later, and very little change in the structure of the dunes is detectable.

If you make the climb to High Dune, you'll climb about 800 feet in elevation, Although the dune top is 700 feet above Medano Creek, you have to walk up and down several smaller dunes along the way. There's almost no way to avoid the up-and-down stuff. I hiked about 1.1 miles to get to High Dune (one way). You could get there with a shorter or longer route. Most people will gravitate toward a slightly longer route meandering along more ridges rather than the straighter route that involves some very steep pitches that will have you down on all fours.

This is far from an easy hike. It'll have you huffin' and puffin'. It will blast you in the face with sand. (Wear some eye protection.) It'll fill your shoes with sand. In the end it'll make you laugh and smile.

Notice how most of the families and casual hikers tend to come out into the first 100 meters or so of the dune field and have their fun there. Because walking up and down sand dunes is very hard work.

Don't hike dunes during thunderstorms!

The San Luis Valley is amazing on multiple levels. Great Sand Dunes National Park is just one of its many fascinating and unique features. For those who like to toodle around writing about history, the valley has more stories to tell than anywhere else in Colorado. This is already the longest chapter in the book, and I have touched on just a few of the historical wonders contained between these two mountain ranges. Others include the new-age cluster of Crestone; the sandhill cranes; Fort Garland; the Japanese migrants; the military's use of the valley, and associated testing of various vehicles, airborne and otherwise; the UFO sightings, many of which are probably related to the testing; the alligator farm; the cattle mutilations. Yes, cattle mutilations, verified and unexplained. The mysterious helicopters and shootings. It's a very interesting place.

Miles and Directions

0.0 Start from the big parking lot and walk into the sand. Medano Creek is right there in front of you, although there is some possibility that the creek will be dry. Aim for the highest dune you see.

1.1 Reach the top of High Dune (by the most direct route); turn around. (**Option:** Keep going!)

2.2 Arrive back at the parking lot (mileage assumes direct route).

Accommodations: You can camp at the Dunes in Piñon Flats Campground, or in the dune field! To camp in the dunes, first get a backcountry permit from the Park Service. www.nps.gov/grsa/planyourvisit/permitsandreservations.htm.

Southeast

Mountain lion track in the dried mud, Picketwire Canyon

19 Picketwire Canyon

Visit North America's most impressive dinosaur track site, and several other fascinating historic sites, on this long walk into Picketwire Canyon in extreme southeast Colorado.

Start: Picketwire Canyon Trailhead
Distance: 11.2 miles out and back
Approximate hiking time: 4 to 5 hours
Difficulty: Moderate to difficult
Trail surface: Jeep roads, moderately rocky; quite steep at the very beginning and end, otherwise flat
Best seasons: Spring and fall
Other trail users: Mountain bikers, hikers, and horses; possible motor tours on Sat
Canine compatibility: Leashed dogs permitted
Land status: Comanche National Grassland

Fees and permits: None
Schedule: Daylight only
Map: USGS Riley Canyon and Beaty Canyon quads
Trail contact: Comanche National Grassland; (719) 553-1400; www.fs.fed.us/visit/destination/picket-wire-trail
Special considerations: To reach the best dinosaur tracks, you will have to wade across the river. The trailhead is located at the end of a fairly rough dirt road that becomes very difficult to navigate when wet.

Finding the trailhead: From La Junta go south on CO 109 a bit over 12 miles and turn right onto David Canyon Road/CR 802. At a T-intersection take a left onto CR 25/Rourke Road. Go south on CR 25 until it turns 90 degrees to the west. There, turn left (east) onto an unmaintained dirt road (Road 500A). Drive 3.2 miles, turning left at the fork, and park at the informal parking area. GPS: N37 39.58' / W103 34.25'

The Hike

Picketwire is possibly the most fruitful history hike in the entire state. Not only is there a mind-blowing wonder of the world at the far end of this out-and-back—the most impressive dinosaur tracks you'll ever see—hikers also pass a variety of other historic sites along this jeep road, spanning several hundred years: a crumbling homestead, an old Hispanic mission, and some seriously cool prehistoric rock art.

If that wasn't enough, the canyon holds additional delights for those who can stand a very long and hot hike (or have some wheels at their disposal). The significant Rourke Ranch is at the end of the canyon, and a side canyon was once the home of a "hermit" who painted beautiful portraits of animals on the canyon walls, some of which are still visible. We won't see those two attractions on this route, but we'll have our hands (and feet) full and be totally satisfied with the basic out-and-back to the dinosaur tracks.

Picketwire Canyon is a deceptively extreme place. The canyon walls aren't very high, and the canyon is luxuriously wide. After the initial steep drop from the trailhead into Withers Canyon, the trail is wide and almost flat. But the weather is a killer, and

Petroglyphs on a trailside rock, Picketwire Canyon

there are very few people out here, relatively speaking. There are no visitor centers or other outcroppings of civilization and wealth. Just space. Alone with the elements.

When the Spanish explorers and dragoons came up this way, venturing beyond the comfortable enclave of Santa Fe, they sometimes starved to death and didn't make it back. They were resigned to leave the Great American Desert to the Comanches and Kiowas who roamed it with impunity.

The Spaniards' fearful reverence for the unforgiving grasslands of southeast Colorado was reflected in their name for the nearby river, which they called (in Spanish) the River of Souls Lost in Purgatory. Later, French trappers simplified it to the Purgatoire, and Anglos mangled it, tongue in cheek or otherwise, to Picketwire.

There's a lot of confusion about the origins of the names of the Purgatoire and Animas Rivers, both of which share similar names and legends for their naming. Lost souls. It may be too late at this point to sort it out.

Once you get acquainted with this canyon (it takes an hour or two to really get a feel for it), you'll gain much respect for the people who chose to live here. Or, depending on the weather that day, you'll be shaking your head at their folly. It's difficult to imagine how anyone could make it work without modern comforts like running water and refrigerators. You'll have an opportunity to think about it when you pass the old homesite on the right as you enter Picketwire itself. Whoever lived here was not excited about being near a bunch of other humans.

Speaking of other humans, plenty of large rocks between the ruined homestead and the ruined mission are adorned with petroglyphs of uncertain origin. It's not known exactly which prehistoric tribes or groups made the rock art, or when, but there was probably a wide variety in both artists and times of creation. Some of the petroglyphs in this part of the state are thought to be more than 4,000 years old.

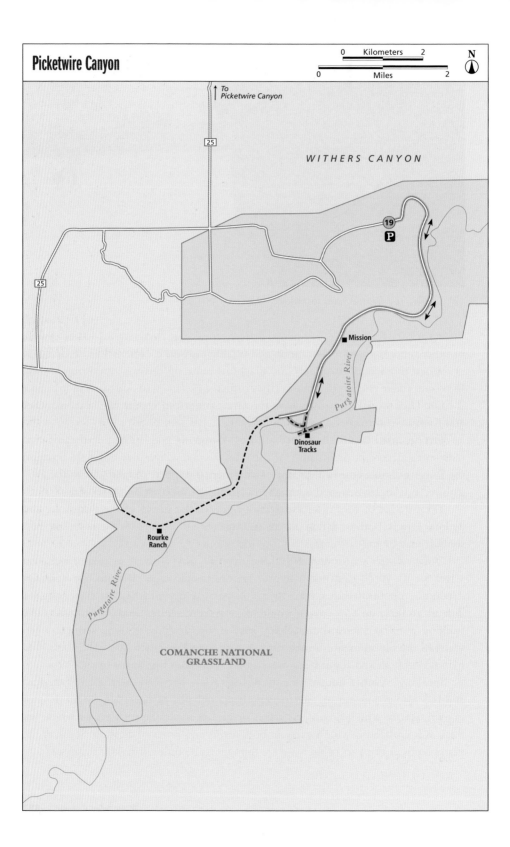

Picketwire Canyon

0 Kilometers 2

0 Miles 2

N

To Picketwire Canyon

25

WITHERS CANYON

25

19

P

Mission

Purgatoire River

Dinosaur Tracks

Rourke Ranch

Purgatoire River

COMANCHE NATIONAL GRASSLAND

Dolores Mission

The Dolores Mission sits at mile 3.9, with a tiny crumbled church and attached graveyard with hand-pecked stones. There are some foundations of residences in the field on the other side of the road. The little community consisted of eleven or twelve families and dates to the 1870s.

From dust to dust, from dust to dinosaur tracks, keep moseying on down the road. After a desolate, straight stretch of jeep road, you'll see the marked turnoff to the dinosaur tracks. There's a little parking area/trailhead here, with a bathroom. The parking area is used on Saturdays during the Forest Service's guided tours, the only way to see Picketwire in a motorized vehicle. (Tour guests must provide their own four-wheel drive and water and pay a fee. Contact the Forest Service for details.)

A short walk brings you to the river and a little bank of tracked-up sandstone. The really good stuff is across the river, and (as long as it's warm) it's worth getting a little wet to get over there. On the opposite slab there are long and obvious trackways made by huge brontosauruses strolling across what was, 150 million years ago, a lakeshore. Also look for smaller tracks made by meat-eating allosauruses. More than 100 separate trackways and about 1,300 individual tracks have been revealed by the river.

Miles and Directions

0.0 Start from the trailhead and begin walking downhill.

5.3 Turn left toward the dinosaur tracks on the river.

5.6 Check out the tracks and head back the way you came.

11.2 Arrive back at the trailhead.

Four Corners

What's left of Hovenweep Castle

20 Petroglyph Point Trail

Adventure-seekers will love this ruggedly gorgeous hike with many fascinating features, including a visit to Mesa Verde's best-preserved cliff dwelling and a panel of rock art. Hardly a hidden gem, this is a popular hike in a popular national park.

Start: Chapin Mesa Archaeological Museum, Chapin Mesa, Mesa Verde National Park
Distance: 2.3-mile loop
Approximate hiking time: 2 hours
Difficulty: Moderate
Trail surface: Rocky, rugged trail with many steep rock stairs and some scrambling. After the trail mounts the mesa, it is much smoother, wider, and flatter.
Best seasons: Spring, fall, and winter
Other trail users: Hikers; no dogs or bikes allowed on trails
Canine compatibility: No pets permitted on the trails

Land status: National park
Fees and permits: Per-vehicle fee to enter Mesa Verde National Park
Schedule: Sunrise to sunset
Map: Mesa Verde National Park map, National Park Service
Trail contact: Mesa Verde National Park, PO Box 8, Mesa Verde, CO 81330-0008; (970) 529-4465; www.nps.gov/meve
Special considerations: This trail is much more rugged than the park's literature lets on. Bring water, sunscreen, and a hat. Be prepared to spend a few hours out there.

Finding the trailhead: From US 160 turn south into Mesa Verde National Park. Drive all the way to the southern portion of the park at Chapin Mesa (not Wetherill Mesa) and park at the Spruce Tree House/Museum parking area. The trail begins next to the Chapin Mesa Archaeological Museum. GPS: N37 11.06' / W108 29.30'

The Hike

The near-universal reaction of the tourists who attempt to hike this loop is *fascinoyance*. What's fascinoyance, you ask? Fascinoyance is the perfect combination of two seemingly exclusive emotions, fascination and annoyance.

On the Petroglyph Point Trail loop, people expect the fascination. There is much here that fascinates. The annoyance, on the other hand, sneaks up on you. Hikers here tend to get annoyed when they find out that the route is much more strenuous and much trickier, and so takes a lot longer, than they expected. These same people might enjoy a tough hike as much as the next person, but in this case the Park Service literature has led them to expect a quick jaunt around the area. So, fascinoyance.

In fact, you may be experiencing fascinoyance right now as you read this.

No doubt about it, this is a great little hike. Start from the Chapin Mesa Archaeological Museum—better yet, start in the museum. The museum is filled with amazing artifacts and information and is a bit of a historical artifact in its own right. In 1924 John D. Rockefeller Jr. came to Mesa Verde National Park with his three sons and toured the biggest dwellings with the park superintendent guiding. Rockefeller was impressed and amazed. In such a mood, when he learned that Congress had appropriated nothing for the park's new museum project, he offered some of his private fortune to make it happen.

The massive area of Mesa Verde National Park contains over 600 cliff dwellings among almost 5,000 separate archaeological sites, according to the Park Service. Ancient structures at Mesa Verde, including cliff dwellings, pit houses, dams, walls, reservoirs and farming terraces, among other things, were created from around 600 to 1300 AD. The Spruce Tree House and other spectacular cliff dwellings were built and occupied during the final century of occupation.

At some point very late in their existence here, the people of Mesa Verde decided to pack themselves into these alcoves hanging over the canyons. They moved into the rocks, like pigeons. Why? The obvious answer is fear. Defense.

Some have wondered if the reason for the move could be even simpler. Might the truth be kinder and gentler? Maybe they found it was cool, as in awesome, to live in the cliffs. It is cool, you can see. Cozy. Neat. Even today people enjoy living in houses that are perched on cliffs and mountains, for no apparent practical reason. Not for defensive purposes, that's for sure. Maybe they enjoy the solitude or pretty views. And there is status associated with living in such places.

It is also literally much cooler in these alcoves. This is particularly obvious at Spruce Tree House. When it's 95 degrees on the sunbaked mesa top, it's about 20 degrees cooler tucked into the cliff in a shady canyon. There are real advantages to living in the shade in a place like this.

Living down here also brought people much closer to a great water source, a seep spring at the head of the canyon. Springs and canyons go together around here. Spruce Tree House residents would have had easy access to the spring but would have also been safe from flash floods that periodically washed through the canyon.

Despite these happy thoughts, real evidence suggests that violent conflict was widespread when the Ancestral Puebloans created the cliff dwellings and then left— or were eliminated from—the Four Corners area during the thirteenth century. There are signs of desperation in the archaeological record. We can see from their trash heaps that they went from eating their favored domesticated turkeys to smaller wild game, as the drought of the late 1200s strangled their agricultural production and ability to support domesticated animals. In this state of depleted resources, we see clear signs of violence. Skeletons found in the Mesa Verde area showed not only violent deaths but healed tomahawk wounds, indicating a state of ongoing warfare. Looking at other less glamorous cliff dwellings, precariously perched in cramped alcoves, it seems clear that the builders were very afraid of something.

This hike combines a visit to Spruce Tree House cliff dwelling, which is just across a shallow little canyon from the Chapin Mesa Archaeological Museum, with a surprisingly physical walk along, then up, the side of the canyon on a solid, well-established, but very up-and-down trail.

The Petroglyph Point Trail does some interesting things. PHOTO BY JERRY HURST

The Petroglyph Point Trail isn't your best choice if you want to crawl through ruins and climb rickety ladders and such (try the Balcony House guided tour), but it does have some payoff for history buffs. Those of us seeking historical intrigue will enjoy surprises like the ancient ax sharpening stone next to the trail—while hiking to the petroglyphs, look for a strange boulder on your left in front of a long alcove.

The boulder is gouged with several sharp troughs that were used to sharpen ax blades. Of course, at the far end of the loop is the petroglyph panel—at the poorly named Pictograph Point (pictographs are a different sort of rock art, painted on; petroglyphs are etched into the rock). Best of all, the hike begins with an up-close-and-personal look at Spruce Tree House, which will give you plenty to think about as you're working your way up the trail.

Spruce Tree House was named in the 1880s by one of the Wetherills, ranchers who were poking around Mesa Verde in amazement along with a Swedish scientist named Nordenskjold. The name for the site came from the huge Douglas fir trees that rise up in the canyon below, several of which are still standing today—Douglas firs can live for many hundreds of years. Douglas fir (*Pseudotsuga*) is a strange sort of evergreen, not really fir, nor spruce. During the 1800s the tree was commonly called the Douglas spruce, which is about as correct as its modern moniker Douglas fir. And that's why it's not called Fir Tree House. Watch for massive versions of whatever-you-call-it as the Petroglyph Point Trail begins. (And here's a weird but almost entirely off-topic side note: The botanist for whom the Douglas fir/spruce is named, David Douglas, was found dead in 1834, on Mauna Kea, at the bottom of a pit intended to trap wild bulls. Gashes in his head and his missing purse seemed to indicate that he had been murdered for his cash, then dumped in the pit.)

Spruce Tree House was the third-biggest cliff dwelling at Mesa Verde, with 120 rooms. The estimated population was under 100, about 20 families. Though Spruce Tree House is the least crumbled of all the cliff dwellings, you can see from the exposed beams where structures have fallen. The T-shaped openings are considered to be doorways to public spaces, plazas and such, while the rectangular doors led to private dwellings. It's easy to imagine from the placement of second-story doorways how they were accessed from the rooftops of one-story buildings that once stood below. The beams sticking out on the third floor are the remains of balconies. One of the big walls was reconstructed, but the vast majority of what you see at Spruce Tree House is original construction, 1200–80.

This little village in a cave was first excavated in the early twentieth century. Archaeologists found all kinds of pottery, bowls and ladles and whatnot, stone and bone tools, and sophisticated sandals made of yucca.

Beyond the big questions about the cliff dwellers that remain unanswered, researchers have wrestled with a smaller mystery at Spruce Tree House. There is a large area behind the structures, against the back wall of the alcove, that was left open. Archaeologists uncovered all kinds of weird items back there that seemed to indicate it was a sort of dump. However, others think the area was used for dancing and ceremonies. Either way, it's sacred space to the Pueblo and Hopi.

When you're checking out Spruce Tree House, watch for signs of the plaster coating that covered the stone walls, and the designs that were painted on the plaster. At twelve sites around Mesa Verde, including Spruce Tree House, archaeologists have found a familiar painted pattern on the walls. It consists of a row of triangles, pointed up. Around the edges of the triangles are dots. It certainly looks a bit like an abstract representation of a mountain range, and most researchers lean toward that interpretation. Local archaeologist Sally Cole has another—corn mountains: "My research suggests that in addition to mountains and skies, triangle-mound imagery represented ears of corn and mounds of soil in which corn was planted. It shared the symbolism of late Pueblo II and Pueblo III stone artifacts from Mesa Verde that Jesse Walter Fewkes, an anthropologist with the Smithsonian Institution in the late 1800s and early 1900s, interpreted as representing the end of an ear of corn and 'corn hills' symbolic of fertility." [Sally J. Cole, "Imagery and Tradition: Murals of the Mesa Verde Region," in David Grant Noble, ed., *The Mesa Verde World: Explorations in Ancestral Pueblo Archaeology* (2006), p. 98.]

If you choose, you can climb a ladder down into a *kiva* (a Hopi word), one of eight at Spruce Tree House, and check out its unique architecture. Often there is a line for the kiva during busy times.

And so the hike begins. Not too bad, right?

The Petroglyph Point Trail escapes the cluster of tourists, heading down-canyon. Not on the canyon floor, though, but up on the side, skirting along just under the band of sandstone. The trail isn't very exposed—you won't fall off a cliff—but it rises and falls sharply, using small footholds and rock steps that will keep you literally on your toes. It's slow going, not the quickie hike it appears to be on maps of the park. Hikers will need sturdy footwear, sturdy legs, and some grit. Also bring plenty of water, sunscreen, and a hat.

The park's booklet, "Petroglyph Trail Guide," is worth the fifty-cent donation, but most of the thirty-five or so waypoints described in it relate to plants and trees. Note also that the booklet does not include a route map. It does have a little "map" of the petroglyph panel, giving some interpretations of the meanings of different markings. Inferring from the booklet, much of what has been etched into the rock here was made not by the Ancestral Puebloans but by people who came later.

The petroglyph panel consists of a few spirals connected by a long, wandering line. Along the line are several glyphs representing animals: eagle, mountain sheep, parrot, lizard, mountain lion. The panel itself is a sort of map. The spiral at the upper right corner is said to represent a sipapu, the hole where the Pueblo people emerged from the earth—the starting point. The other spiral down toward the left, according to the "Petroglyph Trail Guide," which relates the interpretation given by "four Hopi men from Northeastern Arizona" in 1942, could represent the prophesied end of migration, in the land of the Hopi. This seems like a rather four-Hopi-men-centric interpretation. Another possible interpretation given in the pamphlet is that the spiral represents Mesa Verde. At other times and places, spirals are interpreted as representing springs, or an act of migration.

The animals are said to represent different clans and their locations where they dropped out of the group and settled along the route. For instance, the Eagle and Mountain Sheep clans apparently settled very near their point of origin. The lizard

The petroglyph panel at Pictograph Point is a jumble of older and newer markings. PHOTO BY JERRY HURST

symbol near the bottom of the panel, with the circle for a head, could represent the Horned Toad clan or, more interestingly, a crazy-making lizard spirit "whose influence upon the people led them into a period of wandering without direction—almost approaching lunacy." You can see where the line goes nutty as it passes the lizard symbol.

Over on the bottom right, there are several humanlike figures grouped together. Notice how one of the figures has one oversized hand raised, while the rest have both hands raised as if to say "Don't shoot!" Notice also the figure on the far left of the "map" who also has one hand raised overhead. These two waving figures are reportedly "whipping kachinas" who keep the people on the correct path—literally by whipping them. The other figures represent the Pueblo people.

The face on the far right with what appears to be a Fu Manchu mustache is reportedly the Kachina clan symbol. The pamphlet doesn't mention or picture the

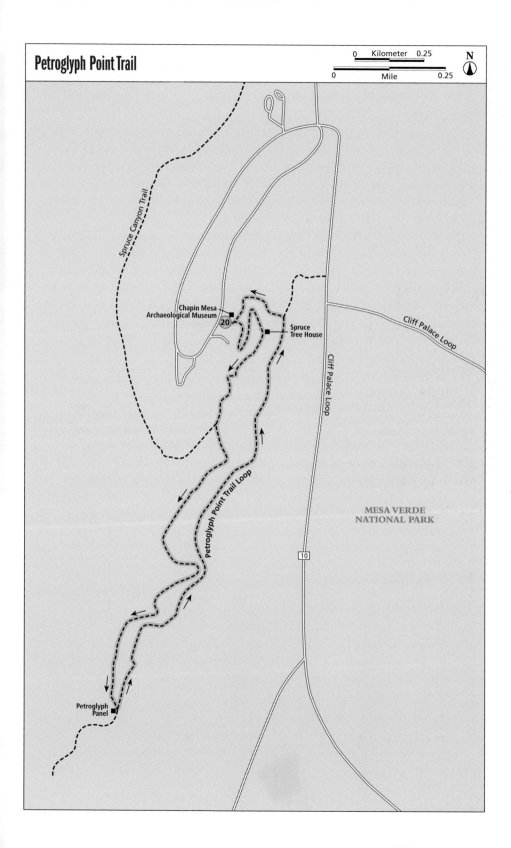

Petroglyph Point Trail

Kilometer 0.25

Mile 0.25

N

Spruce Canyon Trail

Chapin Mesa
Archaeological Museum

20

Spruce
Tree House

Cliff Palace Loop

Cliff Palace Loop

Petroglyph Point Trail Loop

MESA VERDE
NATIONAL PARK

10

Petroglyph
Panel

handprint glyphs at the top of panel, but these types of markings have been identified at many sites around the Southwest. Nobody is entirely certain when any of this rock art was created, but it seems likely that it wasn't all scratched into the rock at the same time.

Dating rock art is sketchier, if you'll pardon the pun, than dating ancient structures. Certain styles of rock art are considered to be older than others, so that is one way of narrowing down the time of origination. The *patination* of an etching can also tell us something about its age. Chemical reactions between bacteria and minerals in the rock create dark layers of "desert varnish" that grow darker over time. The darker the petroglyph, the older it is, generally speaking.

The loop continues from the petroglyphs, believe it or not. For some hikers this will look very much like the end of the line. A sign points the way up the cliff, a seemingly very tall order. *Fascinoyance!* Upon closer inspection, you'll find nicely placed little steps and handholds that will let you climb to the top of the small sandstone cliff without too much trouble (my 75-year-old dad did it, and he actively avoids such things). The remainder of the hike is flat and easy, but hot, as the trail loops back around to the museum.

Miles and Directions

0.0 Start from the Chapin Mesa Archaeological Museum and begin hiking down the asphalt path toward Spruce Tree House.

0.2 Check out Spruce Tree House; then, while exiting the cliff house exhibit with the crowds, turn left onto the Petroglyph Point Trail. The intersection is just below the cliff dwelling.

0.4 Continue on the Petroglyph Point Trail as the Spruce Canyon Trail intersects on the right.

1.2 Arrive at the petroglyph panel, aka Pictograph Point. From here the trail ascends sharply to the top of the canyon. Not as bad as it looks!

2.2 The trail arrives back near Spruce Tree House, popping out onto the asphalt path at a stealthy intersection near the museum (the Park Service deliberately keeps this intersection somewhat hidden to discourage clockwise travel along the loop). Turn right onto the path.

2.3 Arrive back at the museum.

Accommodations: Mesa Verde Motel, W. 191 Railroad Ave., Mancos, CO 81328; (970) 533-7741; www.mesaverdemotel.com. Affordable, clean motel in Mancos.

White Eagle Inn, 2110 S. Broadway, Cortez, CO 81321; (970) 565-3333; http://whiteeagleinn.com. Clean rooms and hospitality at this no-frills budget motel on the highway south of Cortez; pool out of commission.

21 Soda Canyon Overlooks

This short hike on Chapin Mesa, to three tightly spaced and possibly redundant over-looks, gives you a different perspective on life in the canyons.

Start: A small parking pull-off on the east side of the Cliff Palace Loop, Chapin Mesa, Mesa Verde National Park

Distance: 1.2-mile lariat loop

Approximate hiking time: 40 minutes to 1 hour

Difficulty: Easy

Trail surface: Wide, flat trail with some rocks and minor steps

Best seasons: Spring, fall, and winter

Other trail users: Hikers

Canine compatibility: No pets permitted on the trails. Please do not leave pets in vehicles while you hike.

Land status: National park

Fees and permits: Per-vehicle fee to enter Mesa Verde National Park

Schedule: Sunrise to sunset

Map: Mesa Verde National Park map, National Park Service

Trail contact: Mesa Verde National Park, PO Box 8, Mesa Verde, CO 81330-0008; (970) 529-4465; www.nps.gov/meve

Special considerations: This hike visits no ruins or historic sites, but gives you a cool view of the Balcony House cliff dwelling from afar. To tour Balcony House, tickets must be purchased ahead of time at the park visitor center or at a few other locations. There are no self-guided tours of Balcony House.

Finding the trailhead: From US 160 turn south into Mesa Verde National Park. Drive 15 miles to Far View Terrace; then turn left toward Chapin Mesa. Drive another 5 miles; then turn left onto the Cliff Palace Loop. The trailhead is on the east side of the Cliff Palace Loop, north of Balcony House. Since Cliff Palace Loop is one-way, you must drive almost all the way around the loop to reach the Soda Canyon Overlook Trailhead, which is just a small parking area on the right side of the road. GPS: N37 10.05' / W108 28.20'

The Hike

This is a quick little jaunt to the edge of a canyon, where three small overlooks pro-vide a nice yet unspectacular view of the adjacent area. From the first two viewpoints, you can gaze across the canyon at Balcony House and its ever-present swarm of giddy tourists. Balcony House is named for fairly obvious reasons.

The middle overlook has a viewfinder with a powerful lens. This will give you a good chance to zoom in on the otherwise distant scene at Balcony House and decide if you want to join one of the guided tours. Notice that visitors to Balcony House must climb down several fairly serious ladders and through a tunnel to reach the dwelling. It's the most adventurous tour available at Mesa Verde. Unforgettable, but not for everybody.

The view from up here is stark, severe, beautiful: canyons with piñon-juniper-spotted slopes of shale, ramping up to sandstone cliffs, topped with more piñon and

Ancestral Pueblo thrived in these canyons for 700 years.

juniper and shrubs and angry cactus, as far as the eye can see. The continuity is broken only by the jagged canyon walls and an apocalyptic-looking area of blackened junipers, caused by a fire in 2000. Not a drop of water in sight. With some minor tweaks, these are the same conditions under which the Ancestral Puebloans thrived for more than 700 years. Is this entity we call the United States going to last that long? Maybe, but we've got a long way to go before the duration of the nation is even half as long as the duration of the Ancestral Puebloans' existence in the Four Corners region.

The first (known) people to live at Mesa Verde, in around 550 AD, were "Basketmakers." Numbering just a few hundred, they lived in pit houses and used the atlatl, a combination spear and slingshot; they were just learning about ceramic pottery and the bow and arrow. Slowly but surely they were completing the transition from a nomadic lifestyle to a settled farming lifestyle.

"Mesa Verde was a good choice for settling down," notes paleohydrologist Kenneth Wright in *The Water Mysteries of Mesa Verde*. "It had loess, a wind-blown deposit of 3 feet of soil that had blown in from Monument Valley about fifteen thousand years earlier. In the sixth century Mesa Verde was a fertile place for growing crops. Thick forests of pine and juniper provided privacy, security, isolation, building materials, and fuel. Sunshine warmed the south-facing canyons and tablelands. The people adapted so well that their descendants stayed for 750 years."

About 400 years after the first settlements, the population around Mesa Verde was well into the thousands. Agriculture had advanced, and the art of building structures with stone was established and advancing fast. Perhaps most important to their continued habitation, the Ancestral Puebloans of Mesa Verde had already developed canal systems and reservoirs to deliver a stable water supply.

Researchers are primarily concerned with the mystery of this civilization's end, the sudden exodus or disappearance or massacre of the ancient ones. Another tantalizing area of study is their mastery of this difficult environment (which was not much different than we see today, although the land may have been substantially deforested then). Archaeologists noted check dams and farming terraces around the pueblo ruins, and the fact that maize, a new creation, grew with relative ease here in the loess. It wasn't until the turn of the twenty-first century that the full extent of the Ancestral Puebloans' civil engineering prowess came to light.

In 1995 Kenneth Wright and a team of researchers began studying a handful of relatively large-scale engineering projects completed and maintained by the Ancestral Pueblos. In particular, park officials were stumped by a mysterious mound on the floor of Morefield Canyon. Wright was able to prove that the mound was once an ancient reservoir, the first of at least four dug out by the Pueblos of Mesa Verde. He estimated the reservoir came on line around the year 750. The pond eventually became a mound due to the Pueblos' building up of berms to keep up with sedimentation, and the sedimentation's eventual takeover.

When the researchers sliced deep into ancient dirt of Morefield reservoir, it told some cool stories. "The sand layers reveal 21 periods of flooding over the 350 years of the reservoir's operation, and layers of charcoal mark some 14 forest fires," according to Wright.

Fifty years after building their first big reservoir, they built another in Box Elder Canyon. Then they created two mesa-top reservoirs, one at Far View and another at Sagebrush. Each was about 90 feet across and lined carefully with stone. Each had been frequently mistaken for some kind of dance pavilion by modern researchers.

It took a while for scientists and historians to come to grips with the idea of Mesa Verdeans' engineering such sophisticated hydro projects. As Wright says, "These four archaeological sites represent a remarkable legacy of public works engineering, continuity of technology, and the organizational skills needed to keep the reservoirs operational for hundreds of years."

Far View Reservoir (Chapin Mesa Reservoir) and the accompanying village ruins are worth a look. The site—not a cliff dwelling but a mesa-top settlement—is on Chapin Mesa Road, so you can drop by on your way out.

The people of Mesa Verde lived in the canyons and on the mesas into the thirteenth century; then, for reasons not completely understood, many of them moved into the cliff dwellings. They lived in the cliff dwellings for maybe 50 years before departing en masse for points south and east, leaving their ghostly and magical little

Why Do Civilizations Fail?

The question of why societies end, fail, or collapse gets a lot of attention, and the Ancestral Pueblo are often used as an example. Some researchers have introduced a very compelling take on it. They argue that a sort of pathology, perhaps just an expression of human nature, took hold among the Ancestral Pueblo that kept them from adapting to changing conditions. Instead of deftly changing strategies and directions, the group remained committed to the strategies that worked before, when conditions were different. Groupthink took over: "Once members of a group reach consensus, the easiest way to maintain consensus is to stay committed to the group's decision." For many reasons change becomes difficult for societies on obvious approach to the edge of an abyss. Sound familiar at all?

> "We think we can discern evidence that people with large invest-
> ments have, as a result of those investments, a tendency to rather
> rigidly attempt to maintain a previously successful way of life in areas
> and times when they are experiencing severely reduced returns on
> those investments—even to the point where they make additional
> investments in trying to maintain what perhaps ought to have been
> perceived as a lost cause. As a result, local depletion becomes more
> severe than would have been the case, had they chosen to leave ear-
> lier, or otherwise changed the nature of their adaptation. In turn the
> final collapse appears all the more dramatic, given the more impres-
> sive nature of the final structures left behind in a desolate landscape."
> [Marco Janssen, Timothy Kohler and Marten Scheffer, "Sunk-Cost
> Effects Made Ancient Societies Vulnerable to Collapse," 2002.]

Joseph Tainter, in his famous work *Collapse of Complex Societies,* put it this way: "If a society cannot deal with resource depletion . . . then the truly interesting questions revolve around the society, not the resource."

But Mr. Tainter, can any society deal with resource depletion?

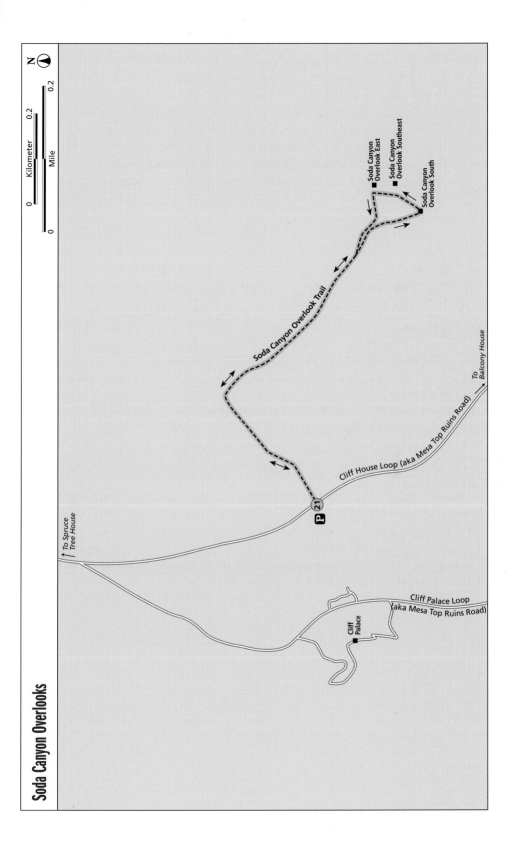

Soda Canyon Overlooks

N

Kilometer
0   0.2   0.2

Mile
0   0.2

To Spruce
Tree House

To
Balcony House

P 21

Cliff House Loop (aka Mesa Top Ruins Road)

Soda Canyon Overlook Trail

Soda Canyon Overlook East
Soda Canyon Overlook Southeast
Soda Canyon Overlook South

Cliff Palace Loop
(aka Mesa Top Ruins Road)

Cliff Palace

villages behind. Or so it seems. In Mesa Verde, as at Castle Rock and elsewhere, there is evidence that the last thing that occurred in these small communities was a devastating attack by some mysterious enemy. Current research has anthropologists thinking that the Ancestral Puebloans turned on each other when things got desperate. Other evidence suggests that they were massacred by invaders, possibly ancestral Utes. Not surprisingly, modern-day Utes push back against that hypothesis, and modern-day Pueblos and Hopis push back against the theory that it was an inside job.

Hundreds of years later Spanish explorers entered the zone of empty stone hamlets around the big plateau and called it Mesa Verde. Where'd everybody go? they wondered.

The Spaniards' name for this place is telling: Green Table. Green Mesa. Does it seem green to you? If you're coming from almost anywhere north of here, it probably won't. It might seem impossibly dry. But if you just crossed the Mojave Desert like a Spanish explorer, it might seem like some kind of green oasis. It proved plenty verde for the Ancestral Pueblo, until it wasn't.

Miles and Directions

0.0 Start from the trailhead at the pull-off along the Cliff Palace Loop.

0.5 The trail veers right here as another subtle trail intersects on the left. The first overlook is dead ahead.

0.6 Enjoy the overlook; then continue north to the next one.

0.6 The middle overlook has a cool viewfinder.

0.7 After enjoying the northernmost overlook, find the trail looping back to the main trail.

0.75 Turn right, returning on the Soda Canyon Overlook Trail.

1.2 Arrive back at the car.

Accommodations: Mesa Verde Motel, W. 191 Railroad Ave., Mancos, CO 81328; (970) 533-7741; www.mesaverdemotel.com. Affordable, clean motel in Mancos.

White Eagle Inn, 2110 S. Broadway, Cortez, CO 81321; (970) 565-3333; http://whiteeagleinn.com. Clean rooms and hospitality at this no-frills budget motel on the highway south of Cortez; pool out of commission.

22 McElmo Loop

More than a mere leg-stretcher, this hike from the Sand Canyon Trailhead tours Ancestral Puebloan ruins in ruggedly beautiful canyon country.

Start: Sand Canyon Trailhead
Distance: 7.5-mile loop
Approximate hiking time: 2.5 to 5 hours
Difficulty: Moderate to difficult
Trail surface: Slickrock and sandy dirt; many rugged, rocky sections
Best seasons: Spring, fall, and winter
Other trail users: Hikers, bikes, and dogs
Canine compatibility: Dogs allowed
Land status: Canyons of the Ancients National Monument
Fees and permits: None
Schedule: None
Map: Canyons of the Ancients National Monument Sand Canyon & Rock Creek trails map, Bureau of Land Management

Trail contact: Canyons of the Ancients and Anasazi Heritage Center, 27501 CO 184, Dolores, CO 81323; (970) 882-5600; www .blm.gov/co/st/en/nm/canm.html
Special considerations: Don't disturb the ruins. (**Note:** This route does not lead to Sand Canyon Pueblo. The remains of Sand Canyon Pueblo [for the most part covered in dirt by archaeologists] are located at the other end of Sand Canyon Trail.) This is a fairly serious route through an extreme desert landscape. Bring water! Wear sunscreen and long-sleeve shirts and hats.

Finding the trailhead: From Cortez drive south on US 160; then turn right (west) on CR G. Drive 12 miles to the Sand Canyon Trailhead on the right side of the road. GPS: N37 20.49' / W108 49.06'

The Hike

As you emerge from your vehicle at the Sand Canyon Trailhead in McElmo Canyon, you are standing at a massacre site.

Known to archaeologists as Castle Rock Pueblo, the village that arose on and around the area's most prominent sandstone landmark was attacked and destroyed by invaders in the late 1200s. So too was Sand Canyon Pueblo, on the north end of Sand Canyon. Other villages in the area were also attacked.

The evidence of a massacre was pretty obvious: dashed-in skulls, and skeletons that had been speared and dumped in awkward positions (an "abandonment state"). They found at least forty-one victims at Castle Rock—with all the dismemberment it was difficult to tell exactly how many. Archaeologists also found evidence of non-lethal head injuries on at least four skulls at Castle Rock and several more at Sand Canyon, indicating that a significant degree of warfare or violence had been ongoing before the final massacre.

Two hundred years before the arrival of Columbus, a massacre occurred here. But who were the killers?

Beyond the massacre itself, archaeologists found evidence of something even more fascinating here. They call it *anthropophagy*, so as not to alarm the ignorant masses too much. We ignorant masses know it as cannibalism. But that word has such a, well, negative connotation that scientists avoid applying it to the Ancestral Pueblo, because they don't know exactly what circumstances led people to dine on other people at Castle Rock and Sand Canyon and other sites where this phenomenon is evident. Whether it was pure desperation or if there was some religious or other motivation, for instance, nobody knows for sure. Nor do they know exactly who was eating whom. But eat they did. Archaeologists found utensil marks on human bones at these sites, human feces with the remains of other humans in it, and other irrefutable evidence.

Many researchers point out that the period of violence in Ancestral Pueblo lands corresponded to a big drought, which is apparent in tree ring data and corroborated by the types of bones found in their middens (what we might call kitchen trash). If they couldn't grow maize, their primary source of food would have disappeared, along with their secondary source, domesticated turkeys.

Kristin Kuckelman, an archaeologist who has studied the area about as much as anyone, sums up the prevailing majority opinion in a 2006 article:

Recent evidence from Sand Canyon Pueblo indicates that when the climate deteriorated in the late 1200s, maize crops failed and turkey flocks, which were fed maize, were decimated. People were forced to search out and eat both a wider variety and less preferred types of wild plants and animals and to compete with residents of other communities for these dwindling resources. Social, political, or religious problems might have caused conflicts during this time, but increasing violence in other parts of the Southwest and of the entire continent during the late 1200s and early 1300s suggests that the cause was a wide-ranging one such as a climate shift, instead of societal problems particular to the Pueblo people of the Mesa Verde region.

That might explain the why of it. But who attacked Castle Rock Pueblo? Was it some distant enemy? From the mountains? From the south? A neighboring Pueblo, people from Mesa Verde itself? It's a subject of much debate. Kuckelman points out that there isn't much evidence (so far) that would suggest the attackers came from far away. "I believe the invaders were warriors from other Pueblo communities in the region," she writes. "Severe shortages of food or water might have provided ample motivation for Pueblo people in the Mesa Verde region to go to war against neighboring Pueblo communities."

On the other hand, the apparent one-sided nature of the engagement might indicate an invasion by some "foreign" group with superior tactics or technology. Interestingly, Hopi oral tradition implicates "savage strangers from the north" (see sidebar).

In the 1800s, when the Castle Rock site was located by archaeologists, there were many other structures here that have since disappeared. We know this at least from the photographs of William H. Jackson, who in 1874 set up his camera very close to where you'll be standing at the Sand Canyon Trailhead. There were buildings and kivas on top of the rock and all over its flanks. Almost all of the structures in the immediate vicinity tumbled down or were manually destroyed.

Start the hike by heading up to the left of Castle Rock, following the cairns. Soon the trail splits. Veer right to begin a counterclockwise loop.

The hike begins and ends atop an exposed slab of white sedimentary rock: Navajo sandstone, the remains of windblown dunes. Castle Rock and the orange cliffs that line the canyons, in the alcoves of which the Ancestral Puebloans built houses, kivas, and granaries, are composed of Entrada sandstone, which was also born as sand dunes. During the Jurassic period, when these layers were formed, the Four Corners region looked like the Bedouin-and-camel-tracked set of a Hollywood movie.

The first third of this hike is bedecked with ancient sites. Much of the fun here involves sniffing out the ruins for yourself, so I won't spoil it with too much direction. Simply watch for the spur trails that are (at time of this writing) well marked but not named. Each one leads to something interesting if not mind-blowing. In a few cases the spurs merely lead to natural viewing platforms along the canyon rim. From some of these it is possible to spy more cliff dwellings on the other side of the canyon.

Other than the little side trails that are highly recommended, the route is a basic loop with a handful of important intersections. The intersections have been clearly marked with maps on signs, but don't count on it—these signs have a habit of disappearing. Bust a left from the Sand Canyon Trail onto the East Rock Creek Connector Trail before the Sand Canyon Trail gets into Sand Canyon. It might not be a great idea to give you a mile marker for this turn, because of all the little side trips hikers are likely to have made leading to this point (GPS: N37 21.53' / W108 48.19').

The East Rock Creek Trail is thin and twisty as it works its way northwest. This trail isn't about getting anywhere in a hurry. It darts around junipers and boulders and twists in and out of countless drainages so its users, primarily mountain bikers,

Invaders from the North?

During the Hayden Survey in 1874, a journalist named Ernest Ingersoll recorded a legend about Castle Rock, which was told to him by a white man who had served as the first Indian agent to the Hopi (then commonly called Moqui) and spoke their language. There doesn't seem to be much in the archaeological record that would refute the version of events that he told. In the Hopi oral tradition, the Ancestral Pueblo farmers manage to beat back the invaders after a month-long battle, but decided to leave the area anyway:

> They cultivated the valley, fashioned whatever utensils and tools they needed very neatly and handsomely out of clay and wood and stone, not knowing any of the useful metals; built their homes and kept their flocks and herds in the fertile river-bottoms, and worshiped the sun. They were an eminently peaceful and prosperous people, living by agriculture rather than by the chase. About a thousand years ago, however, they were visited by savage strangers from the North, whom they treated hospitably. Soon these visits became more frequent and annoying. Then their troublesome neighbors—ancestors of the present Utes—began to forage upon them, and, at last, to massacre them and devastate their farms; so, to save their lives at least, they built houses high upon the cliffs, where they could store food and hide away till the raiders left. But one summer the invaders did not go back to their

can savor the rugged landscape. The trail may have been built with bikes in mind, but it makes a great hiking trail as well. Don't feel bad about hiking here. It's open to everyone, and there aren't likely to be enough cyclists to make the trail feel crowded in the slightest.

There are some points out there where you might lose the trail for a second here and there and begin wandering aimlessly into the outback. Keep checking to make sure you're following the path, usually marked by at least a few mountain bike tracks. Route-finding can be especially tricky on desert trails after a big rainstorm or heavy winds wipe out all the tracks on the trail and make all the surfaces look the same.

mountains as the people expected, but brought their families with them and settled down. So, driven from their homes and lands, starving in their little niches on the high cliffs, they could only steal away during the night, and wander across the cheerless uplands. To one who has traveled these steppes, such a flight seems terrible, and the mind hesitates to picture the suffering of the sad fugitives.

At the *cristone* they halted, and probably found friends, for the rocks and caves are full of the nests of these human wrens and swallows. Here they collected, erected stone fortifications and watch-towers, dug reservoirs in the rocks to hold a supply of water, which in all cases is precarious in this latitude, and once more stood at bay. Their foes came, and for one long month fought and were beaten back, and returned day after day to the attack as merciless and inevitable as the tide. Meanwhile, the families of the defenders were evacuating and moving south, and bravely did their protectors shield them till they were all safely a hundred miles away. The besiegers were beaten back and went away. But the narrative tells us that the hollows of the rocks were filled to the brim with the mingled blood of conquerors and conquered, and red veins of it ran down into the cañon. It was such a victory as they could not afford to gain again, and they were glad, when the long fight was over, to follow their wives and little ones to the south. There, in the deserts of Arizona, on well-nigh unapproachable isolated bluffs, they built new towns, and their few descendants, the Moquis, live in them to this day. [Quoted in *Geological and Geographical Survey of the Territories* (U.S. Government Printing Office, 1876), p. 380.]

Saddlehorn Pueblo

For the final leg of the hike, there is the option of taking either of two trails. Both lead back to the trailhead. One is open to mountain bikers but not horses; the other is open to horses but not mountain bikers. The mountain bike trail is routed more creatively, whimsically you might say, with fun surprises all the way back to the trailhead.

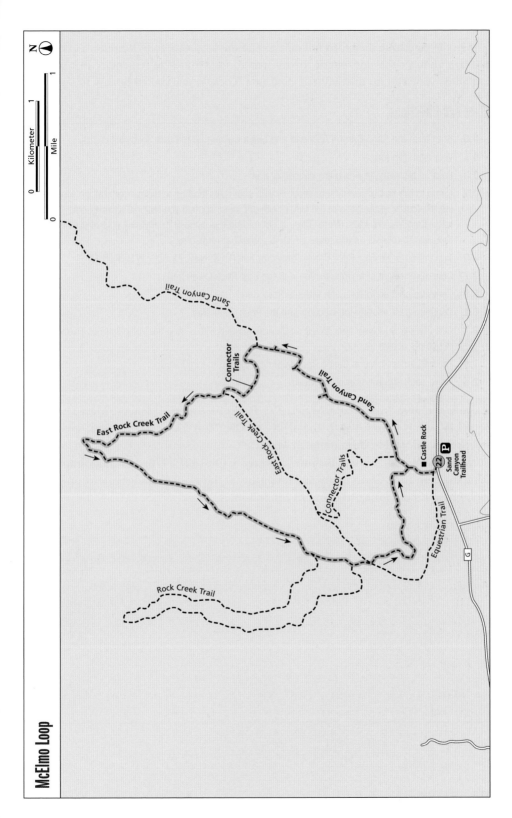

McElmo Loop

East Rock Creek Trail

Sand Canyon Trail

Connector Trails

East Rock Creek Trail

Sand Canyon Trail

Connector Trails

Rock Creek Trail

Equestrian Trail

Castle Rock

Sand Canyon Trailhead

22

G

N

Kilometer
Mile

0   1

0   1

On the sandstone shelf for a full mile to end the loop, the "trail" becomes a cairn-to-cairn connect-the-dots puzzle. If you start to lose your way, remember that you can guide yourself into the trailhead via Castle Rock, which should be easy to see.

Miles and Directions

0.0 Start from the Sand Canyon Trailhead and begin walking up the rock, following cairns.

0.1 Veer right at a fork.

0.3 Pass an intersection with a tiny connector trail.

0.7 Come to the first of several intersections with spur trails leading to the canyon wall on your left to alcoves at the base of the cliff. Check out these spurs if you feel like touring some interesting ancient sites. (***Note:*** There is not interpretive signage or anything else to explain the ruins to tourists on this route, which is somewhat refreshing.)

2.0 Turn left onto the East Rock Creek Connector Trail (GPS: N37 21.53' / W108 48.19').

2.7 Continue straight at an intersection with the East Rock Creek Trail.

5.9 Continue past an intersection with the Rock Creek Trail.

6.1 Continue past another intersection with the Rock Creek Trail.

6.2 At a three-way intersection, go left on the trail marked with a mountain bike symbol. Follow the cairns across the rock.

7.4 The trail arrives back at Castle Rock. Veer right toward the trailhead.

7.5 Arrive back at Sand Canyon Trailhead.

Accommodations: Mesa Verde Motel. 191 Railroad Avenue, Mancos. Mesa Verde Motel, W. 191 Railroad Ave., Mancos, CO 81328; (970) 533-7741; www.mesaverde motel.com. Affordable, clean motel in Mancos.

White Eagle Inn, 2110 S. Broadway, Cortez, CO 81321; (970) 565-3333; http:// whiteeagleinn.com. Clean rooms and hospitality at this no-frills budget motel on the highway south of Cortez; pool out of commission.

23 Hovenweep

An amazing short hike around a seemingly desolate canyon that once teemed with human life. The "tower" ruins at Hovenweep are among the most impressive and best preserved in the Southwest, and defy tidy explanations.

Start: Hovenweep National Monument Visitor Center
Distance: 1.7-mile lariat loop
Approximate hiking time: 1 to 2 hours
Difficulty: Easy to moderate
Trail surface: Moderately rocky and rugged; includes a short but steep descent to the bottom of the canyon, on rock steps, and a quick climb back out
Best seasons: Spring, fall, and winter
Other trail users: Hikers and lizards
Canine compatibility: Leashed dogs permitted
Land status: National monument
Fees and permits: None
Schedule: Trails open from sunrise to sunset. The visitor center open from 8 a.m. to 6 p.m. during the summer months. During the winter the visitor center hours are a little shorter, and it is closed on major holidays.
Map: Little Ruin trail guide, National Park Service
Trail contact: Hovenweep National Monument, McElmo Route, Cortez, CO 81321; (970) 562-4282, ext. 10; www.nps.gov/hove/index.htm
Special considerations: This is a desert hike with potential for serious sunburn and dehydration. Wear hats, sunscreen, or a bedouin robe. Bring water. Please stay on the trails. Don't approach the ruins. Note that the hike includes a steep rock staircase. If this is too much for some hikers, simply do an out-and-back, turning around at some point before the trail dives into the canyon. This portion of Hovenweep National Monument is actually in Utah. Don't be alarmed.

Finding the trailhead: From Cortez drive south for about 2 miles on US 491; then turn right (west) onto CR G/McElmo Canyon Road. Stay on CR G/McElmo Canyon Road for about 30 miles; then turn right onto CR 401 (follow the signs). After about 4 miles on CR 401, take another right on CR 413. Drive about 6 miles on CR 413 and then turn right toward the visitor center. GPS: N37 23.14' / W109 04.52'. (**Note:** GPS users take note—the Park Service issued the following alert in 2015, "Using GPS to find your way to Hovenweep is not recommended. Since Hovenweep has 6 different units with numerous paved and dirt roads intersecting each other, GPS will send visitors to unknown locations other than to the park. Using a map is recommended.")

The Hike

Hovenweep National Monument is not to be missed if you're a history buff. Though you might have to travel ever so slightly into the state of Utah to experience this unique hike, don't let that scare you off.

The Antiquities Act was signed by President Roosevelt in 1906, a response to decades of rampant plundering of ancient sites. The new law made it illegal to disturb or remove artifacts from federal land and gave the president power to create national

Stronghold House from below PHOTO BY JERRY HURST

monuments at his/her whim. Hovenweep, named by photographer William H. Jackson in 1874, became a national monument in 1923. (According to the Park Service pamphlet, *Hovenweep* is Ute for "deserted valley.")

By the time the Antiquities Act was signed into law, it was too late. Much of the archaeological value of the most important sites was already destroyed. Some of the destruction was perpetrated by professional artifact thieves and dealers who mined ancient sites like prospectors searching for flakes of gold. Much of the destruction can be blamed on clueless tourists who engaged in pot-hunting as a form of family entertainment.

After the law's passage, bold criminal attacks on southwestern archaeological sites continued. At Hovenweep in 1983 some unknown perpetrator(s) systematically dug

Hovenweep Castle

out artifacts from around one of the structures. It's not overly dramatic to say that whatever was taken then might have altered our understanding of Hovenweep, or even the Ancestral Pueblo in general.

This hike around Little Ruin Canyon is a ghost town tour like no other. The trail loops past the remains of several structures built right on the edge of the small cliff, giving hikers close-up views as well as equally intriguing cross-canyon views. The trail goes around the head of the spring-carved canyon—the spring being the whole reason for this community's existence—returns on the other side, and finally dives in and out of the canyon itself to complete the loop. The section within the canyon has some short, vertical sections that require much more careful footsteps and might be beyond the limits of some hikers. In that case an out-and-back along the canyon rim is a worthy substitute for the complete loop.

To our modern eyes the architecture at Hovenweep is among the most impressive in the Ancestral Puebloans' former stomping grounds. The "towers" of Hovenweep and elsewhere in the region were created during the last period of their 700-year occupation, during the thirteenth century, concurrent with the cliff dwellings of Mesa Verde. The fact that so many of the towers were built on the edges of cliffs from hand-carved stone and are still standing, more or less, about 800 years after their construction is testament to the skills of the builders. Huge piles of sandstone bricks down in the canyon are testament to the fact that time always wins, no matter how good of a builder you are. But there are a lot more interesting questions here than those involving masonry techniques.

Most modern observers think the towers, sometimes round, sometimes square, and sometimes D-shaped, were defensive lookouts and battlements, but they may have served other important functions. Towers may have been used for signaling, ceremonial purposes, storage of grain or even water, or some combination. The groundbreaking southwestern archaeologist Jesse Walter Fewkes uncovered some support for the storage theory in his excavations of ground-level rooms of southwestern towers. "In support of the interpretation that some of these rooms are granaries," he noted in 1923 in *American Anthropologist*, "we find rows of vases in which corn is stored still standing in them." Lately experts have leaned toward the ceremonial explanation, pointing to attached kivas at many towers and the similarities in round tower and kiva construction methods. Some researchers have focused on the towers' placement in alignment with astronomical features and events and have called them observatories. Some researchers argue that the placement of towers sent a simple message to others that the adjacent areas, often relatively prime farm fields, were already owned and under control—functioning sort of like the placeholder cabins of homesteaders. This is the least uplifting explanation, and probably the one we are least likely to believe.

You'll see a handful of fine towers and several other world-famous ruins on this short hike around Little Ruin Canyon at Hovenweep National Monument. Embarking straight from the visitor center on a counterclockwise sweep through the Square Tower Group of ruins—one of six scattered clusters of ruins that comprise the national monument—the first point of interest is Stronghold House. Stronghold House was probably not a stronghold at all, but nobody is real sure what exactly was going on there. The original structure was built on timbers out over the ledge and connected to a larger complex below, and all of that has collapsed into the canyon.

From this viewpoint you also get a good look at Eroded Boulder House, down in the canyon. This is one of the most unusual-looking cliff dwellings ever found. Fewkes described the ruin in 1919:

> *The front walls are somewhat broken down, but others built in the rear of the cave still remain intact. On the top of the bowlder is the debris of fallen walls, suggesting a former tower, but not much remains in place to determine its outlines. Where the walls are protected the mortar shows impressions of human hands and at one place there are the indentations of a corncob used by the plasterers to press the mortar between the layers of stone. There were formerly at least two rooms in the rear of the cave, the front walls of which have fallen and are strewn down the talus to the bottom of the canyon."* [Jesse Walter Fewkes, Prehistoric Villages, Castles, and Towers of Southwestern Colorado.]

Continuing down the trail, the next ruin is Unit Type House, the generic name reflecting what archaeologists believe was the generic purpose of this little compound. It was a common house for a family or two, with kiva. Nice view for a common house, though.

Take a left at the intersection and walk out to Tower Point. Prime tower action here. The placement of this tower lends credence to the argument that towers were intended as lookouts, to see and be seen. All of the structures here at Little Ruin Canyon seem like they might have been placed, directly or indirectly, to guard the precious spring.

Rejoin the main trail and continue the counterclockwise loop. Next up is the excitingly named Hovenweep Castle. This structure is dated to 1277 by the tree rings in the timbers found inside, making it one of the freshest ruins in the Mesa Verde region. It is also one of the most famous of the countless stone ruins in the American Southwest. On the ground floor there is a single door on the cliff side of the big structure—the only way in was from the roof of a building that was in the canyon. Seems like classic defensive architecture, but there is also normal residential-type architecture here. Maybe this "castle" was a simple outburst of neighbors trying to outdo each other? Probably not, considering the context of the times, but it's fun to wonder about.

Hovenweep Castle had some cool features, like a built-in "light and shadow calendar." Like many structures of the Ancestral Pueblo, Hovenweep Castle was designed, through precisely placed portholes in the walls, to serve as a calendar for the farmers who lived there. Portholes in the cliffside rectangular room of the structure let the sun's rays into the room at sunset. By tracking the movement of the small patch of sunlight across an interior wall day by day, the solstices and equinoxes would be easily recognized and anticipated. Residents would know exactly when to plant their crops.

The portholes at Hovenweep Castle were some of the first features to be discovered that showed the Anasazis' sun-tracking abilities. This doesn't mean Hovenweep Castle was some sort of sun temple. The lowliest of farmers were known to build such calendars into their houses, maybe to inform their own decisions, or just to check on the proclamations of the village priests.

Some might argue that the alignments created by sunlight shining through the holes in the wall were coincidental, mere accidents. In his book *Living the Sky: The Cosmos of the American Indian*, "archaeoastronomer" Ray Williamson calculates the chances of accidentally occurring complementary alignments at Hovenweep Castle at 1 in 216,000. "So we can assume with considerable assurance that the alignments we have found were intentional."

Moving reluctantly along, you come to the remnants of a little "check dam" that the people here used to create a tiny reservoir. It's difficult to say how much of something like this is original and how much has been reconstructed by successive waves of archaeologists over the past 130 years.

Down in the canyon, close to the spring itself, is Square Tower House, which gives this group of ruins its name. Unlike the tower up on the edge of the cliff, overlooking all, this tower's placement does not suggest a lookout function. This particular tower, which includes a kiva, seems to have a deeper purpose. In their paper "Mesa Verdean Sacred Landscapes," William Hurst and Jonathan Till note that the towers of the Mesa

The mysterious Rimrock House (right) and oddly shaped Twin Towers

Verde region are found "almost always close to water sources. At some level, they might represent the architectural formalization or incorporation of spring-related shrines." Square Tower House seems like a good candidate for that sort of thing.

Next up, Hovenweep House, a mere fraction of its original stature, stands atop the head of the canyon. What remains was the core of a much larger pueblo complex. This was the largest building in this area.

Walking now on the other side of the canyon, you'll find the interesting Rimrock House. This one has really vexed the experts. Vexperts. The two-story building has no discernible rooms. Notice also the portholes in the walls here. Unlike at Hovenweep Castle, the holes at Rimrock House have no obvious calendar function. What was this place?

Finally, the Twin Towers. These could be the most intriguing ruins in Little Ruin Canyon. One of the towers is oval, the other like an elongated horseshoe. There were sixteen rooms total between the two very carefully constructed towers, built on their own promontory apart from the canyon rim. The elaborate use of weirdly curved walls on these structures implies either a lot of forethought or a sort of what-the-heck aesthetic. Researchers tend to go with the former interpretation. Speaking of the Hovenweep towers in general, William Hurst and Jonathan Till argue that "The

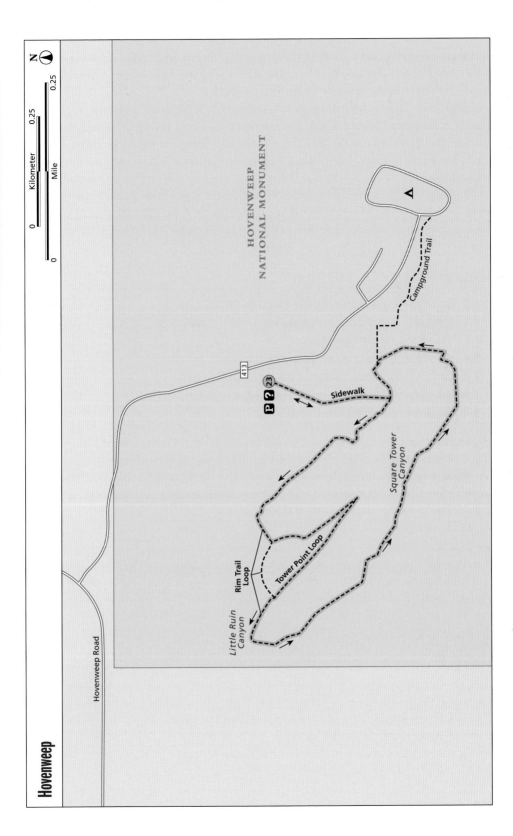

Hovenweep

N

0   Kilometer   0.25

0   Mile   0.25

HOVENWEEP
NATIONAL MONUMENT

Hovenweep Road

413

P ? 23

Sidewalk

Rim Trail
Loop

Tower Point Loop

Little Ruin
Canyon

Square Tower
Canyon

Campground Trail

mixing of circularity and squareness has a conscious, formal quality that suggests symbolic significance, perhaps related to balance between male and female principles or similar opposites in the universe." Informed conjecture.

After Twin Towers the trail drops into the canyon itself, using a slightly precarious set of rock steps. It's not a long descent, or a long ascent up the other side, but it does require dexterity. On the way down notice the change in the rocks. Below the sandstone layers is a layer of chunky conglomerate, formed when a stream flowed through the area.

The Square Tower Group in Little Ruin Canyon is only one of six clusters of ruins scattered around Hovenweep National Monument. So if this hike piqued your interest, grab a map and spend the rest of the day visiting more Ancestral Pueblo ghost towns.

Miles and Directions

0.0 Start from the visitor center and walk toward the Rim Trail Loop.

0.2 Turn right to begin the counterclockwise loop.

0.5 Turn left onto the Tower Point Loop.

0.8 Continue straight, back on the Rim Trail Loop.

1.4 Continue straight at the intersection with the campground trail.

1.5 Turn right and head back toward the visitor center.

1.7 Complete the hike at the visitor center.

Accommodations: Mesa Verde Motel, W. 191 Railroad Ave., Mancos, CO 81328; (970) 533-7741; www.mesaverdemotel.com. Affordable, clean motel in Mancos.

White Eagle Inn, 2110 S. Broadway, Cortez, CO 81321; (970) 565-3333; http:// whiteeagleinn.com. Clean rooms and hospitality at this no-frills budget motel on the highway south of Cortez; pool out of commission.

Central Mountains

I-70 below, rain closing in on Mount Royal in Summit County (hike 24)

24 Mount Royal

Visit the avalanche-blasted ghost camp of Masontown on this short but very steep hike to the top of Mount Royal, looming over Frisco.

Start: Tenmile Canyon Trailhead at the extreme southwest corner of Frisco, just east of I-70 exit 201

Distance: 3.5 miles out and back

Approximate hiking time: 2 to 3 hours

Difficulty: Difficult

Trail surface: Rocky and steep

Best season: Summer

Other trail users: Hikers, runners, and some dogs; bikes allowed but unlikely

Canine compatibility: Dogs permitted

Land status: National forest

Fees and permits: None

Schedule: None

Map: Mount Royal Trail System map, Dillon Ranger District

Trail contact: White River National Forest, Dillon Ranger District, 680 Blue River Pkwy., Silverthorne, CO 80498; (970) 468-5400; www.dillonrangerdistrict.com/trails/Mt_Royal_Area_TS.pdf

Special considerations: Don't attempt this one if you have a low tolerance for steep trails. The hike has been characterized as "family friendly" by some other guides, which may be true if your family likes steep, rocky trails.

Finding the trailhead: The Mount Royal Trail rises from the Blue River bike path on the west edge of the town of Frisco (against the mountain rather than the lake). There is no parking where the trail starts, but there are trailheads and parking areas along the path a half mile on either side of the trail's start point. The easiest trailhead to find is very close to I-70's exit 201, the southernmost of Frisco's two highway exits. Take exit 201 and drive down Main Street toward town for approximately 1 half block and turn right into the parking area. Start the hike by crossing Tenmile Creek on the footbridge; then turn left onto the paved bike path. GPS: N39 34.48' / W106 06.65'. (**Caution:** Approaching the trail's start usually involves a short walk from one of the trailhead parking areas on a busy bike path. Stay very alert and check for approaching riders before making any turns.)

The Hike

This is one of those grit-your-teeth hikes. No casual wander through the forest, the Mount Royal Trail starts off moderately steep. Before long, however, moderately becomes ridiculously.

You'll likely see some runners flagellating themselves on the mountain. It's common for the local fitness fiends to run up and down Mount Royal multiple times in a single outing. On a trail this steep, the workout doesn't end on the way down. But you'll also see plenty of families on this tough trail. It's a good boot camp for your fifth-grader.

About a half mile up, the trail enters the area that was once occupied by Masontown, a tiny nineteenth-century town built around a mine and mill. One of the lessons of Masontown is to pair your mill with an established railroad. Masontown didn't, at least not in time to make a difference. The venture fizzled after a few decades, and Masontown emptied.

Like cosmic punctuation, the mill was smashed by an avalanche in 1912, according to local historians. The structures were abandoned shells when another avalanche wiped most of the camp away in 1926. Another lesson of Masontown—don't build your town in an avalanche chute.

The few remaining cabins of Masontown were appropriated by moonshiners during the Prohibition era, according to local legend. From mill to still on Mount Royal.

There isn't much left of Masontown, but you'll know it when you get there. Watch for various manifestations including the remnants of a brick floor, cabin foundations, and some old bits of iron machinery scattered around the overgrown site. As always, leave these historical relics where they lie. If you're really into it, there are some pseudo-trails wandering farther south through the town site.

The trail turns to the right, passes directly over some tailings and ruins, and starts a determined chug to Mount Royal's rocky summit. Before the final stretch there is a connection to Peak 1 and lesser mountains that overshadow Mount Royal.

A little over a mile from the bottom, a big rock cairn marks a false summit where you can look down on I-70 and Tenmile Creek; Frisco is still out of view. A rustic and rocky singletrack, thinner and less defined than the wide trail you were just on, winds around some snarly old-growth trees and up to another cairn, closer to the mountain's true summit. Photo ops are about equal from either cairn. There are big drop-offs up there, so keep kids well wrangled.

With much of the hike over 10,000 feet, prepare for harsh weather. Other than the hill itself, the most probable antagonist on this hike would be lightning. If thunder is cracking or storms are threatening, summiting the very prominent and pointy Mount Royal would be a big no-no. The common advice holds that starting such an adventure early in the day is the best way to avoid thunderstorms. That's probably true, but there is no guarantee that mornings will be storm-free; there is also a strong chance of blue skies in the late afternoon after storms blow over. So *there*, early risers.

On the way back—if you parked at the west trailhead near I-70—about halfway between the trail and the parking lot, another historical treasure is hiding in the trees: Recen's powder magazine. You'll know it when you see it—if you can find it, which is not an easy feat (GPS: N39 34.44' / W106 06.44'). Watch for a clearing, an area of man-made disturbance, on the non-Frisco side of the path. This is not far from the tailings pile of the Frisco Tunnel. The powder cache is just southeast of the clearing, at the end of a very short trail, hidden under some big rocks. Look for a little wooden door—it looks like the front door of a hobbit house. There is a sign nearby with some explanation of the unusual site. The info on the sign is taken from a book by Charlotte Clarke, a local history nut who discovered the door's significance.

There is—or was, at least—a crushed can inside the door that is thought to be a black powder can, although it might have held carbide, used in miners' lights. Miners sometimes kept their powder stashed away in such spots to prevent catastrophic

Recen's powder stash looks like a hobbit's front door.

explosions. Around 1875 dynamite replaced black powder as the weapon of choice for blasting holes in mountains.

Henry A. Recen was one of the first white guys to try living in the immediate vicinity, dropping anchor in 1873. Although it is generally accepted that the town's name is an homage to San Francisco, it's difficult to determine who named the place

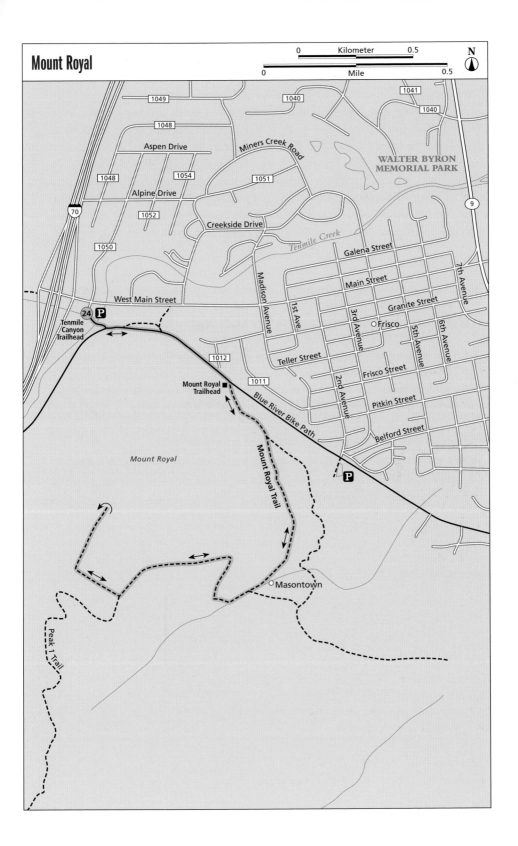

or when Frisco became a recognizable town. According to a January 1941 article in *Colorado Magazine*, "a Captain Lennard, who was doing government scouting work in the region, wrote 'Frisco City' over the door of Recen's cabin" in 1875.

Two narrow-gauge railroads, the Denver & Rio Grande and the Denver, South Park & Pacific, stopped in Frisco on their way to more glorious destinations. As the get-rich dreams faded, the railroads pulled up their tracks and Frisco became about as sleepy as a little town could be, with several dozen residents holding down the fort.

The view you catch of Frisco as you climb down Mount Royal is younger than many of the people reading this book! It's not anything like the view that was enjoyed by residents of Masontown back in the day. Aside from a few fuzzy black-and-whites, we can only imagine what the valley looked like then.

Miles and Directions

0.0 Start from the Tenmile Canyon Trailhead at the extreme southwest corner of Frisco. Walk across the footbridge and take a left on the paved bike path. Watch for bikes! Ack!

0.4 Turn right onto the dirt Mount Royal Trail. There has been substantial signage at the intersection (GPS: N39 34.35' / W106 06.27').

0.5 Stay straight, avoiding trails coming in on the left. If your trail isn't getting steadily more difficult, you're on the wrong one.

0.8 Watch for remnants of Masontown and the Victoria Mine complex, and stay right at trail intersections here. (***Option:*** Explore the site on several faded semi-trails.)

1.3 Turn right at the intersection with the Peak 1 Trail.

1.5 Reach a big rock cairn. Veer right, continuing on a more rustic trail.

1.8 Reach something akin to a mountain summit. Turn around and (carefully) retrace your steps.

3.5 Arrive back at the trailhead parking area.

How Denver Dunked Dillon

In 1963, after a half century of talk, a giant dam was completed that would collect Ten Mile Creek, Blue River, and Snake River all at once. It was one of many audacious projects to secure mountain water and transfer it across the Divide for Front Range development. The resulting mega-reservoir, owned by Denver Water, covered the largest community in the valley, the town of Dillon, eliminating it and several smaller hamlets from the map. Denver Water named the reservoir after the drowned town, sort of like the Colorado tradition of naming local landmarks for Indians who were killed or driven away.

As you might imagine, Denver's dam project did not sit well with many old-time residents of Dillon. Some relocated to higher ground; others left the area in disgust. Denver Water offered lots for displaced Dillonites at the town's new location but wouldn't pay the cost of moving any houses or businesses. Some of Dillon's nicer buildings ended up in Frisco, Breckenridge, and Silverthorne.

Soon after the reservoir filled, developers began their project to transform the area into a tourist zone. Although without a ski mountain of its own, the new condo-encrusted Frisco was perfectly situated to capitalize on the Summit County outdoor sports boom, which is ongoing. No railroads chug through the valley these days, but the highways are choked with travelers.

The town of Dillon in 1906. Currently under water. DENVER PUBLIC LIBRARY, WESTERN HISTORY COLLECTION

25 Iowa Hill

This is a short but sweet little history tour of a hydraulic placer mining operation near Breckenridge. History buffs will get a kick out of the curated exhibits on this micro-adventure, but hiking enthusiasts might fail to get their ya-ya's out satisfactorily, and nature lovers will be even more disappointed in the human race than they were before.

Start: Iowa Hill Trailhead off Airport Road in Breckenridge
Distance: 0.9-mile lariat loop (with option for slightly more)
Approximate hiking time: 1 to 1.5 hours
Difficulty: Moderate
Trail surface: Some steep sections; rocks
Best seasons: Summer and fall
Other trail users: Hikers and dogs; bikes not allowed

Canine compatibility: Leashed dogs permitted
Land status: Town of Breckenridge Open Space
Fees and permits: None
Schedule: Sunrise to sunset
Map: Town of Breckenridge trail map
Trail contact: Town of Breckenridge Open Space, 150 Ski Hill Rd., Breckenridge, CO 80424; (970) 453-3160; www.townofbrecken ridge.com/index.aspx?page=426

Finding the trailhead: From Breckenridge go north on North Park Avenue (the thoroughfare paralleling Main Street to the west); then turn left and continue north on Airport Road. Pass the cemetery and then turn left onto a dirt road, possibly with a sign indicating Iowa Hill. Drive about a block to the end of the road and park in a small parking lot. GPS: N39 30.14' / W106 03.14'

The Hike

Sheer volume. That's what hydraulic placer mining was all about.

They destroyed the mountain in order to get at some specks of sparkly metal buried in the dirt. And they got rich doing it.

This pressure-blasted canyon has become an outdoor museum of sorts, for those with a minimum of strength to get up the hill. The route is fairly well manicured and straightforward. There are several spurs to "exhibits" off the main trail. Mining history buffs think Iowa Hill is one of the finest exhibitions of hydraulic placer mining in the world.

If you indulge in all the spurs, you'll see a reconstructed flume and various types of sluices and gyrating boxes designed to separate the gold from everything else. Then you'll be able to check out the blacksmith's tools, an old cabin ruin, a derrick (small crane), an ore cart, and the big pressure-washer nozzles called giants. The metal nozzles blasted the hillside and washed as much ore-bearing material as possible down to the sluice boxes. Only partially visible here is the extensive network of canals, flumes,

Iowa Hill: a good family hike

and pipes—not to mention the reservoir—that enabled the delivery of such huge amounts of water to the nozzles, day after day.

Notice the shaft that has been sunk into the hillside. If you're like me, you'll be confused at first to see a mine shaft amidst a placer operation. This was a test shaft, so the engineers could check the makeup of the deposits and determine if the hill was worth blasting with water. Apparently it was!

Of course, you'll also see the destruction wrought by the process, as the entire gully was ripped to shreds, and 130 years of recovery time hasn't been nearly enough.

The finale of the hike is a restored and very lovely bunkhouse set in the woods, apart from the destruction. The house, as you can see with a peek through the windows, is accurately furnished as it might have been when built, and quite inviting. It's not open to the public, except during special guided events given by the local historical mavens, the Breckenridge Heritage Alliance.

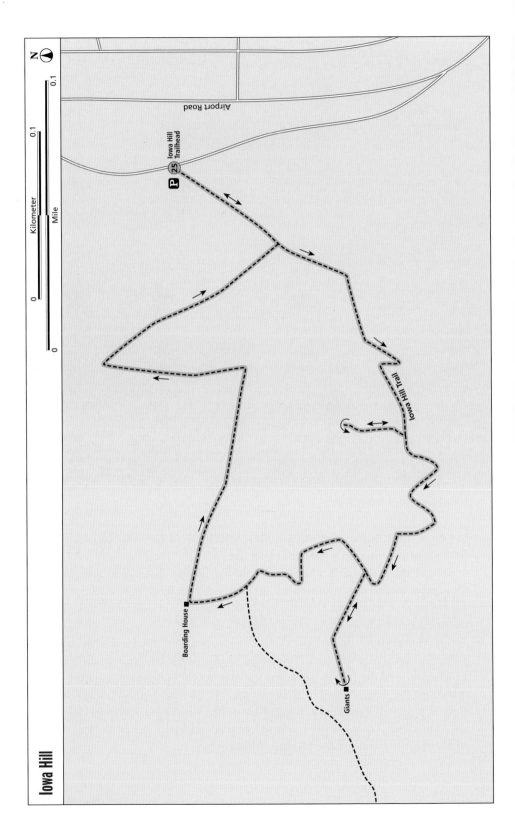

Iowa Hill

N

Kilometer
0   0.1   0.1

Mile
0   0.1

Airport Road

Iowa Hill
Trailhead

P 25

Iowa Hill Trail

Boarding House

Giants

The restored bunkhouse on Iowa Hill

The rest of the hike is a breezy descent, without mining paraphernalia. The elevation profile for this one is somewhat pointy and rude for a casual hike. Though it is undeniably a short loop, some people might be unpleasantly surprised at the steepness of the climb.

Miles and Directions

0.0   Start from the Iowa Hill Trailhead and begin walking up the Iowa Hill Trail. Shortly you will pass the intersection with the trail coming down from above, on which you'll be returning in a bit.

0.2   Check out sluice boxes and other mining relics on spurs to the left, then right.

0.3   Head up the spur that goes into the canyon to see giants and other placer mining machinery. Return and continue.

0.5   Pass another spur that heads up to the pressure box of the placer operation. (***Option:*** Take the spur! It's about 0.3 mile out and back.)

0.6   The main trail leads to the nicely preserved bunkhouse. Continue down and to the right (east) from here.

0.8   Turn left, headed back to the trailhead.

0.9   Arrive back at the trailhead.

26 French Gulch

Take a walk around the dredge piles; then see the beast that made the mess. French Gulch is one of Breckenridge's most abused mining districts but still retains its beauty. The hike visits several shafts, mill sites, and other points of historical interest.

Start: B and B Trailhead in French Gulch near Breckenridge

Distance: 2.6-mile loop (with several options for more)

Approximate hiking time: 2 hours

Difficulty: Moderate

Trail surface: From rocky doubletrack to smooth singletrack

Best season: Summer

Other trail users: Mountain bikers, hikers, and dogs

Canine compatibility: Leashed dogs permitted

Land status: Town of Breckenridge Open Space

Fees and permits: None

Schedule: None

Map: City of Breckenridge trail map

Trail contact: Town of Breckenridge Open Space, 150 Ski Hill Rd., Breckenridge, CO 80424; (970) 453-3160; www.townofbrecken ridge.com/index.aspx?page=426

Finding the trailhead: From Breckenridge go north on Main Street; then turn right on French Gulch Road/Huron Road. Drive 2.3 miles and turn right into the trailhead parking area. GPS: N39 29.00' / W106 00.58'. *Note:* There is alternate parking available up French Gulch Road at the Reiling Dredge Trailhead/parking area, a small dirt patch across the road from Reiling Dredge.

The Hike

In 1859, as the Pikes Peak gold rush cranked up (having very little to do with Pikes Peak), a party of several dozen outfitted itself in the brand-new, burgeoning camp called Denver City and started for the mountains. They dropped into South Park, then disagreed about where to go next. Half the group wanted to cross Hoosier Pass and prospect around the Blue River valley; the other half wanted to keep poking around South Park. So they split up.

The group that dropped into Blue River found a band of Utes already there. The gold-grubbers immediately built a relatively elaborate log fort (Fort Mary B.), which proved unnecessary, as the Utes weren't hostile at all. Had they seen what was coming, they might have been.

There were some experienced miners among the group who knew how to read the land. Their first prospecting efforts met with success. One member of the party took $7,000 in gold out of the first section of stream he tried. When word got out, it meant instant competition and hassle for the group, but also opportunity. The value of the squatters' chosen parcels skyrocketed as gold-hunters streamed in.

Breckenridge was a Thing. All the streams were doomed.

French Gulch: All the streams were doomed.

Actually, the name was Breckinridge, with an *i*. Here's the story there: Looking for an edge over competing town sites in the Blue River valley—town-building was a cutthroat, competitive enterprise—the developers of the would-be town named their settlement after the vice president, John C. Breckinridge, hoping this would help them secure a US post office. The plan worked, but backfired. Breckinridge got its post office, the only one in the Rocky Mountains. However, Mr. Breckinridge, who had become a US senator, pledged his allegiance to the Confederacy when the war broke out. He was expelled from the Senate, and the town of Breckinridge became Breckenridge to show its fealty to the Union.

Anyway, that's the story. A nice tidy story, which helps us forget uglier aspects of Breck's heritage. But there was reportedly somebody named Breckenridge among the founding party, so the old story about the post office and the expelled senator might actually be a work of fiction.

The Reiling Dredge, the centerpiece of this hike, might be the only historic dredge still sitting in its pond. The dredge was built in 1908 and processed untold amounts of rock and earth until it sank in 1922. Crude but effective, the Reiling Dredge was said to have captured $9,000 worth of gold in its first week in French Gulch.

A satellite view of French Gulch shows clearly the monster's snaky path, as wide as a football field. Standing on the dredge pile itself, you can see that the effect on the

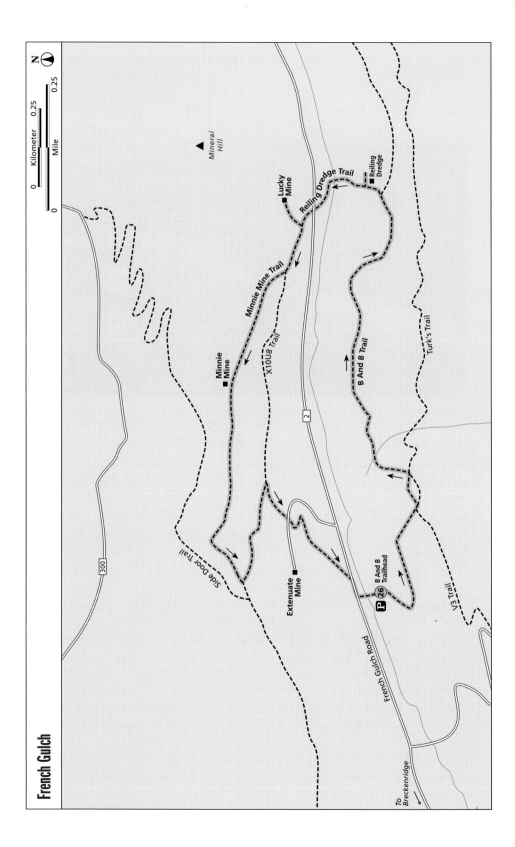

French Gulch

Mineral
Hill

Lucky
Mine

Reiling Dredge Trail

Reiling
Dredge

Minnie Mine Trail

Minnie
Mine

X10U8 Trail

B And B Trail

Turk's Trail

Side Door Trail

Extenuate
Mine

2

300

B And B
Trailhead

P 26

V3 Trail

French Gulch Road

To
Breckenridge

N

Kilometer
0   0.25

Mile
0   0.25

local environment was apocalyptic. Every stream in the vicinity got the same treatment. The Reiling Dredge was the eighth dredge to run near Breckenridge, and one of four or five that were operating at the same time in different streambeds. Dredges carved the gulches of Breckenridge until just prior to World War II.

Finally the Reiling Dredge encountered a rock that was more determined than the dredge, causing it to sink. It had sunk and been resurrected before—being a dredge is hard work—but economic conditions weren't as favorable this time, and the dredge was down for the count.

There are many little points of interest along this loop, with options to walk up side trails to see old mines, mills, and sluices, with plenty of interpretive signs. French Gulch is packed with remnants of nineteenth- and twentieth-century extraction efforts. You might also notice leftovers from the time these crumbling structures were taken over by "hippies" and other transient residents, beginning in the 1960s.

For those who just want to see the dredge, do an out-and-back along the B and B Trail or a much shorter out-and-back on the Reiling Dredge Trail.

Miles and Directions

0.0 Start from the B and B Trailhead on French Gulch Road and begin walking up the B and B Trail. (*Option:* You can also take the B and B Spur Trail that takes off from the same trailhead; the two trails will meet up shortly.)

0.2 Pass the intersection with the B and B Spur Trail on the left.

0.3 Pass the intersection with the V3 Trail on the right. Soon after, you'll see a little singletrack off to the right. This trail cuts across the green space and rejoins the B and B Trail shortly.

0.4 Pass the intersection with Turk's Trail on the right.

1.0 Stay left where the B and B Trail goes right (this connects to Turk's Trail). Now you're on the Reiling Dredge Trail. Not long after this junction, you'll see a viewing platform overlooking the Reiling Dredge. Turn right and visit a second viewing platform on the other side. There are good photo ops from both.

1.1 Cross French Gulch Road. The trail continues on the other side as the Minnie Mine Trail, an old wagon road.

1.2 Turn right to see a little exhibit of the Lucky Mine and a mill jig at the top of the hill. Return to Minnie Mine Trail and continue.

1.4 Pass the intersection with the X10U8 Trail on the left. (*Option:* Take a left here and rejoin at mile 2.2.)

2.0 Take a left here, staying on the Minnie Mine Trail. (*Option:* Go straight ahead to reach the Side Door Trail, which provides a good climb and view of the whole valley.)

2.2 Turn right onto the X10U8 Trail.

2.5 Cross French Gulch Road.

2.6 Arrive back at the B and B Trailhead.

27 Barney Ford Trail

Walk from Breckenridge to Ford Gulch on this moderately strenuous out-and-back to a mining district with extra historical significance. This is a "civilized" hike on trails that cut through the neighborhood above Breckenridge.

Start: Carter Park, Breckenridge
Distance: 4.7 miles out and back
Approximate hiking time: 2 to 3 hours
Difficulty: Moderate to difficult
Trail surface: Somewhat rocky singletrack
Best season: Summer
Other trail users: Mountain bikers, hikers, runners, and dogs

Canine compatibility: Leashed dogs permitted
Land status: Town of Breckenridge
Fees and permits: None
Schedule: None
Map: Town of Breckenridge trail map
Trail contact: Town of Breckenridge, 150 Ski Hill Rd., Breckenridge, CO 80424; (970) 547-3155; www.townofbreckenridge.com

Finding the trailhead: From Main Street in Breckenridge, go east on East Adams Street (away from the ski mountain), turn right on South High Street, and you'll run smack into the Carter Park Trailhead parking area, adjacent to Carter Park. GPS: N39 28.71' / W106 02.41'

The Hike

Barney Ford was born into slavery, his mother a slave, his father a plantation owner. At age 25 he was slaving on a riverboat crew and managed to escape to Chicago, where he met his wife, Julia.

Ford came to Breckenridge by way of Nicaragua, strangely enough. He and Julia had embarked for California via ship, but got sidetracked in Central America, setting up a hotel there. When Nicaragua passed a pro-slavery law and the Fords' hotel was bombed, collateral damage in the local political violence, the couple went back to the United States.

In 1860 Ford was looking, successfully, for gold in a small, steep gulch that drained into French Gulch, just east of the new town called Breckinridge. As a former slave Ford wasn't allowed to own a claim himself, so he had a Denver lawyer file for him. Predictably, the lawyer had the local sheriff order Ford and his handful of African-American helpers off the claim as soon as they struck gold, giving them 24 hours to vacate. Even before the 24 hours were up, some of the local white supremacists galloped up to the site on horseback, shooting their guns. Ford and his men escaped up the hill as the terror squad scoured the claim for the gold they had heard about. Remember Barney Ford when people start talking about the "Miner's Code" of justice. Until 1964 the gulch was known as Nigger Gulch, and the hill above Carter Park was called Nigger Hill.

From Barney Ford Hill, looking across the valley toward the Breckenridge ski area

Turning away from mining, Ford became a successful restaurateur and hotelier in Cheyenne, Denver, and then Breckenridge, returning to town in the 1880s. During the Civil War he used his establishments and whatever assets he had to aid escaped slaves. Ford became a state legislator and steered Colorado toward protection of civil rights. Despite his legacy of service and ultimate bootstrap story, the only memorials he has ever received are the renamed gulch and hill, Ford Gulch and Barney Ford Hill, a public school or two named in his honor, and this trail.

I've been reading about Barney Ford for many years, so it's interesting to actually stand in the gulch where he found gold and was chased away by the local welcome committee. Note that the cabin ruins you see here in the gulch were probably not made by Ford and his crew, but by those who worked the claim later, but nobody is too sure about that.

For more Barney Ford action, visit his house in Breckenridge (Main Street and Washington Avenue). The house is restored and maintained as a small museum, with knowledgeable guides who can answer your questions. Visiting the Ford House gives you a great feel for nineteenth-century domestic life. For still more Barney Ford action, visit his restaurant in lower downtown Denver. Near 15th on Blake Street, the building that once housed Ford's People's Restaurant and barber shop still stands, marked by a small plaque on the front. There was an Indian restaurant in there last time I checked.

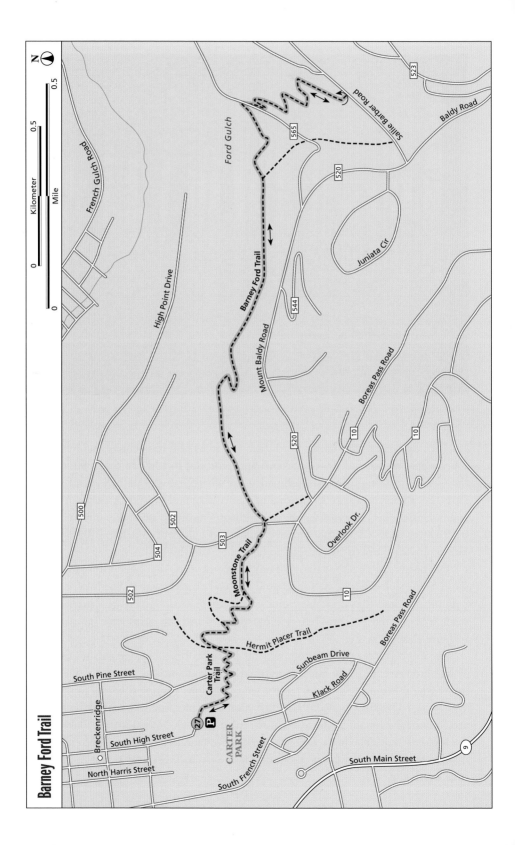

Barney Ford Trail

There are several options for enjoying the Barney Ford Trail. You could skip the early climbing and begin where the actual Barney Ford Trail begins, at CR 503—if you can get somebody to drop you off, as there's strictly no parking there. You could start from the top, near Mount Baldy Road and Sallie Barber Road. You could do it as a one-way shuttle, uphill or downhill. It's also possible to make a loop with the nearby Juniata Trail. But this option, in addition to being not as exciting as it sounds, involves some prickly route-finding and is not recommended for unguided locals or junior-level map readers. Not that getting lost would be that dire in such a developed zone, but it would be very annoying and make your loved ones worried.

One of the many prospect holes that dot the region like bomb craters

Miles and Directions

0.0 Start from Carter Park and begin switchbacking up the Carter Park Trail. Keep climbing, avoiding all social and side trails and neighborhood connector trails, until you've hiked through nine switchbacks.

0.3 The Carter Park Trail ends at the Hermit Placer Trail, which follows an old ditch on a contour around the mountain. Turn left onto the Hermit Placer Trail briefly; then turn right onto the Moonstone Trail. Continue moderate climbing.

0.8 Cross CR 503. The Barney Ford Trail begins on the east side of the road.

1.6 Veer left at a fork in the trail. (The right fork also climbs to the same road as the Barney Ford Trail but goes through private property to get there. Mountain bikers often use it as a downhill trail.)

1.7 This is Ford Gulch. Notice the remains of a few cabins. (*Option:* Turn around here.)

2.4 Arrive at the Barney Ford Trailhead, Sallie Barber Road. Turn around and retrace. (*Option:* Turn left and continue up Sallie Barber Road, which is closed to cars, to the Sallie Barber Mine.)

4.7 Arrive back at Carter Park.

Local Events/Attractions: Barney Ford Victorian House, 111 E. Washington Ave., Breckenridge, CO 80424; (970) 453-9767

28 Buffalo Cabins

On this low-key but potentially strenuous forest hike, starting from an easily accessible trailhead near I-70 and Silverthorne, walk a rugged mile to what's left of an old cabin.

Start: Buffalo Mountain Trailhead outside Silverthorne
Distance: 2.1 miles out and back
Approximate hiking time: 1 to 2 hours
Difficulty: Moderate
Trail surface: Roots. Rocks and roots. And roots. Some steep climbing and descending.
Best season: Summer
Other trail users: Hikers and dogs; bikes not allowed in wilderness area

Canine compatibility: Leashed dogs permitted
Land status: National forest
Fees and permits: None
Schedule: None
Map: USGS Dillon quad
Trail contact: White River National Forest, 900 Grand Ave., Glenwood Springs, CO 81601; (970) 945-2521; www.fs.usda .gov/recarea/whiteriver/recreation/ohv/ recarea/?recid=41285&actid=91

Finding the trailhead: From I-70 and CO 9 in Silverthorne, go west on CO 9 and take the first left onto Wildernest Road. Turn left and continue to the trailhead parking lot. GPS: N39 37.21' / W106 06.59'

The Hike

Admittedly it's not a super-exciting hike and doesn't have the most compelling story, but Buffalo Cabins Trail is worth a go. Cabin ruins near mile 1 make a natural turn-around for a quick but blood-pumping hike with some steep, rooty sections. Those who need more than that have come to the right place. The trail continues from the cabin to the top of Buffalo Mountain, picking its way steeply through a boulder field, then perusing gently sloped alpine tundra to get there. Views, of course, are outstanding from the summit trail; below the cabins the trail is ensconced in the dark forest.

In the 1880s, according to an article in the *Summit County Journal* in 1915, "considerable prospecting was carried on along the course of the Ten Mile Range and in the peaks surrounding Frisco to the north, notably on the sides of Buffalo, which rises to some 13,000 or 14,000 feet, the immense form of which so resembled the buffalo which roamed the plains in an early day that the Indians christened it Buffalo Mountain. Some rich silver ore was quarried from this mountain and quite extensive work carried on for a time. Then came the slump in silver and these workings and others in the vicinity were all but forgotten." And that's pretty much the size of it.

Historians guess that the cabins here were used by miners or prospectors, but nobody is very sure.

There is some confusion about who exactly named the mountain, the Utes or the miners who pushed them out. Either way, it was far from the only mountain around

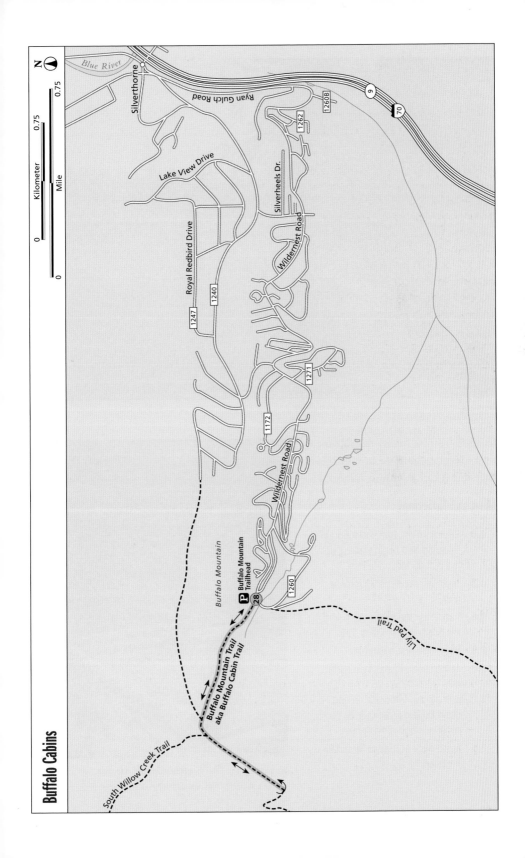

Buffalo Cabins

The hike starts in typical Summit County loveliness.

that was named for its resemblance to a sleeping buffalo. Just be glad they didn't call it Mount Baldy.

Miles and Directions

0.0 Start from the Buffalo Mountain Trailhead and begin walking up the Buffalo Mountain Trail.

0.3 The trail enters the wilderness area.

0.6 Turn left at the intersection with the South Willow Creek Trail.

0.9 Reach the first cabin ruin.

1.0 At the second cabin ruin (GPS: N39 37.14' / W106 07.41'), turn around or buckle up and climb Buffalo Mountain, a strenuous and difficult hike.

2.1 Arrive back at Buffalo Mountain Trailhead.

Spoiler alert! The Buffalo Cabins are not super exciting, but the scenery is nice.

29 Meadow Mountain

Hill climbers will enjoy this steady grunt to the line shack on Meadow Mountain, an old ski area and lettuce farm near Minturn.

Start: Meadow Mountain Trailhead on US 24 just south of the intersection of I-70 and US 24, near Minturn

Distance: 9.4 miles out and back

Approximate hiking time: 3 to 4 hours

Difficulty: Moderate to difficult

Trail surface: Varies from four-wheel-drive-style doubletrack to singletrack; moderately lumpy and rocky

Best season: Summer

Other trail users: Bikers and dogs

Canine compatibility: Dogs are allowed, but they must be under voice control or leashed. (With so many mountain bikers around, leashes are probably best. For the dogs, I mean.)

Land status: National forest

Fees and permits: None

Schedule: None

Map: USGS Minturn quad

Trail contact: Holy Cross Ranger District, 24747 US 24, Minturn, CO 81645; (970) 827-5715; www.fs.usda.gov/detail/whiteriver/about-forest/districts/?cid=fsbdev3_001247

Special considerations: This route is popular with mountain bikers. They are generally of the considerate sort, but be aware, especially if you are hiking with wandering children or dogs.

Finding the trailhead: Take I-70 and use exit 171 to go south on US 24. Almost immediately south of the exit, turn right into the trailhead parking lot, near the Holy Cross Ranger District ranger station. GPS: N39 36.39' / W106 26.67'. *Note:* There is another, separate trailhead a few blocks farther south on US 24 (West Grouse Creek Trailhead), and it's easy to get the trailheads confused.

The Hike

This conveniently located hike, starting from a trailhead right on US 24 near its intersection with I-70, makes for a satisfying mountain trudge, if you're into that sort of thing. After the initial steep, rugged pitch that rises from the dirt parking area, the incline settles down considerably as you join an old road snaking its way up Meadow Mountain.

A lettuce farm thrived here on Meadow Mountain during the 1920s, after operators cut two ditches from West Grouse Creek to irrigate the hillsides. Nearby Minturn was the self-proclaimed "Lettuce Capital," but it seems that other locations, particularly the San Luis Valley, were growing and shipping much more lettuce. Colorado lettuce farms eventually found they couldn't compete with California's yearlong growing season in an era of refrigerated rail cars.

From 1964 through 1969 Meadow Mountain was a ski area, with two lifts. In a shrewd business move, Vail Associates bought out the little ski area in 1969. Instead of developing Meadow Mountain, they more or less shut it down and developed Beaver Creek instead. In 1971 Vail Associates sold Meadow Mountain to the Forest Service.

Line shack from Whiskey Creek Trail

And so here we are, ready to hike up this really fantastic hunk of public land. The three ski slopes are still there for those with a wild urge.

The road to the top is quite gentle, for the most part, and the surface is a bit chunky but not too challenging. The scenery is very nice in this part of the world, and it only gets better as you get higher.

On the way up you'll pass two trail intersections on your left. These routes both head over to connect with the West Grouse Creek Trail, which you can take back down to Minturn (it pops out at another trailhead closer to town) or up into the Holy Cross Wilderness. (A loop starting at Meadow Mountain Trailhead, heading up Meadow Mountain to Forest Service Road 747, down West Grouse Creek Trail, and then looping back to Meadow Mountain via the Connector Trail is around 6.5 miles.)

Not quite to the top of Meadow Mountain, but high enough, you'll probably agree, sits the old line shack. The hike doesn't necessarily turn around here. You can go to the top of the mountain (the old trail is faded away) or start along the Whiskey

Meadow Mountain

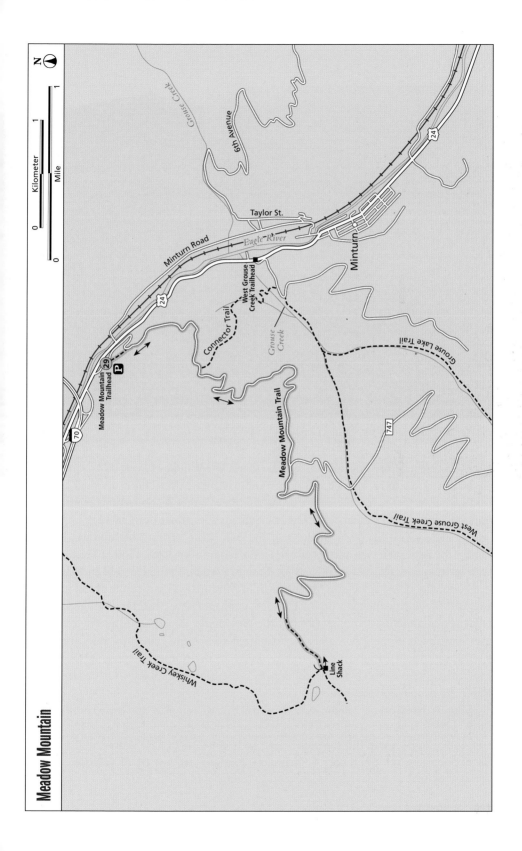

Not the top of the mountain, but high enough

Creek Trail, which tops out right there at the shack. The Whiskey Creek Trail descends all the way down to I-70 and leaves several miles of bike path to finish a loop. That's hardly ideal, but if you're still feeling strong and the weather is cooperating, consider walking a few miles of gorgeous Whiskey Creek for a lengthier out-and-back.

Mining activity has been subdued in the immediate vicinity of Minturn, but just up the road there was plenty of extraction action. Red Cliff, another awesome little town, was established in 1879 as local mines started to produce gold and silver. Anybody who drives up Battle Mountain from Minturn will notice the abandoned twentieth-century settlement on the hillside—Gilman. From 1912 the mines around Gilman were purchased and operated by the New Jersey Zinc Company. The complex shut down in the 1980s and was designated a Superfund site. Like the famous Gold King Mine that spilled toxic orange fluid into the Animas River in 2015, the Eagle Mine here is flooded and promises to cause a lot of problems for the Eagle River and people downstream.

Minturn residents have approved a developer's plans to replace the eerie company town, with its cluster of abandoned residences and offices on the side of Battle Mountain, with a fancy resort. But the pesky toxic waste issue might have shoved all that to the back burner, as it often does. Gilman now continues its slow transformation to a unique twenty-first-century ghost town. The place seems a bit creepy now, but the people who lived here midcentury all seem to have cherished memories of Gilman.

Minturn itself is not a mining town. It's really a railroad town. The town developed around the railroad facilities that were necessary to house and maintain extra locomotives and other equipment needed to push heavy trains over Tennessee Pass.

Miles and Directions

0.0 Start from the Meadow Mountain Trailhead and begin walking up the Meadow Mountain Trail.

0.9 Continue past the intersection with the Connector Trail.

2.5 Continue past the intersection with another trail (Forest Service Road 747). (The trail also leads to West Grouse Creek Trail.)

4.7 Arrive at the line shack. (**Option:** Continue onward for a bit on the out-and-back Whiskey Creek Trail, which eventually drops to I-70.)

9.4 Arrive back at the trailhead.

Accommodations: Minturn Inn, 442 Main St., Minturn, CO 81645; (970) 827-9647; www.minturninn.com. A bed-and-breakfast with cozy rooms and comfortable beds; friendly hosts.

Hotel Minturn, 167 Williams St., Minturn, CO 81645; (970) 331-5461; www .hotelminturn.com. Four sleek, modern rooms available in central Minturn; good value.

30 Camp Hale

Join the beautiful Colorado Trail as it drops out of the subalpine forest into the wide expanse known for hosting Camp Hale and continues up the valley toward Tennessee Pass. Camp Hale is one of the most interesting historic sites in Colorado.

Start: Camp Hale Trailhead of the Colorado Trail, Camp Hale, off US 24 north of Tennessee Pass

Distance: 13.2 miles out and back

Approximate hiking time: 5 to 7 hours

Difficulty: Moderate to difficult

Trail surface: Fairly easygoing: all the challenges associated with subalpine forest single-track, but at a manageable level

Best season: Summer

Other trail users: Bikers, hikers, and dogs

Canine compatibility: Dogs allowed

Land status: National forest

Fees and permits: None

Schedule: None

Map: USGS Pando and Leadville North quads

Trail contact: Holy Cross Ranger District, 24747 US 24, Minturn, CO 81645; (970) 827-5715; www.fs.usda.gov/detail/whiteriver/about-forest/districts/?cid=fsbdev3_001247

Special considerations: Unexploded ordinance! Can't say that very often. Needless to say, don't pick up anything that might explode. Read more below.

Finding the trailhead: From I-70 turn south onto US 24 (exit 171). Drive about 17 miles and turn left into Camp Hale at the northernmost entrance, onto Road 702. As Road 702 approaches the mountainside, veer right onto Forest Service Road 714/East Fork Eagle Road. Stay on the road until after it curves to the east and passes the old rifle range. Turn left into the Colorado Trail Camp Hale Trailhead. GPS: N39 25.45' / W106 17.92'

The Hike

Camp Hale was born in the urgency of World War II.

The basic details of its beginnings are explained in an article by Army Corps of Engineers public affairs officer Eileen Williamson: "In 1940, after learning that Finnish troops held off Soviet invaders for 3 months using winter warfare tactics, National Ski Patrol founder, Charles "Minnie" Dole, penned a letter to the War Department offering to help train U.S. soldiers. Training for six U.S. Army divisions was ordered to prepare troops to fight in cold weather and mountainous regions."

The site of Camp Hale was chosen not only for its consistent snowfall but also for its accessibility. Such a massive construction project would be impossible without nearby US 24 and the Denver & Rio Grande rails. On the other hand, the Army considered the site's proximity to Leadville to be a liability. They saw Leadville as a pit of immorality. The town was happy to enforce gambling and prostitution laws in exchange for the Army's supplying a huge boost to its economy. With the Climax molybdenum mine ramping up production to meet wartime demand, and Camp Hale's construction keeping tens of thousands of workers busy with 70-hour

Approaching Tennessee Pass on the Colorado Trail

workweeks, unemployment seemed to be a thing of the past on the upper Arkansas. In August 1941 an article appeared in the Leadville *Herald Democrat*: "Leadville is Whooping it Up in Wartime Boom." World War II became Leadville's lifeblood.

The valley, already somewhat park-like when the Army took over (and known as Eagle Park), was engineered to a table-like profile. The Eagle River was rerouted into a straight channel down the center, and swampy areas were filled in; dead-straight roads were strapped across the expanse in both directions; and a biblical amount of concrete was poured to make bunkers, gas chambers, barracks, latrines, and firing ranges for various types of weapons, in addition to a massive field house, theater, bowling alley, and other civilized structures that might be found in a small city. Facilities to feed and hold about 13,000 mules were also built. These large-scale efforts are still very evident in the valley, despite the slow progress of nature in overgrowing the place.

In 1943 about 16,000 soldiers began training at Camp Hale, including the entire 10th Light Division (Alpine). Many of the recruits were kids who had grown up in the Colorado mountains. Through the winter they learned not only how to fight and blow things up but how to ski (both downhill and cross-country), climb rocks, and survive in the snowy mountains. Camp Hale's altitude (9,200 feet) was worrisome to some officials but would give the troops a major advantage when push came to shove.

Their training at Camp Hale was quick but intense, occasionally brutal. Hugh Evans, who went on to earn the Silver Star for bravery as well as a Purple Heart,

Caricatures typical of the times on a motivational billboard at Camp Hale, 1943 DENVER PUB-
LIC LIBRARY, WESTERN HISTORY COLLECTION

remembered every detail of the deliberately harsh backpacking test the men had to
undergo, slogging through the deep snow for days while carrying 90-pound packs.
The recruits were worked to the point of exhaustion while soaked to the bone.
Nighttime temperatures approached 50 below. Evans spent the coldest night walking
around the camp to stay alive.

In June of 1944 the division transferred to Fort Swift in Texas. The 86th Regiment of the 10th Mountain Division, as it was now called, was deployed to Italy in
December 1944, and within weeks sustained casualties. The rest of the division was
on its way.

The 10th went to Italy with the objective of breaking the German "Gothic Line,"
a 108-mile-long zone of heavily fortified positions, observation posts, and minefields
strung all the way across the rugged Italian Alps. Allied forces were O for three in
previous assaults on the ridge.

The 86th set up shop in villages below German strongholds Riva Ridge (Monte
della Riva), a rugged, 1,500-foot-tall slope, and the adjoining Mount Belvedere. Riva
Ridge had proved to be a very effective observation post for German artillery, so it
was the 10th's first target. (Riva Ridge may ring a bell for a different reason: A race-
horse by that name won the Kentucky Derby and Belmont Stakes in 1972.)

For some reason almost none of the skis and other specialized equipment belonging
to the 10th Mountain Division made it to Italy, so the men had to scrounge to equip
themselves. Through January the makeshift ski troops of the 86th Regiment mapped
several approaches and probed German positions. Some of these forgotten scouting
expeditions achieved epic status. Meanwhile, the 85th and 87th Regiments arrived
and snuggled into villages at the base of Mount Belvedere, waiting for the green light.

On the night of February 18, 1945, a detachment of 900 men from the 86th
Regiment began climbing single-file up an unlikely route on Riva Ridge, concealed

by a helpful blanket of fog. According to some of the soldiers who were there, the troops' guns were empty—no bullets! They were ordered to fix bayonets and climb with unloaded guns to prevent any discharge, accidental or otherwise, that would reveal the attack. The rest of the 86th, along with the 85th and 87th regiments, were ordered to wait silently at the base of Mount Belvedere.

The Germans had mistakenly assumed that the Americans' chosen route was unclimbable. So their silent arrival at the top of Riva Ridge was quite unexpected. They overwhelmed the German gun positions and attacked the sleeping troops with grenades. Riva Ridge belonged to the Americans, but they would have to defend against multiple counterattacks and constant artillery fire to keep it. Quickly but not easily, engineers set up a tram to evacuate wounded and send supplies to the top of the ridge.

The remainder of the 10th attacked up Mount Belvedere the following night and possessed the stronghold by dawn. More artillery barrages and counterattacks followed. The force started to suffer steady losses. The troops pushed onward, taking more stronghold peaks at high cost. Hugh Evans took out two machine gun nests almost singlehandedly to earn the Silver Star. Finally the 10th stopped for a decent rest, at which point many of the men ventured to Florence and various villages, where they were treated like kings.

It was an important rest, as the toughest fighting was yet to come. In April the mountain troops attacked onward toward the Po Valley, directly into the teeth of two dug-in German divisions. On April 14 the Americans sustained over 500 casualties in a 24-hour period, their worst day of the campaign. Overall the 10th suffered more than 4,000 casualties, including almost 1,000 fatalities. Other divisions had taken more hits, but none fighting in Italy suffered so many casualties in such a short time. Concluding their incredible work, the 10th fought a final battle around Lake Garda and forced a surrender from the German forces in Italy.

Hitler wasn't a surrender type of guy. He believed in an extreme strategy of forts and strongholds, in which the holders of a fort were expected to fight to the last man, thus exacting the maximum toll on the enemy and bringing glory to the motherland and all that. Of course his generals were too smart for that, and preferred to utilize tactical retreat instead of sacrificing themselves and troops, and so came frequently into conflict with Hitler. Hitler threw most of his generals into prison camps at one time or another for neglecting to follow his militarily self-destructive orders.

A day after the surrender of German forces in Italy, Hitler committed suicide in his bunker, true to his bluster.

As the victorious 10th shipped out, some of the men thought they would soon be fighting in the South Pacific, but that was never really in the cards. The war was over. The 10th came home, to Camp Carson this time. Camp Hale had been officially decommissioned almost as soon as the soldiers had left for Texas.

The military wasn't done with the valuable base yet, however. In 1945 Camp Hale was being used as a POW camp for Germans captured in Africa. In the 1950s soldiers from Fort Carson trained here sporadically; then, from 1959 to 1965, the CIA used Camp Hale to train Tibetan guerrillas who were fighting the Chinese, a fact now openly acknowledged. To scare people away from the area, the Agency circulated the story that the base would be used for atomic testing. The whole valley was razor-fenced and patrolled by military police. The Tibetan rebels were transported back and forth from Denver's Stapleton Airport in buses with blacked-out windows—not suspicious at all.

More than 1,000 structures that composed the built environment of Camp Hale were dismantled and removed about 50 years ago, but this wide valley below Tennessee Pass is still dominated by the unique mountain military base and its ghosts.

Along with the physically obvious vestiges of Camp Hale, the concrete pads and roads and such, the camp also leaves a more important, invisible legacy: unexploded projectiles, grenades, practice land mines, white phosphorus, asbestos, lead, and chemical weapons. The unknowns are particularly disconcerting. It's doubtful that any single person ever knew about everything they were shooting into the mountainsides here, especially when the base was secretly taken over by the CIA.

In the late 1990s the Army embarked on the project of trying to find the leftover nasty stuff, removing it from the area or blowing it up on site. The first phase of the search was in the records, trying to figure out exactly what happened out there, and where. The task might be impossible to complete, but they've discovered a lot of interesting things.

After Camp Hale was built, the military had unlimited access to the public land around the base for training purposes. As such, the 10th was all over the place. Troops shot artillery into the Homestake Valley, in the Holy Cross Wilderness. They used poison gas and fired mortars high up the headwaters of Resolution Creek, maneuvered on top of the Ten Mile Range above Breckenridge, and even threw hand grenades at pretend Germans on Copper Mountain. Between 1942 and 1965, the claimed end of training activities at Camp Hale, about 250,000 acres were used in one way or another. In 2014 the Army Corps of Engineers reported that they had narrowed down the potentially munitions-tainted area to about 100,000 acres, or about 150 square miles.

In the meantime, as research further focuses the search, some limited forays into the field have taken place, particularly in the heavily blasted East Fork Valley. These searches produced a few dozen live munitions and countless fragments. Searchers have found plenty of unexploded ordnance just lying on the ground, although most of the dangerous shells are presumed to be buried a few feet below the surface. Basically, it's all still out there, and some of it is still dangerous. The freeze-thaw cycle will heave long-buried projectiles to the surface, adding another layer of frustration to any cleanup effort.

It is hoped that education of the public will partially make up for the shortcomings of the cleanup. You'll see signs along this hike warning you and other trail users about some of the potential hazards you might encounter. The "Three R's" are

Remains of the rifle range and ammo depot

emphasized—recognize, retreat, and report. That is, if you see something, don't pick it up; tell somebody else, and let the people with special gear and training come out and deal with it. It's a shudder-inducing reminder that people had been hiking through here for decades without any kind of warning whatsoever.

Although no hikers have been hurt, the infestation of unexploded ordnance has had some real-world effects (beyond the expensive cleanup). In 2002 a lightning-sparked fire started burning in the East Fork Valley, on a slope above "Nazi Village," the mock village targeted in so many training exercises. The firefighters wouldn't go fight the fire on foot for fear of blowing themselves up. On the other hand, the Army Corps of Engineers recommended that planes flying over remain at least 500 feet above the ground, which nixed the possibility of slurry bombing. They let the fire burn itself out.

The route described here goes right through one of the most heavily affected areas, the valley of the East Fork of the Eagle River. Then it climbs up on the hill behind the rifle range, and its attached ammo depot fortified with concrete bunkers. The Colorado Trail climbs the hill gently, eventually crossing one of the old ski slopes used for training (overgrown), and then turns the corner and parallels US 24, headed toward Tennessee Pass. At mile 3.3 (and 10.0 on the way back), the trail crosses US 24. There is no parking or trailhead at this crossing.

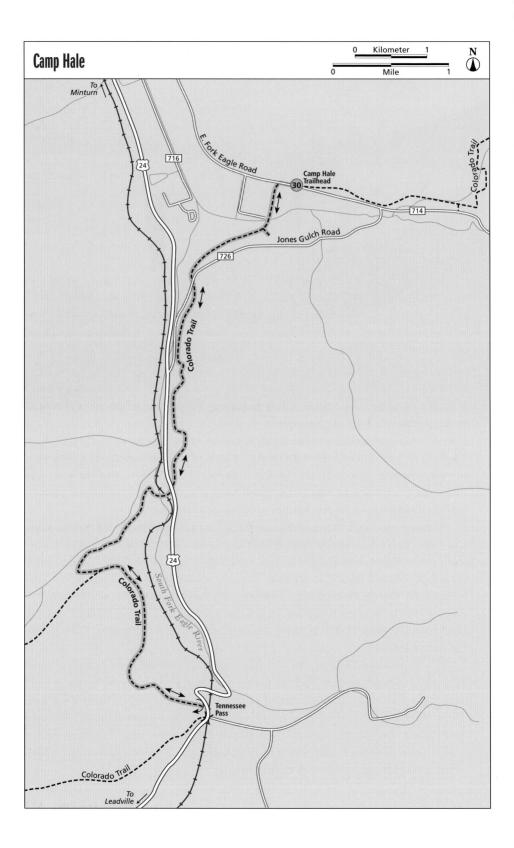

Camp Hale

0 Kilometer 1
0 Mile 1

N

To Minturn

E. Fork Eagle Road

24

716

Camp Hale Trailhead

30

Colorado Trail

714

Jones Gulch Road

726

Colorado Trail

24

South Fork Eagle River

Colorado Trail

Tennessee Pass

Colorado Trail

To Leadville

After crossing the highway and railroad tracks, the route enters a particularly beautiful section where the singletrack rolls gently through an open valley, with high peaks poking up beyond. The trail cuts up through the woods too soon. Before long it joins an ex-railroad grade (the old Denver & Rio Grande) and contours gently to Tennessee Pass. Turn around at Tennessee Pass for a 13-plus-mile out-and-back. Of course the Colorado Trail continues onward from here, so there's plenty of opportunity for even longer hikes—as long as you could possibly want. If 13-plus is too long, turn around where the trail joins the railroad bed, or where it crosses the highway, or even at the bench overlooking Camp Hale, and you'll still have a solid, satisfying hike in the subalpine forest.

Although not quite as historically interesting, the Tennessee Pass Trailhead provides access to some really nice hikes, including lengthy backpacking trips in the Holy Cross Wilderness.

For an even more casual hike from the Camp Hale Trailhead, try going the opposite direction on the Colorado Trail, up the East Fork Valley toward Nazi Village. Eventually this route becomes a serious high-altitude test, but the early miles are easy going. About 1.5 miles from the trailhead is a small waterfall that makes a nice turnaround for a quick hike.

Miles and Directions

0.0 Start from the Camp Hale Trailhead of the Colorado Trail and start walking northwest along the road.

0.1 Turn left onto another old camp road, following the Colorado Trail signs.

0.4 As the trail passes an old firing range, the Colorado Trail diverges from the camp roads onto a singletrack and crosses the river.

1.3 The trail crosses a dirt road (Forest Service Road 726).

3.3 Carefully cross US 24, then the railroad tracks.

4.7 The trail joins what looks like a four-wheel-drive road. Continue, following the Colorado Trail insignia and blue diamond markings on trees. Take note of this intersection so you don't miss it on the way back (GPS: N39 22.75' / W106 19.70').

6.1 Pass old coke ovens.

6.6 Arrive at Tennessee Pass parking area. Turn around here or keep walking along the Colorado Trail.

13.2 Arrive back at the Camp Hale Trailhead.

Accommodations: Minturn Inn, 442 Main St., Minturn, CO 81645; (970) 827-9647; www.minturninn.com. A bed-and-breakfast with cozy rooms and comfortable beds; friendly hosts.

Hotel Minturn, 167 Williams St., Minturn, CO 81645; (970) 331-5461; www .hotelminturn.com. Four sleek, modern rooms available in central Minturn; good value.

31 Mayflower Gulch

This quick but not-quite-easy hike to the ruins of an old mining camp called Boston rewards with a truly impressive alpine vista.

Start: Mayflower Gulch Trailhead on CO 91
Distance: 3.2 miles out and back (with option for more)
Approximate hiking time: 1 to 2 hours
Difficulty: Easy to moderate
Trail surface: An uphill dirt road with some rocks and ruts. The route is open to vehicles, but most people hike from the trailhead.
Best season: Summer
Other trail users: Motor vehicles, bikes, hikers, and dogs
Canine compatibility: Dogs allowed
Land status: National forest

Fees and permits: None
Schedule: None
Map: Mayflower Gulch map, Dillon Ranger District
Trail contact: White River National Forest, Dillon Ranger District, 680 Blue River Pkwy., Silverthorne, CO 80498; (970) 468-5400; www.dillonrangerdistrict.com/summer/maygul_hkg.htm
Special considerations: High altitude. Watch the weather up here, and carry appropriate clothing.

Finding the trailhead: From I-70 turn south onto CO 91 at Wheeler Junction (Copper Mountain). Drive about 6 miles on CO 91; then turn left into the parking area of Mayflower Gulch Trailhead. GPS: N39 25.81' / W106 09.91'

The Hike

Hiking into the Mayflower Amphitheater—a huge, gorgeous natural bowl below Atlantic, Crystal, Pacific, Fletcher, and Tucker Peaks and the stegosaurus ridgeline that connects them—shouldn't be so casual and carefree. It just feels wrong. Typically such sublime locales are tucked away at the end of half-day hikes and multi-thousand-foot elevation gains. Here a moderately inclined half-hour hike puts you right at the heart of the matter.

As you might expect with such an accessible destination, right in the middle of the state next to a major highway, Mayflower Gulch occasionally gets a little crowded. It's great for families and casual walkers but also serves as an access route for hard-core mountain climbers on their way to the crazy-looking ridge and 13,900-foot peaks, and in the winter is thoroughly tracked by Nordic and Alpine skiers headed for the natural ski slopes above.

Mayflower Gulch "Trail" has an unfortunate feature, in my opinion: It's open to motor vehicles (highway-legal only; no dirt bikes or quads). Folks can almost drive right up to the Boston site. Thankfully, they usually don't, opting for the hike instead.

About a mile up from the bottom, there is a collapsed cabin within spitting distance; then, a little farther along the chunky dirt road, the remains of an ore loading

Stout cabins still provide shelter at timberline in Mayflower Gulch.

chute. Around a few more curves you'll see the cabins of Boston and a fork in the road; to the left for a little tour around Boston in the open tundra, to the right to begin a steep, switchbacking climb up the bowl.

Walking among the stoutly built ex-cabins of Boston will make you wonder about life in the camp. Such an uplifting place to live—for part of the year anyway. Would location make up for having to spend every day inside the mountain, huffing rock dust and shoveling ore into a cart? Seems doubtful. And what if you had to sleep in a cramped bunkhouse with a bunch of smelly dudes who hummed Sousa marches nonstop?

Also, try to imagine the basin devoid of the big pine trees that fill the lower part. During the mining camp's heyday, just about every tree nearby would have been cut down for cabins, mining timbers, cooking fuel, and heating fuel, so the view was a bit more desolate than it is now. On the other hand, there were no shockingly huge tailings ponds nearby as there are today (across the highway, below the huge operational molybdenum mine). The landscape is always scarred in the human era, although the scars change with the decades.

Nature is taking over at the top end of Mayflower Gulch, but down at the bottom the landscape is dominated by a brightly colored toxic wastewater pond or three, the least glorious part of the massive molybdenum extraction operation at the top of the pass. A sizable ghost town, Kokomo, is sitting at the bottom of the tailings pond.

The Climax Mine, as the source of the tailings is popularly known, is historic in its own right, the first moly mine in America and one of the first in the world.

Boston, Mayflower Gulch

Molybdenum mining commenced there in 1915, as demand for hardened metal spiked with the war. During the mine's glory years, those decades when war and automobiles were both in fashion, several thousand men and women worked there, mostly underground. In 1982 the Climax Mine closed. Twenty-five years later moly was in demand again and the mine reopened. There was much rejoicing in Leadville, which needed jobs. When it restarted, however, the sleeker version of the Climax Mine employed fewer than 500 workers.

Climax, operated by Freeport-McMoRan in 2015, is now an open pit mine. Large chunks of the mountain are removed, and the raw ore is sent to a nearby mill. The small boulders are crushed to a powder in a multistage process; then the powder is treated with hydrogen sulfide and other chemicals that separate the molybdenum and make it float in a froth on top of the solution for relatively easy extraction. It works nicely but produces large amounts of toxic waste. To see the mine and the brightly colored reservoir of waste, simply drive farther up toward the top of Fremont Pass.

Mining activity in Mayflower Gulch flared up briefly a few times over the past 150 years. Before the Boston Mine opened, there were other small mines in the basin. An 1879 mine directory lists the Silver Blossom, Resumption, and Golden Eagle Mines in Mayflower Gulch, with ore worth approximately $100 per ton. In 1912 the mining industry press reported that thirty men were employed at the "old" Boston Mine, indicating a second try there. A few million bucks worth of silver, lead, gold,

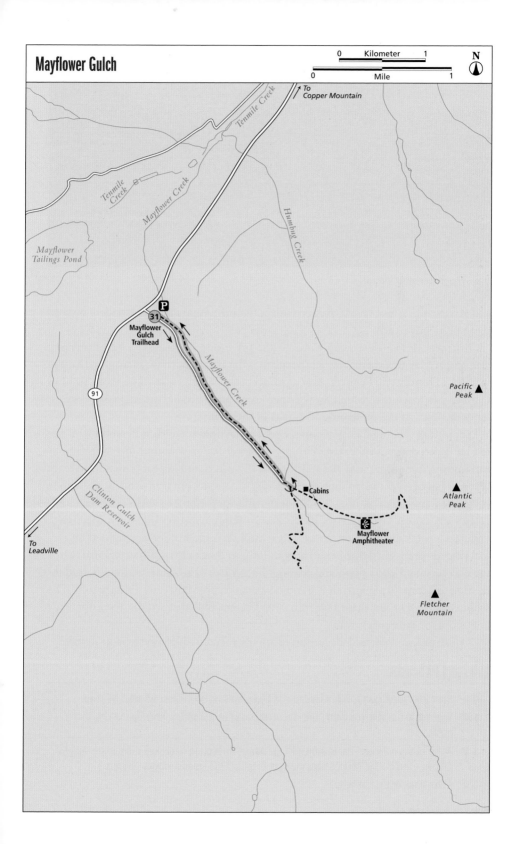

Mayflower Gulch

To
Copper Mountain

Tenmile Creek

Tenmile Creek

Tenmile
Creek

Mayflower Creek

Hunting Creek

Mayflower
Tailings Pond

P

31

Mayflower
Gulch
Trailhead

91

Mayflower Creek

Pacific
Peak

Atlantic
Peak

■ Cabins

♿
Mayflower
Amphitheater

Clinton Gulch
Dam Reservoir

To
Leadville

Fletcher
Mountain

0   Kilometer   1

0   Mile   1

N

The Mayflower Amphitheater

and zinc was dug out of Mayflower Gulch; then the mineral-seekers faded away to more productive areas.

In recent decades the steep climb in the price of gold sparked a bit of sidelong glancing at Mayflower Gulch from speculators, but there's been no indication that the well-loved retreat will be given over again to private interests anytime soon. Summit County purchased the ground for the open space program, and the mine owners gave up their rights to dig underground as part of the deal.

Sort of like the miners, geologists look at Mayflower Gulch differently than the rest of us do. Among other interesting geological features around here, the famous Mosquito Fault comes into the gulch from the south and appears to end suddenly, where it has been cut by an intersecting fault, "a conspicuous iron-oxide stained zone of crushed and silicified rock 90-300 feet wide," according to a 1971 US Geological Survey report. "The rocks of the Kokomo-Tenmile district [of which Mayflower Gulch is a part] show the effects of an eventful tectonic history highlighted by several periods of plastic deformation and faulting in Precambrian time, regional warping accompanied by faulting and folding during Paleozoic time, and uplift, folding, faulting and large-scale intrusion in post-Paleozoic, probably early Tertiary time. The sedimentary rocks are deformed into broad open folds that overlie the complexly contorted Precambrian terrain."

Deformed, faulted, folded, contorted, uplifted. Translation: awesome mountains.

Miles and Directions

0.0 Start from Mayflower Gulch Trailhead and begin walking up the four-wheel-drive road.

1.4 Veer left at the fork. (**Option:** Continue up the road as it climbs farther up the side of the basin.)

1.6 Arrive at the cabins of the Boston mining camp. Turn around or explore more of the Amphitheater. (The road continues past the cabins toward the steeper slopes above.)

3.2 Arrive back at the trailhead.

Roaring Fork

Well, they don't call it Oak Hollow. (hike 34)

32 Doc Holliday Trail

This is a steep but short climb to an old cemetery above Glenwood Springs. The cemetery is—possibly—home to some very famous residents.

Start: Doc Holliday Trailhead at 12th Street and Bennett Avenue in Glenwood Springs
Distance: 0.8 mile out and back, depending on amount of wandering around the graveyard
Approximate hiking time: 0.5 to 1.5 hours
Difficulty: Moderate
Trail surface: Moderately rocky and steep wide-track trail
Best seasons: Spring and fall
Other trail users: Hikers and dogs
Canine compatibility: Dogs allowed
Land status: City of Glenwood Springs

Fees and permits: None
Schedule: None
Map: *DeLorme: Colorado Atlas & Gazetteer*
Trail contacts: City of Glenwood Springs, 101 W. 8th St., Glenwood Springs, CO 81601; (970) 384-6400; www.ci.glenwood-springs .co.us. Frontier Historical Society, 1001 Colorado Ave., Glenwood Springs, CO 81601; (970) 945-4448; www.glenwoodhistory.com.
Special considerations: Please don't disturb or walk on the graves or deface grave markers.

Finding the trailhead: Take I-70 to Glenwood Springs (exit 116). Turn right (south) on CO 82/ Grand Avenue, drive about a quarter mile, and turn left onto 13th Street. Take 13th to the top of the hill and turn left onto Bennett Avenue. Drive 1 block and park. The trailhead is on the right, next to the house. A sign here may point the way to Pioneer Cemetery. GPS: N39 32.48' / W107 19.30'

The Hike

It's interesting what kind of heroes America latched onto as the frontier days came to an end. Shooters, killers. Outlaws. Up to and including murder, the sins of very bad guys were forgiven as long as the bad guys possessed certain manly traits, like the virility to stand to other bad guys.

Doc Holliday is one of those curious American heroes, loved primarily for his fearlessness, coolness under fire, loyalty to his friends, and perceived willingness to take out anybody foolhardy enough to insult his manhood for any reason. Nobody knows exactly how quick to murder Doc Holliday really was. It's not known exactly how many men he shot and killed, or how he felt about it. In some versions of his legend, he killed sixteen, with knives as well as guns, for petty saloon offenses as well as righteous vengeance. In more sober accounts Holliday gunned down a mere pair of individuals and injured a few others, but that won't satisfy the purveyors of legend. How many people did Holliday kill? Not enough! The public demands more.

Born in Georgia in 1851, John Henry Holliday got his nickname because he was a practicing dentist in Atlanta. He also had tuberculosis, and that's not great for building a dental practice. Holliday found himself working harder on his gambling and whiskey drinking than his dentistry, and he drifted west toward drier air and wetter

Grassy grave at Linwood Cemetery

saloons, and soon after he got there abandoned all pretense of being a dentist. It may also be true that Holliday killed somebody and had to leave Georgia, as some versions of the legend say. In any case he was in his element when he arrived in the mining and cattle boomtowns of the west.

"Doc Holliday was a weakling who couldn't have whipped a healthy fifteen-year-old boy in a go-as-you-please fight," wrote Bat Masterson in his later years. According to Masterson, Holliday was about 5'10" and 130 pounds. Photos appear to confirm the description. Physically unimposing yet hotheaded and confrontational, Holliday developed supreme pistol skills. He seemed to lack any fear of death, perhaps because of his illness.

Historians don't dispute the made-for-Hollywood legend that Doc Holliday had a part-time prostitute girlfriend known as Big Nose Kate, a Hungarian immigrant working in Dodge City; or that Holliday and Wyatt Earp were, at the very least, best buddies. The two seem to have met while gambling in Texas. Masterson implies that Earp and Holliday had romantic feelings for each other.

In 1881 Holliday was an eager participant in the Earp brothers' attempts to force law and order on a gang of rogue cowboys in Tombstone, Arizona. Hot lead from Holliday's gun was responsible for at least one of the deaths at the OK Corral shoot-out. Some blamed Doc himself for the trouble in Tombstone, for helping to instigate the conflict and then steering it to its bloody end.

When Wyatt Earp's brother was murdered by members of the gang after the shootout, Holliday rode with Earp on his mission to hunt down and kill every one of them. Full-on vigilante mode. The grisly task was, for all intents and purposes, completed, thanks to help from Holliday. Somewhere in there Holliday gunned down at least one more.

Holliday couldn't escape the 1880s. In 1887 his condition worsened, and he sought relief in the vapor caves of Glenwood Springs. Didn't work. Holliday spent his last weeks drifting toward incoherence in a Glenwood hotel. His last words were "This is funny." He was 36 years old.

"The Doc Holliday of history is an individual seen almost entirely through the eyes of others," writes esteemed Colorado historian Gary Roberts in his biography of Holliday. "He remains, essentially, a man without a voice, a circumstance that makes him at once a compelling subject and a frustrating figure . . . Not a single sample of his writing that would provide insight into how he felt or what he believed appears to have survived. In his lifetime he gave precious few interviews, and they are disappointing—except to the extent to which they reveal Doc's humor and studied disdain for the whole process of interview."

The Doc Holliday of history is buried right here in Linwood Cemetery, as a matter of record. However, nobody knows exactly where his body ended up. It seems a fitting aftermath to such a mysterious life. All they know is that he is somewhere on this mountainside. You'll see a tombstone or two up here with his name on it, but they're just props. Most likely, considering Doc's financial condition at time of death, he was interred in the paupers' graveyard, aka Potter's Field, appended to the main cemetery, and any authentic markers that once existed were removed by Doc-worshippers or souvenir-seekers of the past.

Also up there under the pines lies the skeleton of Kid Curry, another famous outlaw. Curry (real name Harvey Logan) was just getting started with his outlawing when Doc Holliday died of consumption. Kid Curry became a member of the

Harvey Logan and girlfriend Della Moore, aka Annie Rogers LIBRARY OF CONGRESS, PINKERTON DETECTIVE AGENCY COLLECTION. PUBLIC DOMAIN, WIKIMEDIA

"Wild Bunch" with Butch Cassidy and the Sundance Kid, although he proved to be much more cold-blooded than either of his famous outlaw bros. Where Butch would plan heists meticulously and avoid bloodshed, Curry was a shoot-'em-upper. Anybody who stood in his way was going to get blasted. Butch Cassidy is not known to have killed anybody in his criminal life. Logan/Curry killed at least nine lawmen in shootouts.

Kid Curry's taste for killing existed outside of robberies and banditry. Several of the murders pinned on Kid Curry were revenge killings of one kind or another. At one point he snuck onto a Montana ranch and waited all night for the ranch owner, who had shot Curry's brother years earlier, to emerge from his house. When the man stepped onto his front porch in the morning, Kid Curry killed him with a rifle shot from afar.

In 1904 Kid Curry and some members of the gang allegedly robbed a Denver & Rio Grande train near Parachute and, to facilitate their getaway, stole horses from local ranchers. Robbing trains was one thing—the locals could get behind robbers who took money from faceless banks and railroad companies—but stealing a man's horses was something else entirely. The local boys joined the posse and took off after the thieves, and caught them. As the ensuing gunfight turned sour for the train robbers, Kid Curry shot himself in the head. He had vowed never to be taken alive.

That's the story of how Kid Curry ended up in Glenwood Springs, and it's a believable one. But the story is also disputed by reputable sources. For instance, Mike

Doc Holliday Trail

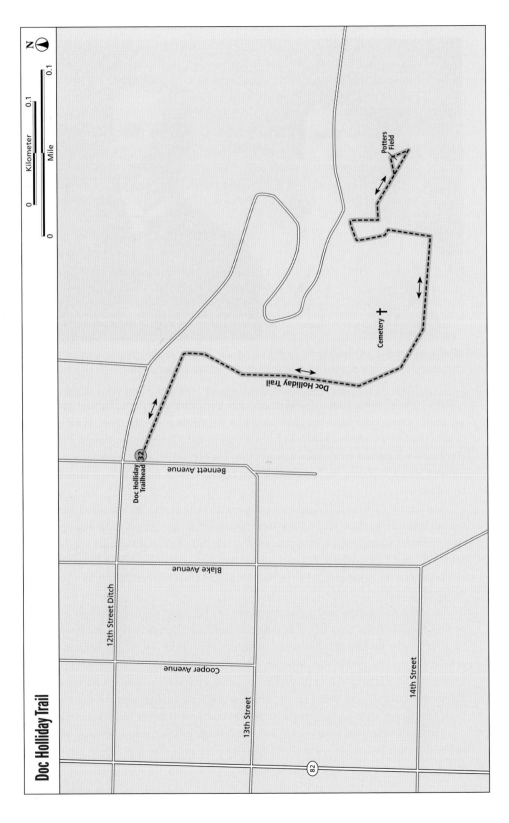

Potters Field

Cemetery

Doc Holliday Trail

Doc Holliday Trailhead

32

Bennett Avenue

Blake Avenue

12th Street Ditch

Cooper Avenue

13th Street

14th Street

82

N

Kilometer
0   0.1   0.1

Mile
0   0.1

O'Niel, who was the fireman on a train that was robbed by Kid Curry and testified against him in court, claimed that he saw him drinking in a bar in Great Falls, Montana, decades after his alleged death. Charley Siringo was a Pinkerton detective who tracked the Wild Bunch all over the west for many years, posing as an outlaw drifter. Siringo's sources told him that the man who killed himself after the Parachute robbery was definitely not Kid Curry, and Siringo trusted them. After chasing many false leads, the Pinkerton Agency declared the case closed and Kid Curry dead. Siringo eventually resigned over the disagreement.

So the end of Kid Curry, like those of Butch and Sundance, remains a delectable mystery. Seems like there's about a fifty-fifty chance that the cadaver under this pine is actually Kid Curry.

One thing that's not disputed is that Kid Curry was a vengeance-fueled spree killer. He was a hardened murderer. And yet here he is, or might be, with the best-maintained grave in the entire cemetery and an expensive marker from the historical society. It's a curious thing, how popular history resurrects these killers and props them up, tidies up their legacies of murder for new generations to smile upon whimsically. Gunslinging bandits are celebrated as much as any aspect of western history. Who else in this cemetery other than Doc and Kid Curry have books written about them? Who else has strangers tidying up their graves? Naturally people are attracted to exciting things like gunfights, but too often the brutal reality is glossed over in order to create cartoonish figures that fit some comforting Old West fantasy. Killers with hearts of gold. Deadly but righteous: If they killed you, you probably deserved it. Butch and Sundance might have been good guys deep down; Doc Holliday and Kid Curry and most of the other well-known outlaws were a different sort. Our obsession with these dark-hearted individuals is not exactly like the legions of people sending love letters to Manson, but it's interesting.

The inherent spookiness of Linwood Cemetery lends itself to dramatization. Every year around Halloween, paying groups are led up the trail by costumed actors and local history enthusiasts, where they meet characters like reanimated Doc Holliday and speaking-from-the-grave Kid Curry. But maybe these two sharpshooters should just stay dead, wherever they are.

Miles and Directions

0.0 From the Doc Holliday Trailhead on Bennett Avenue, begin walking up the Doc Holliday Trail.

0.3 The trail arrives at Linwood Cemetery. Turn right and walk up to "Potter's Field." There lies Kid Curry, to the right. Poke around respectfully, try to find Doc Holliday's grave, and then head back down to the main part of the cemetery.

0.4 Do a slow loop around Linwood Cemetery; then head back down the trail.

0.8 Arrive back at the trailhead.

33 Government Trail

Walk from Snowmass to Aspen on the varied, challenging, and delightful Government Trail. While you're walking, ponder the relatively recent discovery, at a nearby pond, of thousands of bones belonging to ice-age beasts, like mastodons and giant sloths.

Start: Ditch Trailhead at the high end of Snowmass Village, on Divide Road

Distance: 11.2 miles one way

Approximate hiking time: 5 to 6 hours

Difficulty: Difficult

Trail surface: Highly variable, from rugged and steep to smooth and easy; something new around every corner

Best season: Summer

Other trail users: Bikers, hikers, and dogs

Canine compatibility: Dogs allowed; must be under voice control

Land status: White River National Forest

Fees and permits: None

Schedule: Government Trail closed for elk calving from May 15 to June 20

Map: Government Trail #1980 map, Aspen Ranger District

Trail contact: White River National Forest, Aspen-Sopris Ranger District, 806 W. Hallam, Aspen, CO 81611; (970) 925-3445; www .fs.usda.gov/detail/whiteriver/about-forest/ districts/?cid=fsbdev3_001248

Special considerations: The route described here is one-way from Snowmass to Aspen and will require a second vehicle or a bus trip, unless you can convince somebody to drop you off. You can also walk from Aspen to Snowmass, of course. Either way it's a longish hike without nearby services along the trail. Be sure to bring enough food, water, and also foul-weather gear. Note that the Government Trail is off-limits from May 15 to June 20 to give the elk a little space.

Finding the trailhead: From CO 82 turn west onto Brush Creek Road and drive toward Snowmass Village. Veer right and continue on Brush Creek Road at a roundabout by the Snowmass Rec Center. Continue toward the ski area; then turn right onto Divide Road. At the top of the hill, before the road turns to dirt, turn left into the Ditch Trailhead parking area. GPS: N39 12.29' / W106 58.30'. (**Note:** Use the free Roaring Fork Transit Administration bus system to get back to Snowmass Village or drop a shuttle vehicle at the Aspen Rec Center. To reach the Rec Center, take Maroon Creek Road from the roundabout on CO 82 just west of Aspen. Drive up past the high school; then find the large parking lot of the Aspen Rec Center on the right.)

The Hike

The development of the Brush Creek Valley into Snowmass was part of the mid-century rush to cash in on the ski fad. Not long after the creation of Aspen ski area, Snowmass Mountain was scouted and picked as the next big thing. A smart guy named Bill Janss, who knew how to shape the future to his liking, had been buying up as much of the land as he could. In 1962, after lobbying from Janss, the Forest

Brush Creek Valley—ice-age home to mastodons and giant sloths

Service granted a permit to operate snowcats to pull skiers to the top of the hill. A few years later they gave permission to go all out cutting ski runs and developing the valley below. Snowmass ski area came to life in 1968, a joint project of Janss and the Aspen Skiing Company.

But the most interesting history here takes us back about 100,000 years to the late Pleistocene epoch. In October 2010 a bulldozer operator named Jesse Steele was beginning to enlarge Ziegler Reservoir, very close to the start of this hike, when he uncovered something freaky that made him stop work immediately. It turned out to be a bone from a mammoth. Within 2 days scientists from Denver's Museum of Nature and Science were digging at the site, and they quickly uncovered bones from almost thirty different ice-age beasts before winter blanketed the valley.

The scientific community was beside itself over the find. Apparently an ancient glacial lake existed at this improbable location—a ridgetop—for as long as 100,000 years before it was ever so slowly filled by sediment. The lake and the wetland around it became the final resting place for a wide variety of animals—including mastodons, mammoths, a huge ground sloth, an ice-age version of a camel, super-sized buffalo, and many more—from about 140,000 to 75,000 years ago, spanning the last interglacial period, or Marine Oxygen Isotope Stage 5.

The most common question about the site: Why did so many different beasts kick the bucket at this spot? The distribution of bones in specific layers of sediment, while other layers have no large-animal remains, indicates that the lake, for periods of its existence, may have developed into a sort of trap, perhaps with slippery sides or sticky muck from which the animals could not escape. Time is the other answer to this question. Over tens of thousands of years, there were plenty of opportunities for animals to die natural deaths at one of the most popular local watering holes.

Not the typical dig, the "Snowmastodon Project" was in emergency mode, advancing as quickly as possible. Snowmass Village was under contract with the land-owners to complete its reservoir project by a specified date and would otherwise incur financial penalties. Financial penalties! Science didn't stand a chance against the possibility of financial penalties.

The scientists, landowners, and Snowmass Village made a deal—the fossil hunt could continue until July 11; then the construction crews would resume building their dam. This would give the fossil hunters about 2 months of decent weather and unfrozen ground to excavate as much as they could.

By mid-May the following spring, the scientists were back in Snowmass digging up bones at a furious pace. The little lake swarmed with volunteer scientists and graduate students from dozens of different institutions. On any given day about fifty people shoveled into the dirt. With regularity the volunteers unearthed freakishly large femurs, vertebrae, tusks, claws, and entire skulls. Before the cutoff date the dig uncovered almost 5,000 individual fossils.

The site was hugely productive, but not the largest in the world. It was, however, unique due to its high altitude. The thin air helped preserve all the interesting things found here. In addition to the megafauna, countless plant specimens were recovered from the bottom of the ancient lake. "Preservation of organic material at the Ziegler Reservoir fossil site is exceptional," write Kirk Johnson, Ian Miller, and Jeffrey Pigati, who were in the pit every day. "Even after more than 100,000 years of burial, sedge and willow leaves were still green, mollusks and gastropods showed color, beetle parts remained iridescent, fossil conifer cones were intact, and an entire beach of 20-m-long driftwood logs was preserved. The exquisite preservation allowed for detailed analysis of pollen, plant macrofossils, conifer cones, and fossil wood, as well as insects, chironomids, mollusks, ostracodes, and other invertebrates—all in addition to the spectacular faunal remains" [Kirk Johnson, Ian Miller, Jeffrey Pigati, et al., "Intro-duction to the Snowmastodon Project Special Volume," *Quarternary Research*, Volume 82, 2014, p. 473.] (chironomids are a type of fly, and ostracodes are tiny crustaceans).

The treasure trove was welcomed giddily back at the Museum of Nature and Sci-ence, but the fossil windfall would also necessitate a great deal more work, and more funding, to store, analyze, and display all that new material. In the end it would add a great deal to our understanding of the "ice age."

The Government Trail is far less busy than you might expect for such a high-quality stretch of singletrack. This is probably due to the trail's approaches, which are all steep, long climbs. The Government Trail itself is a contouring route, primarily, with some tough climbs and rugged descents along the way. There's nothing too big in between Aspen and Snowmass, but getting up to the trail is an unavoidable grunt no matter which direction you're headed. So the Government Trail lies in a state of sweet preservation for hikers and mountain bikers with a little extra gumption and leg muscle.

Starting out near the top (west) end of Snowmass resort on the wide, rocky Ditch Trail, this hike is wonderfully horizontal—for a few blocks. Then it turns left and *up*. The Connector Trail zigzags up the ski hill, crisscrossing the straight-up access road several times. (Feel free to chug straight up the road and pick up the trail later, for shorter, harder hiking.) A little perseverance here will be rewarded shortly.

When the Connector Trail pops out onto a more established dirt road, turn right and continue uphill. Around the corner you'll find the Connector continuing to the right.

A little more uphill work (I know! I know!), and you're at the thin singletrack of the Government Trail. There may or may not be a sign here. Turn left and cruise in and out of dank aspen forests as you cross Snowmass ski area. (**Note:** For a much shorter hike, turn right on the Government Trail here and descend to the Ditch Trail, and then loop back to the trailhead.)

For the most part the Government Trail is well signed and easy to follow. There are some tricky points, however, places where several trails converge and the route is not obvious. At mile 2.2, for instance, the trail arrives at the top of a ski run; one trail goes left, and another winds directly down the slope. Signs are unhelpful. Head down the latter trail that snakes down the slope. Here and elsewhere the tall grasses and thick undergrowth of the ski slopes have overgrown the trail, making it seem like you took a wrong turn. Occasionally you'll be walking on nothing but stamped-down greenery. Don't be alarmed.

As it makes its way across the ski mountain, the Government Trail crosses several service roads, occasionally borrowing their routes for a short distance. Several other trails cross the Government; some head up higher on the mountain, while others are one-way chutes built for downhill mountain biking. Generally speaking, continuing to contour eastbound will keep you on the Government Trail route. The side trails and apparent alternate routes funnel into a single obvious route before the trail leaves the ski area on the east (around mile 5).

Much later, as the trail crosses the Buttermilk ski area, the route turns into a doubletrack that goes straight down a slope for a short stretch before heading back into the woods. Slightly confusing. The good news is that getting lost up here is not particularly dangerous, unless you share the typical Aspenite's conception of danger—missing out on happy hour. I won't lie to you; that's a real possibility for those attempting this hike.

Finally the trail deposits you on Tiehack Road. A walk across the fantastic ped/bike bridge over Maroon Creek takes you to the back side of the Aspen Rec Center, from which you can catch a ride, perhaps a local shuttle bus, back to Snowmass.

Government Trail

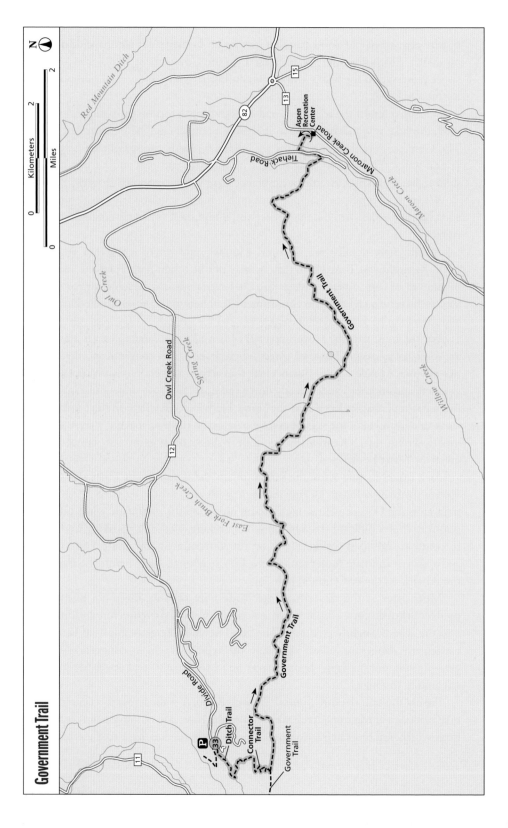

So where'd that name come from—Government Trail? Sounds like a story there, right? Well, if there is one, I can't find it. Let me know.

Miles and Directions

0.0 Start from the Ditch Trailhead near Divide Road and Pinon Drive and begin hiking southwest on the Ditch Trail.

0.4 Turn left and begin climbing the singletrack Connector Trail (aka Campground Connector).

1.0 The Connector Trail spills out onto a dirt road. Unlike the other times it has done this, there is no obvious continuation of the trail on the other side. Turn right here onto the road.

1.1 Veer right, back onto the Connector Trail. (Or just continue up the little road, which heads straight up a steep ski slope as the Connector zigzags across.)

1.6 Turn left onto the Government Trail.

2.2 The route snakes directly down a ski slope here before reentering the woods (GPS: N39 11.83' / W106 58.00').

5.7 Pass the intersection with the Anaerobic Nightmare Trail. This trail leads north to a network of trails on the north side of the mountain.

10.7 The trail spills out onto Tiehack Road. Continue downhill (north) on the sidewalk.

10.9 Turn right onto the pedestrian bridge over Maroon Creek. (There is a parking lot here that would be a fine place to leave a vehicle.)

11.0 On the other side of the bridge, continue straight next to the first base line of the ball field.

11.1 Turn right and walk between the rec center and the ball fields.

11.2 Arrive at the front door of the Aspen Rec Center, with its large free parking area. A great place to drop a vehicle or pick up a ride.

Accommodations: Tyrolean Lodge, 200 W. Main St., Aspen, CO 81611; (970) 925-4595; www.tyroleanlodge.com/. A good value on Main Street, catering to the active traveler. Historic ski gear displayed in the rooms.

Hotel Jerome, 330 E. Main St., Aspen, CO 81611; (855) 331-7213; https://hoteljerome.aubergeresorts.com/. A historic luxury hotel packed with western art. For the full Aspen experience, Hotel Jerome is the place.

34 Sunnyside/Shadyside Loop

To find a better view of the Roaring Fork Valley, you'd have to be in a plane with Don Johnson. The Sunnyside Trail climbs steeply and relentlessly from McClain Flats Road just outside Aspen.

Start: Sunnyside Trailhead on McClain Flats Road (right up the road from the Rio Grande Trailhead on Cemetery Road)
Distance: 10.0-mile lariat loop
Approximate hiking time: 4 to 5 hours
Difficulty: Difficult
Trail surface: Several rocky, very steep sections punctuate a long climb that never eases up for long. Once at the top, in the aspens, the trail remains moderately rocky and generally very rustic for the entire route.
Best seasons: Spring, summer, and fall
Other trail users: Bikers, hikers, and dogs
Canine compatibility: Dogs allowed; must be on leash
Land status: White River National Forest

Fees and permits: None
Schedule: None
Map: City of Aspen trail map
Trail contacts: City of Aspen Open Space, 585 Cemetery Ln., Aspen, CO 81611; (970) 920-5120; www.cityofaspen.com/Departments/Parks-Trails-Open-Space/. White River National Forest, Aspen-Sopris Ranger District, 806 W. Hallam, Aspen, CO 81611; (970) 925-3445; www.fs.usda.gov/detail/whiteriver/about-forest/districts/?cid=fsbdev3_001248.
Special considerations: This hike is for tough nuts, people who feel the need to exercise very strenuously and/or punish themselves for sins of all kinds.

Finding the trailhead: From CO 82 in Aspen, take Cemetery Road until it ends at the Rio Grande River and McClain Flats Road. Continue up the hill on McClain Flats Road and park in a small trailhead parking area. GPS: N39 12.94' / W106 50.53'. (**Note:** There isn't much parking here, but if necessary, there is some more parking available at the bottom of the hill by the river. [There is also a trail that leads from that lower trailhead and the Rio Grande Trail up the hill to the Sunnyside Trailhead on McClain Flats Road.])

The Hike

The beautiful long-distance views and trailside scenery along this hike may not be enough to dominate your memory of it. I think what you'll remember most is the difficulty of the climb.

A good indication of the difficulty of a climb is the willingness of mountain bikers to attempt it (if the trail in question is indeed open to mountain bikers). It's more difficult to pedal up very steep trails on a bicycle than it is to walk up them; if the trail is so steep and rugged that the mountain biker must dismount and push or carry the bike up the trail, then the bike-less hiker has an even bigger advantage. The Sunnyside Trail is open to mountain bikers, but almost nobody in this bike-crazy corner of the

It takes a bit of work to get this view. Aspen (left) and Aspen Highlands ski areas line the Roaring Fork Valley.

world attempts to ride *up* the thing. Word got around. That should give you a good indication of what kind of trail we're dealing with.

The hike starts from a small parking area on McClain Flats Road and makes its way up the very dry, sun-baked south-facing slope; thus the trail's name. The trail is intermittently rough, with boulders and slabs to step on. It joins fading irrigation ditch roads and other confusing tracks here and there, and there are vestiges of an older version of Sunnyside Trail that was rerouted because it invaded somebody's private property (probably a Saudi prince or something). So the route is less clear than we'd like in spots, but not bad enough to cause real problems for the mindful hiker.

Quickly the trail gets high on the hillside, with awesome views of the valley below. A history-rich valley if there ever was one.

Instead of giving you that ol' song and dance about the Utes and prehistoric Indians who lived here, and the birth of Aspen as a mining boomtown, I thought I'd give you a word or two about Aspen in its late-twentieth- and early-twenty-first-century glory, when it became North America's most exclusive mountain town.

Ever since the town entered its glitzy phase, a process that began when the runs were carved on Aspen Mountain after World War II, it's been a magnet for magnates, celebrated by celebrities, lived in by luminaries. The airport below you—you'll notice the planes roaring away for periodic takeoffs and looping in for landings through most of this hike—is a big reason why Aspen became *Aspen*. Other reasons include the cultural institutions started by the Paepckes, modern Aspen's founders, and, of course, the unbelievable scenery.

"Aspen's mission as a center for play served to create in the town a cult of youth," according to Ed Richey, scholar of Aspen cultural history. By the mid-1970s the town had very few residents over the age of 65.

In the 1980s the town began to be defined in the public consciousness by its most well-known part-time locals, and Aspen increasingly defined those residents. Barbie Benton and Don Johnson exemplified the sparkly, cocaine-snorting party crowd, jet-setters who hung out in Aspen on their way to or from LA and the South of France. They came not only to ski and be in the mountains, an end in itself, but with the hope that some of Aspen's cultural mystique would rub off on them. Maybe if they stayed cool and skied with some panache, they would be seen as insiders.

John Denver had some semi-unhinged new age thing going on. Or was it just an elaborate real estate scheme? Always hard to tell around here. Meanwhile, Hunter S. Thompson gave the town a dose of much-needed authentic energy, from his home in Woody Creek and various safe havens around the valley. Thompson, a self-described freak with a liking for truth, justice, and psychedelic drugs, had moved to Aspen as soon as he had the means, as if drawn to the mother ship. His run for Pitkin County sheriff in 1970 was just the beginning of his energetic civic involvement. The association in the public mind of John Denver and Hunter Thompson with Aspen became as strong as their association with the creations that made these cultural icons famous to begin with.

Hunter Thompson had a lot of funny and scathing things to say about Aspen's corporate overlords. In 1970 he wrote an article for *Rolling Stone* called "The Battle of Aspen," about the recent mayoral election that his side, Freak Power, had run entirely from an oak table in the Hotel Jerome tavern. "Aspen is full of freaks, heads, fun-hogs and weird night people of every description," he noted lovingly. But the good people of Aspen were under attack by an evil corporate real estate machine. Same old story: "Freak Power" versus "greedheads." Even if the freaks didn't win, they showed that their power was real. They changed Aspen civic politics for decades.

Thompson became a political rabble-rouser, the voice not only of Aspen's freaks and hippies but of the service employees who wanted to live in the town but couldn't find affordable space. He described accurately the process that was, even in the 1960s, pushing the workers further and further down-valley—"first the tiny midtown apartments, then out-lying shacks, and finally the trailer courts." Thompson became symbolic of a fun-loving (drug-devouring) grassroots movement that empowered low-income locals against out-of-state developers, the Aspen Ski Company, and others with impossibly deep pockets. The movement led to some affordable housing laws and kept the developers more restrained than they otherwise would have been.

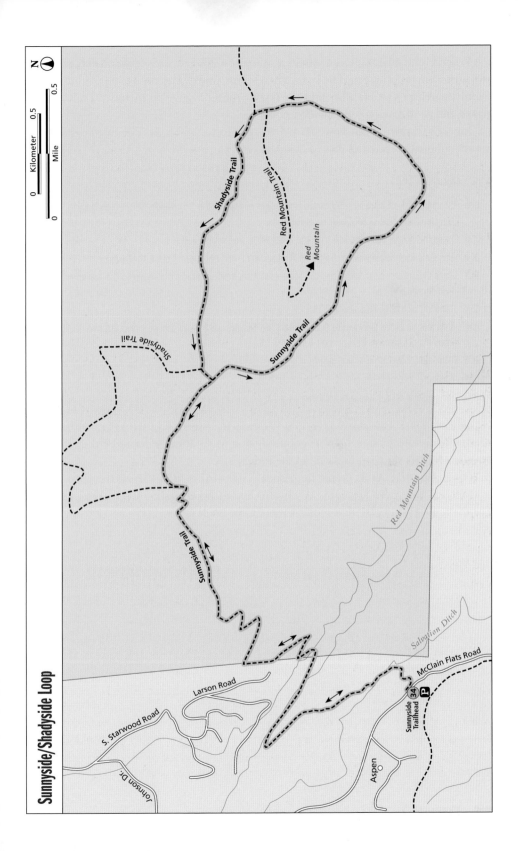

Sunnyside/Shadyside Loop

When Hunter Thompson committed suicide in 2005, by .45-caliber handgun, it was a bad omen for Aspen. His last written words were: "This won't hurt." Untrue. Family members shot his ashes into the sky via rocket to give his memory a suitably freaky and good-natured exclamation point.

In today's Aspen, Freak Power could be at its lowest ebb ever. The fun-hogs and weird night people have all moved down-valley.

Miles and Directions

0.0 Start from the Sunnyside Trailhead and begin hiking up the Sunnyside Trail, which begins on the other side of McClain Flats Road.

3.0 Pass the subtle intersection with the Shadyside Trail on the left.

3.4 Pass the intersection with the Shady Cutoff Trail (we'll be coming back that way).

5.3 Pass the intersection with the Red Mountain Trail, a doubletrack that goes to the top of Red Mountain.

5.4 Turn left onto the Shadyside Trail.

6.4 Turn left onto the Shadyside Cutoff Trail. (The Shadyside Trail continues here and eventually joins the Sunnyside Trail at mile 6.9.)

6.5 Turn right, back on the Sunnyside Trail.

6.9 Pass the intersection with the Shadyside Trail.

10.0 Arrive back at the trailhead. Whew.

Accommodations: Tyrolean Lodge, 200 W. Main St., Aspen, CO 81611; (970) 925-4595; www.tyroleanlodge.com/. A good value on Main Street, catering to the active traveler. Historic ski gear displayed in the rooms.

Hotel Jerome, 330 E. Main St., Aspen, CO 81611; (855) 331-7213; https://hoteljerome.aubergeresorts.com/. A historic luxury hotel packed with western art. For the full Aspen experience, Hotel Jerome is the place.

Rocky Mountain National Park

Kawuneeche Valley: A tragedy of war kept the Utes away from a favorite summer hunting ground (hike 35).

35 Holzwarth Ranch

An easy jaunt to a historic tourist ranch preserved by the National Park Service, located on the less populated west side of Rocky Mountain National Park.

Start: Holzwarth Ranch Trailhead parking area on the west side of Rocky Mountain National Park

Distance: 1.2-mile lariat loop

Approximate hiking time: 30 minutes—add another 30 minutes for poking around

Difficulty: Easy

Trail surface: Wide, flat gravel path

Best season: Summer

Other trail users: Hikers; bikes and dogs not allowed

Canine compatibility: No dogs allowed on trails

Land status: National park

Fees and permits: There is a hefty fee to enter Rocky Mountain National Park, which is paid by the vehicle or, if you're walking or riding bikes, by the individual. The entry fee is good for up to 1 week.

Schedule: None, but overnight parking requires a permit. Trail Ridge Road usually closes in winter; for status call (970) 586-1319.

Maps: Rocky Mountain National Park map, National Park Service

Trail contact: Rocky Mountain National Park, 1000 US 36, Estes Park, CO 80517-8397; (970) 586-1206; www.nps.gov/romo

Special considerations: Hiking inside Rocky Mountain National Park comes with several special regulations. No bikes allowed. No dogs allowed. No camping without a permit.

Finding the trailhead: The trailhead is located on the west side of Rocky Mountain National Park on Trail Ridge Road (US 34), about 7.5 miles from the west entrance. GPS: N40 22.35' / W105 51.27'

The Hike

This is an easy hike inside Rocky Mountain National Park, across the flat Kawuneeche Valley to an old "trout lodge" nestled in the trees on the other side. It's a great little hike for kids or anyone who needs a quick leg-stretcher after a long car ride—a nearly universal condition among tourists moving through this area. History buffs will enjoy the cluster of buildings that make up this establishment, including a number of tourist cabins, an icehouse, and a taxidermy shop. Many nineteenth- and early-twentieth-century tools and other artifacts add interest to the ranch site. There is also a nicely preserved homestead cabin near the trailhead. Both sites are crewed by guides who are happy to share their knowledge of the local history.

With the nascent Colorado River running through it, the relatively flat Kawuneeche Valley, carved by a 20-mile-long glacier, was a prime spot on the itineraries of nomadic Native Americans. They avoided the place in winter, naturally enough, and came to hunt in the spring and summer when the elk were here with their heads buried in the grasses.

Holzwarth Trout Lodge, b. 1917

"Kawuneeche" is an Anglicized version of an Arapaho word meaning "coyote river." We know this because, in 1914, a few members of the Colorado Mountain Club invited some Arapaho elders who knew the area to tramp around the soon-to-be national park, pointing out Indian trails and disclosing the names they had for prominent landmarks. A young man named Oliver Toll earnestly recorded the Arapaho names. Though there was no good way to reproduce Indian names with the English alphabet, Toll did the best he could. His journal was published in 1962 with the title *Arapaho Names and Trails.*

The good-hearted venture may have been flawed from the beginning, and not just because the Indians tended to have several names for a single location. The valley and other places visited were more strongly connected to the Utes than the Arapahos. The Arapahos were traditionally Plains Indians, and the Utes were mountain people who had lived in the area of "coyote river" for many hundreds of years. The Cheyenne-Arapaho and the Utes were blood enemies. If the Arapahos came to the area we now call Rocky Mountain National Park before 1860 or so, it was probably to seek out and battle with Utes who lived around there. The Utes were enthusiastic participants in this ongoing war. In any case a Ute name might be more appropriate for this valley and other park landmarks.

By the time white dudes were swarming around the area of Grand Lake, they noticed that the mountain Utes seemed to avoid the area. The conspicuous absence was explained by a common Ute legend. The Utes told the story of a horrible disaster that occurred while a band of the tribe was encamped near Grand Lake. While the Utes' lookouts had retreated from their rocky posts during an intense thunderstorm, Cheyenne and Arapaho warriors attacked in the night. The Ute elders, women, and children sought refuge on rafts in the lake as the battle and thunderstorm raged. Somehow the surprised and badly outnumbered Utes won the battle. But when the dust settled, they noticed that the rafts and all onboard were gone. There was nothing but mist rising slowly from the water. In overwhelming sadness and fear, the Utes avoided "Spirit Lake" from then on.

You won't see any Ute or Arapaho artifacts on this little hike. The relics here belong to a different time and place.

John and Sophia Holzwarth were German immigrants who homesteaded in the area in the 1880s. They moved to Denver and ran a saloon for many years, but Prohibition put the kibosh on the saloon, and in 1917 the family packed up and moved

The Grand Ditch

Looking at the steep slope high above the Holzwarth Ranch, notice the apparently man-made feature cutting all the way across the mountain. It looks like a railroad cut, but it's a big aqueduct called the Grand Ditch. The 20-foot-wide ditch is fed by no fewer than twelve diverted creeks as it cuts 14 miles north through the hills, across the Continental Divide, dropping just 125 feet in its entire run. Grand Ditch deposits its load in the Cache la Poudre River, which delivers the water to thirsty Front Range farms.

A private company started making Grand Ditch in the 1890s, using many Japanese workers. The remains of a workers' camp are evident near the ditch (above the Lulu City site). Crews extended the ditch southward from the Cache la Poudre little by little. The more they completed, the more they had to maintain. In 1936 the ditch achieved its present form when it was extended to Baker Creek, by a different company. A 40-year project.

The Grand Ditch cut an impressively wide footprint—affecting the wilderness far beyond its 20-foot canal. On May 30, 2003, a big section of the ditch failed catastrophically, sending a massive mudslide down the mountain, uprooting trees, causing a huge scar, and dousing wetlands in sediment. Even when working perfectly, the ditch steals so much water that it has a significant effect on the ecosystem in the valley, but this was something else entirely. In the words of Rocky Mountain National

back to the Kawuneeche. As with so many other ranchers in the area, their early ag aspirations gave way to the business plan of the future—coaxing dollars from tourists. Their decision to open a fishing lodge was nicely timed with the opening of Fall River Road, linking Grand Lake to the Front Range, and their hospitality skills were apparently pretty good too.

There's a lot of confusion about the name of this place. In 1923 the Holzwarths built a more modern dude ranch on the other side of the river, around where the trailhead parking sits today. This was the Never Summer Ranch, named after the rugged mountain range to the north. Both ranches became part of Rocky Mountain National Park in 1975. As part of the deal the Holzwarths made with the Park Service, the buildings of the family's beloved Trout Lodge were preserved, while those at the newer Never Summer Ranch were removed. Adding to the confusion, the Park Service renamed the surviving cluster of buildings Never Summer Ranch.

Park managers, "The breach has resulted in highly unnatural conditions within the project area as a large amount of excess sediment has been deposited into the system and remains in an unstable, erodible state." The ditch broke open up the valley at a spot called Windy Point, above Lulu Creek and the Colorado River headwaters.

The government filed suit against the ditch owners, Water Storage and Supply Company, and the company agreed to pay $9 million. But 10 years after the breach, the Park Service was still mulling public comments and trying to figure out what to do about it all. They're faced with an unsavory dilemma—do nothing and live with damage to the Colorado River headwaters ecosystem while it slowly repairs itself, or try to clean up and restore the affected area with engineering and heavy equipment that will also negatively impact the environment.

The slide zone can be accessed by spirited hikers via the Colorado River Trailhead, just up the road a mile or so from the Holzwarth parking lot. On that hike you can also see where a short-lived but high-hoped town called Lulu City once stood. Lulu City was hot for a few years (1881–82), showing all the signs of a budding silver boomtown. Then people started to figure out that the surrounding hills were not producing paydirt, just regular dirt, and everybody left as quickly as they came. Most evidence of the town's existence has crumbled into the aforementioned regular dirt, but you can still find some wrecked cabins and other structures. Turn left above Lulu City and head up Lulu Creek to where you might find the foundations of the Grand Ditch workers' cabins and various other relics at the site of their historic camp (c. 1900), and Grand Ditch itself.

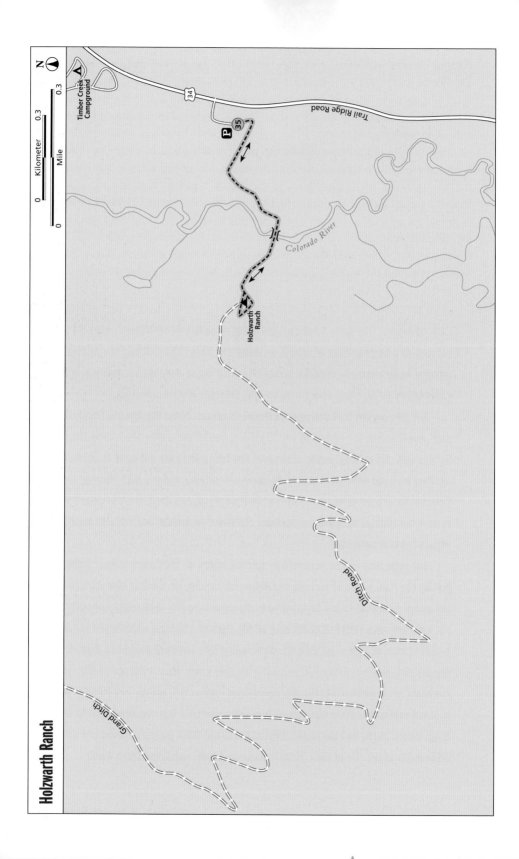

Holzwarth Ranch

Timber Creek Campground

34

35 **P**

Trail Ridge Road

Colorado River

Holzwarth Ranch

Ditch Road

Grand Ditch

N

| 0 | | Kilometer | 0.3 |
| 0 | | Mile | 0.3 |

Nothing here gets out alive: Holzwarth taxidermy shop.

You'll probably see a lot of elk lounging around the glacier-carved Kawuneeche Valley, maybe even some moose. You can see why this would be a prime summer hunting spot for Native Americans. However, the spectacularly awesome and gawky moose are not native to Colorado. They weren't around before the 1970s. Like so many of our nonnative species, moose were injected into Colorado by government wildlife managers to spice things up a bit for hunters and tourists.

Miles and Directions

0.0 Start from the parking lot and begin walking along the wide dirt path. Hang a quick left and check out the little homestead cabin near the parking area and speak with the ranger, who knows a thing or two about what's going on here.

0.4 Arrive at the trout lodge; embark on a quarter-mile clockwise loop of the grounds. The taxidermy shop and icehouse are on the left. Then head back.

1.2 Arrive back at the parking area.

36 Moraine Park

Loop around one of Rocky Mountain National Park's well-known glacier-carved meadows while trying to imagine what it looked like at the turn of the century, when it was covered with dude ranches and fishing lodges.

Start: Cub Lake Trailhead in Moraine Park, Rocky Mountain National Park
Distance: 4.8-mile loop
Approximate hiking time: 2 to 3 hours
Difficulty: Moderate
Trail surface: Horse-stomped singletrack and wide-track, often boggy or muddy
Best season: Summer
Other trail users: Hikers and horses; bikes and dogs not allowed
Canine compatibility: No dogs allowed
Land status: National park
Fees and permits: There is a hefty fee to enter Rocky Mountain National Park, which is paid by the vehicle or, if you're walking or riding bikes, by the individual. The entry fee is good for up to 1 week.

Schedule: None, but any overnight camping requires a permit.
Map: Rocky Mountain National Park map, National Park Service
Trail contact: Rocky Mountain National Park, 1000 US 36, Estes Park, CO 80517-8397; (970) 586-1206; www.nps.gov/romo
Special considerations: Hiking inside Rocky National Park comes with several special regulations. Any overnight camping requires a permit. No pets are allowed on the trails. Please don't leave pets inside cars while you hike. Fishing: This hike passes by some great fishing, which requires a Colorado fishing license. Check with the rangers at Moraine Park Discovery Center for specific regulations for Moraine Park streams.

Finding the trailhead: From Estes Park head west on US 36 to the Beaver Meadows entrance of Rocky Mountain National Park. Take the first left after the entrance onto Bear Lake Road. After Bear Lake Road goes around a few curves, turn right onto Moraine Park Road. Turn left onto Fern Lake Road instead of continuing straight toward Moraine Park Campground. Drive for a bit over a mile on Fern Lake Road and park at the Cub Lake Trailhead. GPS: N40 21.37' / W105 36.95'

The Hike

Who do you think you are, the Earl of Dunraven?
—Traditional northern Colorado insult

Moraine Park is a gently sloping square mile filled with green grasses and wildflowers, just inside Rocky Mountain National Park on the east side. The Big Thompson River winds through, and of course spiky 13,000-foot peaks are popping up on all sides, making this one of the showpiece spots of the state. Colorado road-trippers know the place well but usually drive right past it, gawking. Today we'll become intimately acquainted with this magical meadow, walking most of the perimeter before heading

Once filled with tourist lodges and guest cabins, Moraine Park is going back to nature.

through the tall grasses and even climbing up onto one of the lateral moraines that give the place its name.

When a glacier carves a valley like this one, it doesn't just leave us with a pretty open space and winding rivers where the glacier used to be. Glaciers also create moraines, which are the massive walls of debris—boulders, primarily—pushed to either side by the advancing ice. The lateral moraines are particularly obvious here in Moraine Park.

Moraine Park gives the impression of a place that is almost pristine, a nicely preserved mountain valley that has been encroached upon with a few roads and cabins. In reality, the Moraine Park you see today is more pristine—closer to its natural state—than it's been at any time in the past 150 years. When white settlers discovered the place, they set about building—cabins, lodges, roads, corrals, stables. By the time Rocky Mountain National Park was created in 1915, Moraine Park was almost packed with structures. The establishments continued to operate until the 1960s, when the feds embarked on a controversial project to remove buildings and return the park to nature.

Undeveloping Moraine Park involved a lot more than simply knocking down some old cabins. The largest, best-known operation in Moraine Park at the time,

Steads Ranch, formerly Sprague Lodge, included about twenty separate buildings and a large outdoor swimming pool.

Thomas Sprague went to Colorado aka "Pikes Peak" in 1860 to look for gold. It was a popular quest. Soon Thomas, inflicted with scurvy, realized that finding gold was one of the least likely ways to make a living in this new world. Farming and ranching seemed a better way to go, and Thomas Sprague claimed 160 acres where the Big Thompson River exits the mountains and slithers into the plains, near Loveland. In 1863 he left his tiny cabin (unlocked) and returned to his wife and kids in Illinois. All winter he told them crazy-sounding stories about Pikes Peak Country; then in the spring they all piled into their covered wagon and started for their new home, arriving a few months later, just in time for the Indian hysteria of 1864.

Thomas's teenaged son Abner took to Colorado with a vengeance. As soon as he was old enough to pull it off, he went into the Big Thompson Canyon, cut trees, and floated the timber to a point where he could cart if off and sell it. He raised war parties from the settlers' sons and rode off to attack imaginary bands of hostile Indians during the late 1860s, when every distant horseman became an Indian army in the paranoid rumor mill of the day. In his off time he traveled with his friends to the mountains above Estes Park, camped, fished, and climbed mountains. In 1875 Abner decided to take a bit of that sublimely beautiful land for himself.

During the 1870s settlers in the Estes Park area were embroiled in a wide-ranging battle with an English lord with the impossibly delicious name of Windham Thomas Wyndham-Quin, the Earl of Dunraven. Lord Dunraven was attempting to steamroll his way into ownership of a huge area of land around Estes Park, using nefarious transactions to game the Homestead Act and accumulate acreage.

The earl had come to the area in 1872 to hunt with a party from England and, quite simply, fell in love with the wild mountains. His words of recollection about those days are full of youthful enthusiasm. A man of almost unlimited funds and energy, Lord Dunraven came back to Estes Park in 1873. Not satisfied with a mere rich man's hunting excursion, he apparently decided he would like to own every mountain and river in the vicinity, and everything in between. The popular conjecture was that the lord was trying to create a vast hunting estate for himself and his friends, but cattle ranching was obviously part of the plan.

Curt Buchholz explained Lord Dunraven's methods in his history of Rocky Mountain National Park:

> *Assisted by his new friend Theodore Whyte and several Denver bankers and lawyers, the Earl first arranged to have the park legally surveyed. Once that formality was accomplished, the Earl and his agents used a scheme, common among other speculators, exploiting the Homestead Law to their advantage. They found local men in Front Range towns willing—for a price—to stake 160-acre claims throughout the park. More than thirty-five men filed claims using this ploy. Then, Dunraven's "Estes Park Company, Ltd." (or*

the English Company as it was called locally) proceeded to buy all those parcels at a nominal price, estimated at five dollars per acre. Between 1874 and 1880, the Earl managed to purchase 8,200 acres of land. In addition, the Company controlled another 7,000 acres because of the lay of the land and the ownership of springs and streams. [C. W. Buchholz, Rocky Mountain National Park: A History*]*

In 1876 Lord Dunraven hired the well-known artist Albert Bierstadt to paint a portrait of the park, reportedly shelling out $15,000 for the canvas and hanging it in his castle back home. (The painting now resides in the Denver Art Museum, garnering many a "meh" from the artsy hipsters of today.) Maybe Lord Dunraven loved the place so much that he wanted to look at it even when he was castle-bound. Or maybe the earl just wanted a fancy conversation piece to enable bragging to his snooty buds about his fantastic Rocky Mountain hunting estate.

When the Spragues (Abner and his father) built a homestead cabin in Moraine Park (then called Willow Park) in 1875 and began to clear all the willows and kill all the beavers, as would-be ranchers were known to do, they were under the assumption that the Earl of Dunraven had already filed claim to it. "I went there as a squatter,"

Lord Dunraven as he appeared in a Vanity Fair *caricature, 1878.* PUBLIC DOMAIN, WIKIMEDIA

Abner remembered. He was ready for a fight. One gets the feeling from Sprague, whose writings are tinged with testosterone, that he relished the idea. Later Sprague learned that the Englishman's company had never formally claimed Willow Park in its quest to control the area, which gave Sprague the upper hand. Still, Sprague found himself at odds with Lord Dunraven's reps during those early years.

In the end the Colorado estate proved more troublesome than fantastic for Lord Dunraven. As you might imagine, haughty English lords didn't play too well among the weathered pioneer demographic, while "straight shooters" like Abner Sprague were lionized. Lord Dunraven was widely perceived as the villain, the common enemy, and did little to chip away at this perception. His PR was terrible. The challenges to his claims were supported by strong local sentiment as well as judges. Tax officials piled on. His representatives were always in court, defending against this and that.

And then, of course, there was the matter of a few murders around Estes Park to which the earl was indirectly linked. Most famously, one of his high-strung representatives was present in 1874 when Rocky Mountain Jim Nugent, one of Estes Park's earliest and best-known residents, a man immortalized by Isabella Bird in her dispatches, was shotgunned and killed under still unresolved circumstances. The deadly drama seemed to epitomize the clash of worlds, as Nugent had been one of the prickliest obstacles to Lord Dunraven's vision.

Lord Dunraven ultimately lost his war with the Spragues and other local settlers, and his grand scheme to corner Estes Park real estate for his private use (for whatever purpose, not entirely clear) was downsized to the operation of a single high-end hotel, known to everyone as the English Hotel. The English Hotel was the first serious symptom of a new type of business that would take over this area.

Like many others, the Spragues started in Willow Park with the idea of becoming cattle ranchers. "We soon learned that if we were to make a living, we must turn from calves, butter and milk to tourists," wrote Abner Sprague in his memoirs. Guest ranches sprang up all over the place, in Willow Park, Estes Park, and other obvious locations around what we now call Rocky Mountain National Park.

Though Abner Sprague is commonly remembered as the proprietor of the Spragues' guest ranch, that might be a mistake. His name was on the land, but much of the credit must go to his parents. An early ad for the "Sprague House, Willow Park" names the proprietor as his father T. E. Sprague, while Abner is "and son."

Abner's mother, Mary, might have been the real workhorse of the operation. It's quite possible that she was too busy taking care of business to jot down notes for her memoirs and enable historical glory to be unleashed upon herself.

> *"My mother was taken more than a few times to be my wife by the stray tourists that wandered along," noted Sprague. "I remember meeting a man in the upper end of the park who told me my wife at the cabin had told him so-and-so. 'My wife!' I exclaimed, and started away, saying I must hurry as she might leave before I got to see her as I had never had that pleasure. He thought I was crazy until I explained that he must have seen my mother, who was the only woman I could get to live with me, as yet. My mother did go with me when I was on odd jobs about the place."*

In 1881, when their guest ranch business was just getting under way, Abner Sprague became a railroad engineer and joined a surveying party to document parts of Colorado for the Union Pacific Railroad. The ranch's workload was left to his mother, father, and brother. In 1882 Thomas Sprague died. Working for the railroad, Abner didn't return to work full-time on the ranch for almost 10 years. With two-thirds of the family's males suddenly AWOL, the guest ranch operation continued.

"The building up of the business of entertaining visitors and the success of that business was almost entirely owing to my mother."

"After I married and quit railway engineering," Sprague continued, "I returned to the ranch and with the help of a wife and the continued help of my mother, continued the business until it was sold to J.D. Stead in 1904."

Clearly women were key to the Sprague guest ranch. While Abner Sprague himself gives credit where it's due, the historians who rely on his memoirs tend not to for some reason. It's always *Abner did this, Abner did that...* At the very least he had a lot of help. It seems just as likely that his mother and wife did most of the work.

After selling their ranch to the Steads, the Spragues moved back down to Loveland. But the mountains were calling their name, and within a few years the Spragues were back, putting a cabin in Glacier Basin as a family getaway. In 1914 they set up a new, bigger lodge on the road to Bear Lake. Abner resumed doing what he loved most, guiding guests to the best mountain summits and fishing holes in what would soon be known as Rocky Mountain National Park.

You won't see much if any evidence of the old Sprague guest ranch on this hike around Moraine Park, although the route does go right past the ranch site. Start from the Cub Lake Trailhead at the heart of Moraine Park and walk south across the glacier-scoured park bottom, crossing the meandering Big Thompson River (not so big up here). Hang a left at the other end of the valley and walk east along the South Lateral Moraine. You'll find yourself next to a creek, perhaps heavily involved with it as you move east. Even on the satellite view it's not terribly clear if this is a tributary of the Big Thompson or some sort of side channel; in any case almost all of Moraine Park is a huge marshy island.

That's the nicest part of the hike, in my opinion. If you're not excited about making a big loop, another nice option is to turn around somewhere along the South Lateral Moraine for a sublime out-and-back route.

The South Lateral Moraine Trail eventually veers right and chugs up the moraine unceremoniously, but our route is a little more civilized, continuing straight and flat on a rustic dirt road. (If you wish, you can stay on the trail, but it just goes up the moraine and comes back down to the road, a trail used primarily by groups on horseback.) Here along the road you'll see ten or so cabins that survived the frenzy of unbuilding in the 1960s. Where the road turns north and crosses the river, leave it and go through the gate to begin a trek across the green field. I do believe this is the old road that took travelers to the Sprague place.

The next phase of the hike is quite different. The trail goes up to the paved road, crosses it, and climbs the opposite moraine. For a few moments the hike is tough going on this horse-churned trail. From here on out things are more vertically oriented. The trail isn't necessarily very hilly, but it contours across some steep hills. Foot placement gets a lot more interesting up on the moraine.

The biggest route-finding danger here lies in the loop's second half, in the woods. Several trail intersections add confusion, beckoning hikers toward Beaver Meadows.

Moraine Park

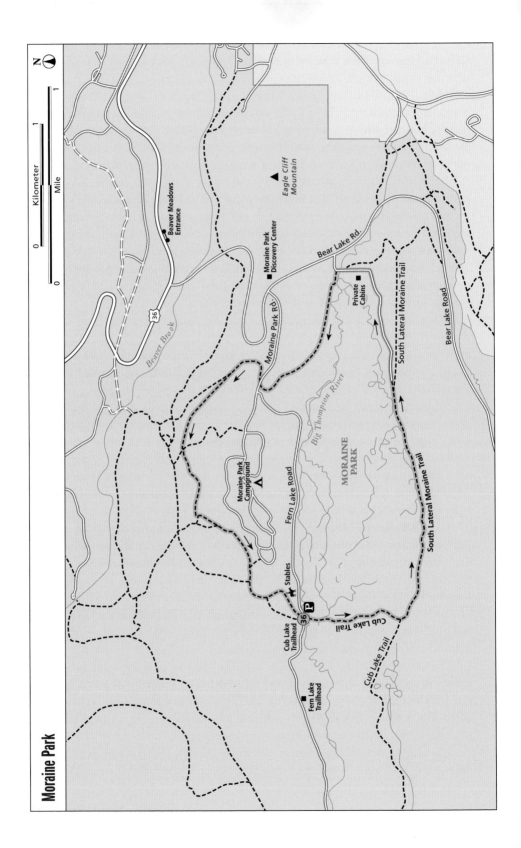

Keep angling to the left without entering the Moraine Park Campground (signs of which are fairly obvious during the route's final miles); toward the end of the loop, stay to the right of the stables, and you'll soon find yourself dropping onto the start point from above.

Much of this route is heavily used by the nearby horseback riding operation. This means the trail is often covered with horse apples and blasted out by hooves, turning it into a very messy sandpit or, if it's wet, mud pit.

While pretty and historic, this is one of the least dramatic hikes in all of Rocky Mountain National Park. If you want more intense terrain and scenery, it's all around. Every basin and glacial lake is accessible by maintained trails, a wonderland for strong hikers with mountain sense. Try the nearby Fern Lake Trail for a long alpine loop that eventually drops right down onto Bear Lake. Or, a bit shorter, climb the Cub Lake Trail for a loop that drops into Hollowell Park, one glacial valley to the south.

Miles and Directions

0.0 Start from the Cub Lake Trailhead in Moraine Park and begin walking south on the Cub Lake Trail.

0.1 Cross the Big Thompson River on a bridge.

0.5 Turn left onto the South Lateral Moraine Trail (GPS: N40 20.98' / W105 36.97').

1.7 Continue straight as the South Lateral Moraine Trail heads right up a hill. Your trail spills out onto Moraine Park Road, lined with several cabins. (**Option:** Veer right and follow the South Lateral Moraine Trail. It simply goes up the hill; turn left at a trail intersection and come back down, rejoining the route at mile 2.2 below.)

2.2 Stay on the road as it turns to the north and passes intersections with trails coming in from the right.

2.4 Cross back over the Big Thompson and immediately turn left, staying on the old road. You may have to open and close a gate (GPS: N40 21.25' / W105 35.04').

3.0 Veer right at a trail intersection.

3.1 Cross Moraine Park Campground Road. (**Option:** If you're not feelin' it at this point, one option is to walk back to the trailhead from here, veering left immediately onto Fern Lake Road. It's basically flat, but it's still quite a walk, over a mile.)

3.4 Take the left fork here.

3.6 The trail spills out onto a dirt road. Turn left briefly; then find the trail continuing on the other side (GPS: N40 21.91' / W105 36.02').

4.0 Turn left again.

4.1 Continue straight through.

4.6 Turn right and follow singletrack or continue straight on the wide-track trail past the stables. Either way will get you back to the trailhead.

4.8 Drop in on Cub Lake Trailhead.

37 Sprague Lake

Abner Sprague made a fishing lake for the benefit of his tourist lodge and its guests that is one of the most beautiful you'll ever see. An easy, flat gravel path rings historic Sprague Lake, creating one of the most accessible hikes in Rocky Mountain National Park.

Start: Sprague Lake parking area on Bear Lake Road in Rocky Mountain National Park

Distance: 0.8-mile lariat loop

Approximate hiking time: 30 minutes

Difficulty: Easy

Trail surface: Wide, flat gravel path

Best season: Summer

Other trail users: Hikers; bikes and dogs not allowed

Canine compatibility: No dogs allowed

Land status: National park

Fees and permits: There is a hefty fee to enter Rocky Mountain National Park, which is paid by the vehicle or, if you're walking or riding bikes, by the individual. The entry fee is good for up to 1 week.

Schedule: No overnight camping without permit

Map: Rocky Mountain National Park map, National Park Service

Trail contact: Rocky Mountain National Park, 1000 US 36, Estes Park, CO 80517-8397; (970) 586-1206; www.nps.gov/romo

Special considerations: This trail is accessible to wheelchairs. Hiking inside Rocky National Park comes with several special regulations. No bikes allowed. No dogs allowed. No camping without a permit.

Finding the trailhead: The trailhead, and a large asphalt parking lot, is located on the east side of Rocky Mountain National Park, 5.5 miles up Bear Lake Road (about halfway between Moraine Park and Bear Lake) on the left side. GPS: N40 19.23' / W105 36.47'

The Hike

One thing you can say about Abner Sprague without any hesitation: He knew how to pick a spot.

After arriving in Colorado as a youngster in 1864, Abner grew up near present-day Loveland, learning the ways of the quasi-frontier. One of his first significant acts as a full-fledged adult was to drop a homestead cabin in spectacular Moraine Park in 1875—nice spot. Later he picked cozy Glacier Basin to build a cabin, then a tourist lodge. Sprague was a lucky fellow who managed to situate himself for life in some of the most visually spectacular locations in Colorado. Living in such beautiful places today is the realm of oligarchs and Saudi princes.

I say "lucky" because Sprague and his pioneer contemporaries benefited from an extraordinary law, the Homestead Act of 1862. Under this law someone could claim 160 acres simply by putting up a tiny cabin, living on the land (supposedly), and attempting to work it. Once established on the land, these homesteaders could gain additional acreage from supplemental laws like the Timber Culture Act of 1873,

A man-made lake—made by a self-made man?

which allotted another 160 acres in exchange for planting trees. Homesteaders were often able to parlay their grants into highly profitable enterprises, expanding their holdings ten- or twenty-fold and passing huge fortunes onto their offspring. The Homestead Act, designed to populate the contested Colorado plains with supporters of the Union and push out both the Indians and the Confederates, was ripe for abuse of various types.

Of course there was a lot more to homesteading than free land. Sprague's family crossed the plains in a covered wagon pulled by oxen during the Indian scare of 1864. For the people coming west just 5 years later, the journey was on a train. Pioneers like the Spragues spent their first years in Colorado in near-constant fear of attack by Indians. The threat was often overblown, sometimes deliberately overblown, but fear is fear. In the absence of state authority, settlers created their own justice systems, for better and worse. And then they had to endure the kind of atmosphere that fosters vicious but intricately planned vigilante attacks in the middle of the night—if the state's apparatus didn't take care of a suspected horse thief quickly enough, there was a strong chance that the "Citizens' Committee" would do it for them, and the alleged perpetrator would be swinging from a tree in the morning for everybody to see. For some pioneers that arrangement felt right and just, and was necessary. For others it must have been a horrifying aspect of pioneer life, but it's not like they could speak out loud of their concerns.

The real pioneers spent a lot of their twilight years guarding their lauded status from pretenders, as shown in this passage from Abner Sprague's memoirs, written when he was more than 80 years old: "Those who came after it was proven that Colorado was a good place to live in, a good place to establish a business and a home, do not belong in the pioneer class and should not be so named, alive or dead, no matter how long they have lived in the state."

But Abner . . . Free land! At what other time in history could people take land like this for their own? That seems lucky, in hindsight.

Abner Sprague versus the US Government

Abner Sprague closed out his memoirs with a story about his related financial conflict with the federal government, to which Sprague Lodge would be inextricably linked:

We were transferred from the Department of Agriculture to the Department of Interior upon the establishment of Rocky Mountain National Park. Our rights secured from the Agriculture Department prior to the passage of the bill creating the park and protected by that bill were denied us. Our acreage was cut from 95 to 20 and the rent more than doubled. I learned no lesson from this; better luck next time.

I owned an interest in 200 acres, which included beautiful Loch Vale and Mills Lake in the center of the park and later, I secured the whole tract. I offered to trade this tract, which by no means should belong to the park, for the land on which my property [Sprague's Lodge in Glacier Basin] was located . . .

The secretary saw the advantage both to us and the national park. He said the Interior Department would sanction a bill authorizing the secretary to make the trade and without doubt, it would pass. Mrs. Sprague and I spent a winter in Washington lobbying the bill through both houses of Congress. I hardly think being a lobbyist is anything to brag about, at least in such a small matter.

After all the red tape was dealt with, the trade was made and we owned 160 acres in Glacier Basin. . . .

I took no interest or part in the establishment of Rocky Mountain National Park. If the region was made a national playground, it

And Sprague admitted in his memoirs that he actually enjoyed most of his family's covered wagon trip from Illinois. The emigrants' arduous journeys became the most celebrated aspect of pioneer suffering, but to Sprague, who fondly remembered falling asleep against trees while the sun fell to the horizon day after day, "two months of travel in a covered wagon were not all grind."

could do us no harm. After it was established, I worked for its success. My holding our property intact, making it easy to transfer, cut no ice when it came to fair dealing on the part of the government, however.

When the government started to purchase stray tracts of land within the park boundaries, its attempts were encumbered by a special law requiring that the landholders receive only 50 percent of a parcel's appraised value. Noted Sprague: "It could not be expected that anyone would donate one half of his hard-earned property to the United States. It was a fool law."

In order to obtain property under this "fool law," the government simply appraised the land it wanted to obtain at twice its real value, thus compensating the landowner for its true value. This was a pretty sweet arrangement for the landowners, although probably more illegal than legal.

When it came time to sell off his unneeded land to the government—he only wanted 100 or so acres to encompass the lodge and his lakes—the fake valuation made Sprague uncomfortable, but he went along with it. After all, he wasn't about to give away half his land. When the sale was made, Sprague reported nothing to the IRS because he claimed not to have profited from the deal.

Well, the IRS examined the deal and, not paying much heed to the Department of the Interior's funky arrangement with landowners, presented Sprague with a tax bill based on what it felt was the true value of the transaction. Sprague felt like he was being robbed. When Sprague squealed about it, repeatedly and as high up the ladder as he could, as such a man was wont to do, the IRS launched an investigation into the whole situation of land transfers in Rocky Mountain National Park.

Eventually Sprague agreed to pay the IRS about half the original bill. He remained bitter about the situation throughout his days. The pioneer refused to accept the notion that he owed the government anything whatsoever.

Sprague Lake: almost owned by the IRS

Sure, taking a train was easier, and the Indian scares were all but over. But the post-pioneer settlers paid dearly for their land, unless it was already deemed useless by those who came before. Life is full of big trade-offs.

Sprague's good taste in spot-picking dictated his vocation, and the vocation of his close family members. Farming and ranching the mountain land profitably was found to be virtually impossible, but tourists from all over the world wanted to experience the Rocky Mountains. So the Spragues and other settlers in the area became inn-keepers and guides for paying guests, first hosting tent campers on their 160 acres and then building rustic cabins and lodges of various sizes. In most of these operations, the men spent a lot of time guiding guests to amazing places while the women were back at the lodges cleaning up and making meals.

Such was the scene at the Sprague Lodge, a set of large but rustic log structures that used to stand where the Sprague Lake parking area is today. The Spragues already had a great deal of hosting experience when they opened their new lodge in 1914. The Spragues operated the place for a few decades, building up a resort that could house sixty guests, and then left it to be managed by a nephew.

When Rocky Mountain National Park was created in 1915, the Spragues and other proprietors who had already been running lodges and guest ranches within the park were granted leases to continue operating. But the terms could be muddy, especially as the governing agencies changed (see sidebar).

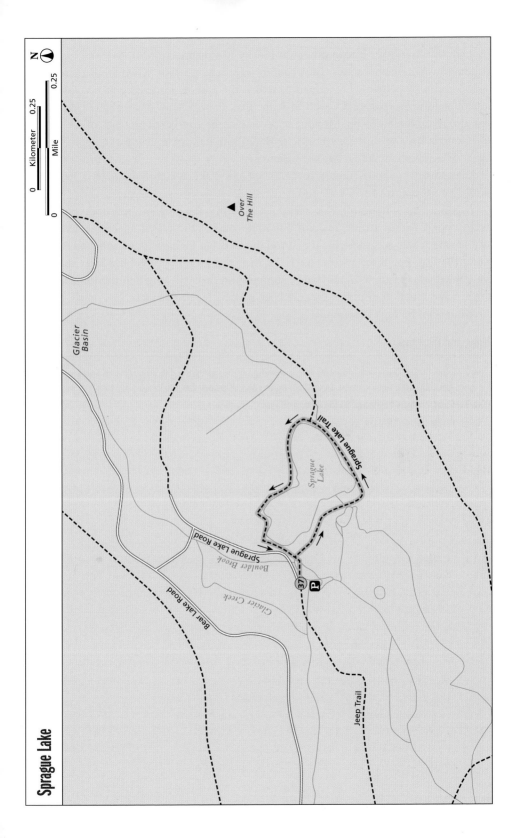

Sprague Lake

Glacier Basin

Bear Lake Road

Glacier Creek

Boulder Brook

Sprague Lake Road

Over The Hill

Sprague Lake

Sprague Lake Trail

Jeep Trail

Like so many other buildings within Rocky Mountain National Park, the lodge buildings were removed about half a century ago, during a time when the Park Service was run by people who wanted to return the park to something more closely resembling its natural state. Over in Moraine Park the Spragues' original guest ranch was also taken out bit by bit. Moraine Park, despite the continued presence of several small cabins, has a pristine feel. In Glacier Basin, with its large asphalt parking lots, the effect of removing buildings has been muted.

Interestingly, nobody wanted to drain Sprague Lake, which is as much a man-made feature as anything else around here.

Man-made, but beautiful. This nearly flat trail rings the gorgeous reflecting pool/fishing pond within a mile, making this route one of the easiest and most accessible—wheelchair-accessible, in fact—in all the land, but giving a lot of oohs and aahs along the way. For those who crave more than this little leg-stretching loop, there are connections to the Glacier Basin Campground that will lengthen the loop, and other trails taking off from the Sprague Lake parking lot that can take you on all-day adventures to the high mountains.

Miles and Directions

0.0   Start from the parking area and begin walking on the Sprague Lake Trail. The trail soon forks. Go counterclockwise around Sprague Lake. (**Option:** Go clockwise.)

0.3   Pass the trail that leads to the Glacier Basin Campground.

0.8   Arrive back at the parking area.

North Front Range

Faded glory: The barricaded entrance to Blue Bird Mine.

38 Caribou Ranch

This mellow hike through forests and meadows above Nederland will take you back 100 years in 4 miles. The well-signed route takes you to the historic Blue Bird Mine and DeLonde homestead.

Start: Caribou Ranch Open Space Trailhead
Distance: 4.0-mile lariat loop
Approximate hiking time: 2 hours
Difficulty: Easy to moderate
Trail surface: Moderately rocky singletrack trail and smooth doubletrack; shallow slopes
Best season: Summer
Other trail users: Hikers; bikes and dogs not allowed
Canine compatibility: No dogs allowed
Land status: Boulder County Parks & Open Space
Fees and permits: None
Schedule: This property is closed from Apr through June, opening to the public on July

1. Visitors are then permitted on the property from sunrise to sunset.
Map: Caribou Ranch Open Space map, Boulder County Parks and Open Space
Trail contact: Boulder County Parks & Open Space, 5201 Saint Vrain Rd., Longmont, CO 80503; (303) 678-6200; www.bouldercounty .org/dept/openspace/pages/default.aspx
Special considerations: No dogs, leashed or otherwise, are allowed at Caribou Ranch Open Space. Don't confuse Caribou Ranch Open Space with the ghost city of Caribou or the Caribou Mine, which are a few miles to the south on Caribou Road.

Finding the trailhead: From the Peak to Peak Highway/CO 72, about 1.5 miles north of Nederland, turn west onto CR 126 and drive for about a half mile to the parking area. GPS: N39 58.95' / W105 31.16'

The Hike

"Can you imagine growing up here?" my dad asked as we took refuge on the porch of the historic DeLonde house in Caribou Ranch Open Space, looking out over the green meadows and sharp pine-covered mountains surrounding us.

We were both shivering after getting caught in a very cold, drenching rain, and more of the same seemed to be rolling in over the hills. I imagined that growing up here would have been quite nice, but frequently challenging. No doubt living at the DeLonde homestead was pretty fantastic on mild, sunny days.

Lightning stabbed out of the sky and crisped a fir on the other side of the meadow, sending the German tourist who was hiding out on the porch with us deeper into his weather-related despair. He did not like lightning, or hypothermia.

We decided to look up the weather prognosis on Dad's iPhone, the way people do these days. The phone shook in Dad's hand as he dialed up the current radar image. We watched a red and yellow blob envelop the "You Are Here" arrow on the tiny screen. More red and yellow blobs seemed to be forming behind it. "Says here it

The Blue Bird Mine near the DeLonde homestead

could rain all night," Dad said, reading his weather app. I could see a little more of the German fellow's morale leaking away.

Dad wanted to get going. Standing around on the porch wasn't doing him any good. So we bid farewell to our porch companion and pushed off into the cold rain, heads down.

Luckily for everyone involved, the distance from the homestead back to the trailhead was not much more than a mile—we made it and lived to tell the tale. Despite the sudden drenching precipitation that afflicts these meadows, it is unlikely that anybody will have to get all Jack London and crawl inside their dog to stay alive. Just hustle back to the car. You'll be fine, probably. Crank up the heater. And would-be Jack Londons should remember that dogs are not allowed at this open space parcel anyway.

Our predicament was a good reminder to always bring rain gear and some thermal wear made of polypropylene or wool even on seemingly casual hikes in the mountains, if there is any possibility of precipitation. Altitude changes the game. Warm summer afternoons turn into shiver-fests real quick up here. It may not kill you, but it will make you very uncomfortable and ruin the hike.

The DeLonde homestead, with its restored red barn, comes into view a little over a mile from the trailhead, sitting pretty in the meadow below the trail. Emery DeLonde was early on the scene, for a Euro-American. The DeLondes were established property owners by 1867. Emery was very active in local politics and civic functions. In 1893 the *Boulder Daily Camera* described him as one of "the staunch Populists of Nederland." The Populists were a, um, popular political party at the time.

The environment around the DeLondes' home was quite a bit different in the nineteenth century than it is today. In some ways it was tamer, more beaten down by the doings of men. Imagine, for instance, dozens of men constantly encamped at the Blue Bird Mine and the sounds of ore trains as well as excursion trains on the Switzerland Trail. Imagine sawmills running night and day, swallowing whole sections of forest. In other ways it was wilder, as illustrated by the following passage from the *Boulder News*, June 1870:

> *Mr. Thomas Cameron, of Central, called on us yesterday. Last Sunday Mr. Cameron and a party were hunting grouse up at the head of North Boulder, and, while camping at noon, a little dog, that was along with them, commenced barking and scratching in the dirt a short distance away. Cameron, thinking it was a grouse, seized his rifle and hurried to the spot, when he was suddenly confronted by a huge grizzly bear. He instantly raised his gun and fired, the ball entered the animal just back of the fore shoulder. A Mr. Jones coming up just then, also fired, sending a musket ball into his brain. This bear was of immense size, a vertible [sic] Rocky Mountain Grizzly. He weighed, when dressed, over nine-hundred pounds, and was killed six miles from Tom Hill's. The Delond boys took the carcass to Central.*

Shortly after the homestead comes into view, you'll find a trail intersection. This is the beginning of the Blue Bird Loop. Taking the left fork puts you on the Switzerland Trail (which is here part of the Blue Bird Loop), an easy doubletrack that contours around the valley.

As you might have guessed from its near-flat disposition, the Switzerland Trail is an old railroad grade. The Denver, Boulder & Western Railroad used the grade between 1904 and 1919, hauling to and from the mines but also, more famously, hauling party-minded tourists on sightseeing trips.

Colorado Grizzlies

Grizzlies once roamed all over Colorado, even the plains. They were pushed higher and deeper into the mountains, to places like the North Boulder Creek headwaters above the DeLonde place, and were finally wiped out—or were they?

Some say there are still grizzlies alive in the southwestern part of the state, south of Pagosa Springs. It was there that a female grizzly was killed by a bowhunter in 1979, after an alleged struggle. It was the last confirmed grizzly sighting in Colorado. Grizzlies were eliminated from the northern mountains much earlier.

One of the stops along the Switzerland Trail was the Blue Bird Mine, located at the far end of the loop. As the roar of North Boulder Creek fills the woods, find a well-signed side trail leading up to the complex. The semi-preserved site will give you a decent idea of the miner's life in the 1870s and beyond. The site is anchored by a large bunkhouse, but also features chicken coops, one anachronistic-seeming mid-twentieth-century structure, and plenty of twisted metal. Rusted rails lead to the mine shaft, hidden behind a corrugated shed. The county has done good work creating some helpful interpretive signs.

Caribou Ranch Open Space has been appropriated a few times by the entertainment business. Director Gordon Douglas used the Blue Bird ghost camp in his remake of *Stagecoach*, the 1939 John Ford classic that made a star out of young John Wayne. The 1966 remake, starring Ann-Margret, Bing Crosby, and Red Buttons, couldn't hold a miner's candle to the much-loved original, despite a good performance by Crosby in his last role. Critics blasted it with black powder. Amazingly, somebody decided to remake *Stagecoach* a third time, for a TV special in the '80s. That one apparently made the '66 version look good.

Some baby boomers and classic rock enthusiasts have heard of Caribou Ranch for a different reason. In 1971, 4,000-acre Caribou Ranch was purchased by a music producer named Jim Guercio. Guercio had been frustrated by his lack of control over studio operations and decided to acquire his own studio, a place where freedom would translate into great music. Until it was destroyed by a fire in 1985, Guercio's Caribou Ranch recording studio hosted legendary artists like Michael Jackson, John Lennon, Chicago, Tom Petty and the Heartbreakers, Rod Stewart, Billy Joel, the Beach Boys, Peter Frampton, U2, and Earth, Wind and Fire. Elton John recorded three albums there, including one that was named after the studio itself.

Imagine all those famous musicians dude-ranching around in the Colorado mountains. According to ranch archivist John Carsello, Michael Jackson dressed up in a fat suit while visiting the ranch during the Jacksons' Victory Tour in 1984, and went

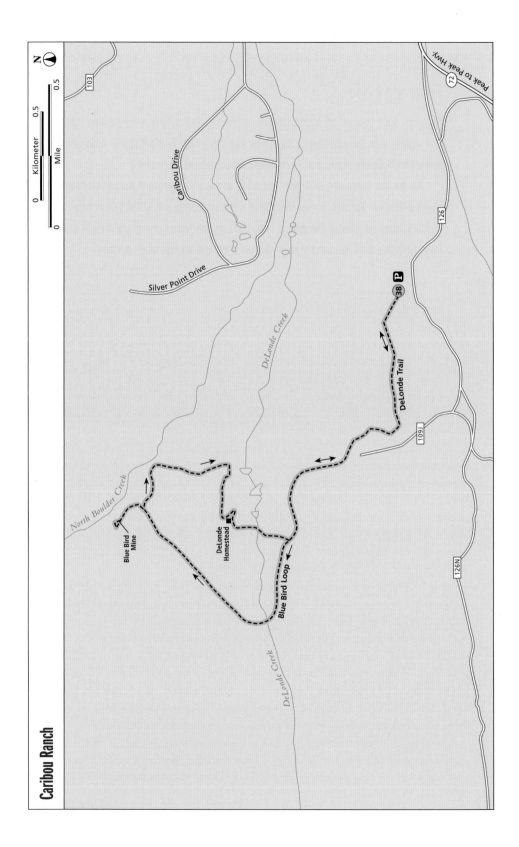

Caribou Ranch

into Boulder to preach door-to-door to fulfill his obligations as a Jehovah's Witness. Do any of you old Boulder residents recall an eerily familiar portly proselytizer with a very gentle voice, and perhaps a single white glove? Numerous photographs show Jackson cruising around Caribou Ranch on a horse and three-wheel ATV and hiking on rocks.

The studio was located in a barn on another ranch site to the south, not the DeLondes', although Guercio's holdings once encompassed the DeLonde homestead as well. Guercio sold this part of his land to Boulder County to be used as open space, and much of the rest is protected by conservation easements. A final 1,600 acres was put up for sale by the Guercios in 2013, price tag $45 million.

The future of the Caribou Ranch is uncertain, although there has been talk of rebuilding the studio to modern standards and cranking it all up again. Considering that the ranch was slated for a housing development when Guercio swooped in and bought it 45 years ago, we can say that music kept this place relatively pristine. Whether it can continue to do so remains to be seen.

With all the different Caribou this or that up here, there's great potential for name confusion. Don't confuse Caribou Ranch Open Space and its associated mine and homestead or Caribou Ranch the recording studio with Caribou, aka Caribou City, an important nineteenth-century mining camp that was located several miles away, up Caribou Road. The remains of that Caribou are worth a look, if you've got the time. There are some fairly dramatic ruins of stone buildings still standing near a popular trailhead at the end of the two-wheel-drive-accessible road, with various options for hiking or biking from there.

Miles and Directions

0.0 Start from the Caribou Ranch Open Space parking area and begin walking along the DeLonde Trail.

0.9 Veer left onto the Blue Bird Loop/Switzerland Trail. (**Option:** Turn right here and go around the loop counterclockwise.)

1.8 Turn left and head toward the Blue Bird Mine complex.

1.9 Peruse the Blue Bird Mine complex; then turn around. **Note:** Be careful not to start walking down the road, which seems like the correct route but will take you the wrong direction. Retrace your steps on the trail.

2.1 Veer left, back on the Blue Bird Loop.

2.7 Walk past the DeLonde homestead. The porch of the house makes a good rain cover during storms.

3.0 Veer left, back on the DeLonde Trail.

4.0 Arrive back at the trailhead.

39 Picture Rock

This hike is a simple out-and-back through a lovely little valley near Lyons. The route turns around at an old quarry site, but anybody who wants more mileage can keep going into the Heil Valley Ranch trail network.

Start: Picture Rock Trailhead near Lyons (aka Heil Valley Ranch North Trailhead)
Distance: 6.4 miles out and back (with option for more)
Approximate hiking time: 1 to 1.5 hours
Difficulty: Moderate
Trail surface: Varies from manicured and wide to thin and loose; top half is moderately rocky
Best season: Fall
Other trail users: Hikers, bikers, and horses

Canine compatibility: No dogs allowed!
Land status: Boulder County Parks & Open Space
Fees and permits: None
Schedule: Sunrise to sunset
Map: Heil Valley Ranch trail map
Trail contact: Boulder County Parks & Open Space, 5201 Saint Vrain Rd., Longmont, CO 80503; (303) 678-6200; www.bouldercounty.org/dept/openspace/pages/default.aspx

Finding the trailhead: From Lyons take CO 7/South Saint Vrain Drive south for about a half mile; then turn left onto Old Saint Vrain Road. Take the second left onto Red Gulch Road. Take the first right into the trailhead parking area. GPS: N40 12.68' / W105 16.37'

The Hike

Picture Rock Trail, one of the newest and sweetest trails in the state, is a personal favorite that just happens to feature a historic site. Between the trailhead and an old quarry, one of many that occupied these hogbacks, the humble trail rises 600 feet in just over 3 miles of flowing curves. The trail builders have been very generous here, literally going the extra mile to keep grades pleasant and subdued.

Almost the entire route is tucked behind the hogback ridgeline in a small valley that stays relatively dry in winter and greens up nicely in the spring. Gambel oak, ponderosa pine, and cactus are common here. The valley is a haven for mule deer, coyotes, mountain lions, black bears, and rattlesnakes, with frequent visits by elk and bighorn sheep. Because it is at the transition zone between mountains and plains, Heil Valley Ranch (to which Picture Rock Trail belongs) gets to see both mountain-loving and grassland-loving species. Classic rattlesnake territory. I would tell you to hold on to your dogs, but dogs aren't allowed on Picture Rock Trail or the other trails included in Heil Valley Ranch Open Space.

As nice as it is, the trail still feels pretty lonely on weekdays. The relatively remote trailhead keeps the Boulder crowds at arm's length. Still, keep your eyes and ears open for approaching mountain bikers and be ready to evacuate the trail if necessary. Mountain bikers are supposed to ride slowly enough that they could stop and yield

The ruins of a very old automobile near the Picture Rock Trail

the trail to any hikers, horses, or other bikers, but reality is more prickly. On a trail like this, with such tight curves and low visibility, it's a good idea for hikers to stay one step ahead and not leave their safety in the hands of speedsters who can't resist letting go of the brakes.

The directions for this route are about as straightforward as you will find. There are no trail intersections or route problems. After about 3 miles of gentle climbing, the trail approaches the quarry complex, passing very close to an old grain silo—the silo isn't part of the quarry, but does mark the point where you're getting quite close to it—then the ruins of a stone boarding house or two. The trail then climbs onto the rock floor of the quarry itself, where a '52 Plymouth (a guess) improbably sits, full of bullet holes. Just beyond is the skeleton of a '24 Ford (another guess). There used to be a road that came up from the Heil Ranch side.

Note that the trail doesn't end at the quarry. It continues up the hill, getting rockier as it goes, and joins with the Heil Valley Ranch trail network. There are several options for turning the hike into a lariat loop, or a one-way shuttle between the Picture Rock and Heil Valley Ranch Trailheads.

The quarry cut here isn't nearly as dramatic as the Kenmuir Quarry's in Red Rock Canyon near Colorado Springs. Here nature has done a lot of work reclaiming the site, which was a more free-form type of quarry to begin with, not a big steam-powered operation like Kenmuir. Low-budget and humble though it may have been, the Lyons sandstone quarried here found its way into the stately buildings of Boulder's university campus. This rock was special because it was "picture rock," a term

Picture Rock

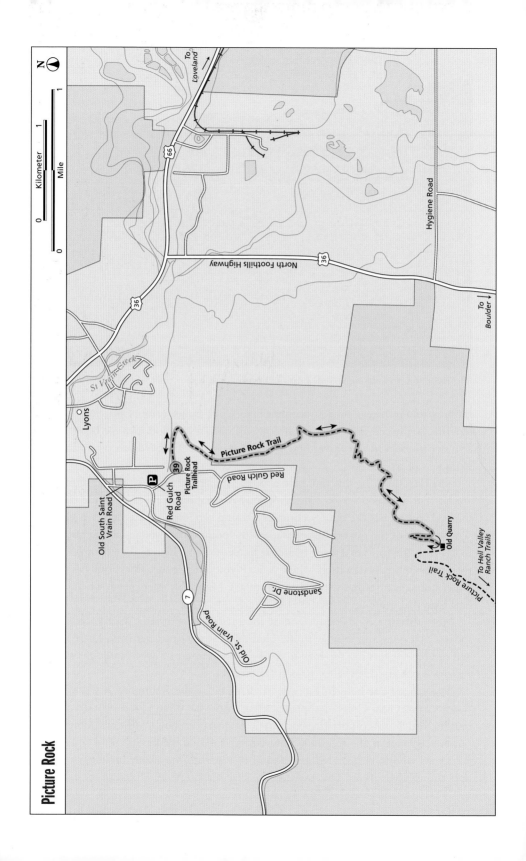

At the quarry a bullet-riddled hulk with suicide doors

that refers to the coloration found on some sandstone slabs that were stained over the millennia by water seepage.

The use of the valley by prehistoric people is almost undoubtable, although scientific proof is scant. There are large collections of prehistoric artifacts that have been gathered from the area, now sitting in the University of Colorado's collections and elsewhere, but labeling has been so spotty that today's researchers can't determine from where exactly they came. The only thing these artifacts can tell us for certain is that local prehistoric sites have been greatly affected by casual collection of artifacts, and that this section of Colorado in general was well populated for the last 12,000 years or so. Most of the artifacts found around these parts date to the Ceramic period, when people were starting to farm and use bows and arrows, as well as making clay vessels of all kinds.

Miles and Directions

0.0 Start from the Picture Rock Trailhead, carefully cross the road, and begin walking up the trail.

3.2 Arrive at the quarry site, marked by the shell of an old automobile. Turn around here. (*Option:* Continue another 2.3 miles to the connection with the other Heil Valley Ranch trails.)

6.4 Arrive back at Picture Rock Trailhead.

40 Bobcat Ridge

Two historic homesteads and a mysterious teepee ring are among the waypoints on this moderate loop in the Masonville area. The eastern portion of the loop, to the Kitchen/Smith Cabin, is wheelchair-accessible.

Start: Bobcat Ridge Natural Area Trailhead
Distance: 4.6-mile lariat loop
Approximate hiking time: 2 to 3 hours
Difficulty: Moderate
Trail surface: On the east side of the loop, a very wide and tame gravel path with moderate gradients—wheelchair-accessible all the way to the cabin. On the west side (particularly the northwest quadrant), the trail is much more rugged, with several short, steep sections and moderate rockiness.
Best seasons: Spring and fall
Other trail users: Bikers and hikers
Canine compatibility: No dogs allowed

Land status: City of Fort Collins
Fees and permits: None
Schedule: Dawn to dusk
Maps: Bobcat Ridge Natural Area brochure, City of Fort Collins
Trail contact: Bobcat Ridge Natural Area, 10184 CR 32C, Loveland, CO 80538; (970) 461-2700; www.fcgov.com/naturalareas/finder/bobcat
Special considerations: Rattlers! The hogbacks west of Fort Collins and Loveland provide more rattlesnake sightings and encounters than anywhere else in the state these days. Watch where you step.

Finding the trailhead: From Denver go north on I-25 and then west on US 34. Go through Loveland; then turn north onto CR 27. Turn left onto CR 32C and follow signs to Bobcat Ridge Natural Area. GPS: N40 28.77' / W105 13.55'

The Hike

Two very different types of "homesteads" are on display at Bobcat Ridge Natural Area. You'll find the familiar log cabins, barns, and sheds associated with late-nineteenth- and early-twentieth-century attempts to work the land. There are old ranch structures near the trailhead, and out along the loop as well.

On the other hand, there's a (probable) Ute teepee ring in the golden grasses above the cabins. The Utes didn't stay in any single place for very long, moving with the seasons and the elk (and according to the necessities of never-ending wars with other tribes), but some of them apparently liked this place well enough to set up a nice teepee ring, with over one hundred stones. Possibly this was a lookout point. Out in the sunny meadow, it would have made a nice spot in winter. George Bird Grinnell, author of *The Fighting Cheyennes*, believed the Indians used stones to hold down the hides that formed their teepees' walls during winter months, when the ground was too frozen for stakes to penetrate. Some contemporary Native Americans suggest that many so-called teepee rings are really prayer circles, without practical origin.

The conglomerate International Harvester manufactured this McCormick-Deering rake in the 1920s.

That's about all we know about this potential teepee ring. Archaeological study of the site has been very limited—imagine a bunch of grad students walking back and forth looking for obvious rock features or artifacts lying on the ground. But the ring of stones exists in the context of several apparent prehistoric campsites that have been found in the general vicinity, as well as countless projectile points and even a burial site near Masonville that is believed to be around 2,000 years old. It is estimated that there are huge numbers—tens of thousands, at least—of teepee rings in Colorado. Most remain undiscovered. While most of the teepee rings found are attributed to Utes and thought to be just a few hundred years old, some 2,000-year-old rings have

Ghosts and rattlesnakes: Kitchen / Smith Cabin

been identified. The age of this particular ring is undetermined, but the depth of the rocks indicates it's been around for at least a few hundred years.

The route described here includes two little side trips to the contrasting homestead sites, adding about 0.7 mile to the loop distance.

After just 1.2 miles of counterclockwise looping from the trailhead, hikers arrive at the turnoff for the Kitchen/Smith Cabin. The site is just around the corner, a single cabin that has been lightly made over and opened up to the public. The structure was built in 1917, most likely, although at first glance it seems much older than that. It ain't fancy but has some low-key twentieth-century features, like concrete chinking. Behind the cabin sits a well and various farming implements representing several decades of agricultural travail.

When I was here, I wandered out back to look at the machinery and poke around. I took a few photos and breathed in some nice clean air on a September day. Walking back to the cabin, I very nearly stepped on a rattlesnake that was stretched out on the trail. I had surprised the heck out of it, so much so that it was doing the ultra-still pretend-to-be-dead-and-maybe-he'll-go-away thing that snakes sometimes do in a last-ditch effort to save their hides from whatever overwhelmingly large beast has swooped down upon them. Either that or I had already squished and killed the creature. The rattlesnake was so still it was impossible to tell which. I watched it intently for a minute or two. It was about 30 inches long, still a young'un. Motionless. If it

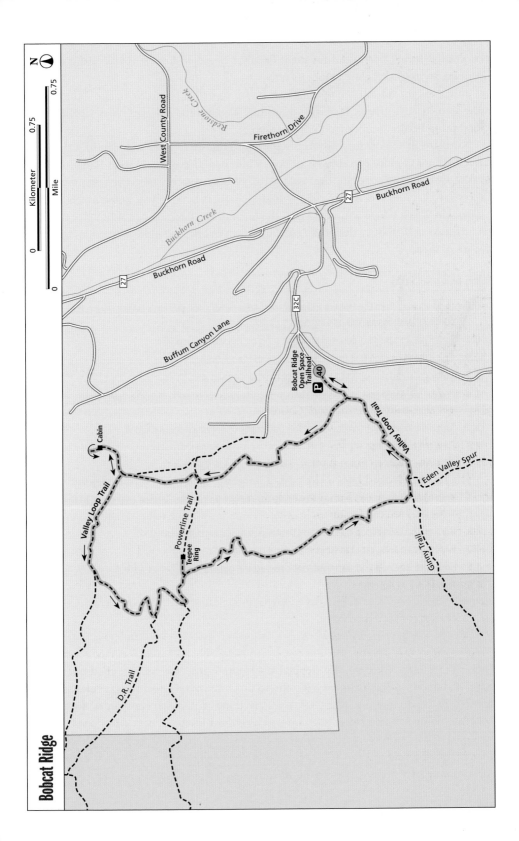

Bobcat Ridge

was dead, it hadn't been dead for long. Finally I began to believe that it really was deceased, an ex-snake, gone before its time.

Sure enough, just as I brought my camera up to snap a photo, he or she slithered away into the tall grasses, hissing and rattling, wedge head hovering like a cobra's. Good thing I didn't lean down for a close-up.

No place in Colorado gets more reports of rattlesnake bites and sightings than these Larimer County parcels west of Fort Collins and Loveland. Bobcat Ridge and nearby Devil's Backbone are the snakiest of all open space parks. Even mountain bikers have been nailed as they ride by trailside rattlers here, so you know hikers are vulnerable. Watch where you step! That's the main thing to remember, although easier said than done. Without a doubt the old cliché is true: They are more afraid of us than we are of them.

Miles and Directions

0.0 Start walking from the Bobcat Ridge Natural Area parking lot. (Mileage begins where the concrete path leaves the parking area.)

0.1 Turn right and begin a counterclockwise loop on the Valley Loop Trail.

0.9 Cross the Powerline Trail (more like a dirt road than a trail).

1.2 Turn right to take a side trip to an old cabin/homestead site.

1.4 Peruse the cabin and immediate surroundings (watch for snakes, though); then retrace your steps back to the main loop.

1.6 Turn right, back on the Valley Loop. The trail starts to get much more difficult.

2.4 Pass the intersection with the D. R. Trail.

2.6 Cross the Powerline Trail at the high point of the loop, 5,759 feet.

2.7 To see the teepee ring, turn left on a little spur trail that heads over to the Powerline Trail, then turn right and descend the Powerline Trail briefly to the site. Retrace your steps to the Valley Loop and continue.

2.9 Back at the Valley Loop after visiting the teepee ring, continue south.

4.0 Pass intersections with the Ginny Trail and Eden Valley Spur Trail.

4.5 Complete the loop and turn right, back toward the parking area.

4.6 Arrive back at the start.

Resources and Further Reading

Roxborough State Park

Gilmore, Kevin. "Analysis of the Artifact Collection from the Jarre Creek Site (5DA541), a Terminal Early Ceramic Period Occupation on the Palmer Divide, Colorado," *Southwestern Lore,* Vol. 70, No. 2, Summer 2004, p. 2.

Gilmore, Kevin, and Shawn Larmore. "The Palmer Divide Archaeology Project: Documentation of Artifact Collections from the Tenth Fairway (5DA123), Rainbow Creek (5DA124), and Jarre Creek (5DA541) Sites, Douglas County, Colorado," University of Denver, Archaeological Research Institute, August 5, 2003, p. 48. http://www.researchgate.net/profile/Kevin_Gilmore2/publication/267867349_The_Palmer_Divide_Archaeology_Project_Documentation_of_Artifact_Collections_from_the_Tenth_Fairway_(5DA123)_Rainbow_Creek_(5DA124)_and_Jarre_Creek_(5DA541)_Sites_Douglas_County_Colorado/links/545bcceb0cf2f1dbcbcb0448.pdf.

Red Rocks: Trading Post Trail

Hendrix, Jimi. *Starting at Zero: His Own Story* (A & C Black, 2013), p. 153.

Mount Falcon

Walker, John Brisben. "The Homestead Object Lesson," *The Cosmopolitan*, vol. 13, May, 1892, p. 572.

———. "The City of the Future—a Prophecy," *The Cosmopolitan*, v. 31, May-October 1901, p. 473-475.

———. "Some Speculations Regarding Rapid Transit," *The Cosmopolitan*, November, 1895, p. 28.

White, Sally L. "John Brisben Walker, the Man and Mt. Morrison," *Historically Jeffco*, volume 18, Issue 26, 2005, pp. 4–8. https://historicredrocks.files.wordpress.com/2011/10/walker05-fin.pdf.

Castlewood Canyon

Castle Rock Journal, May 14, 1897, p. 2.

"Receiver Appointed," *Castle Rock Journal*, July 6, 1900, p. 4.

"A Terrible Disaster," *Aspen Daily Times*, May 3, 1900, p. 1.

Mount Galbraith

"Fix Speed Limit for Parks," *Colorado Transcript* (Golden), Thursday, August 28, 1919, p. 1.

"Golden City," *Colorado Transcript*, December 19, 1866, p. 1.

"How We're Getting Eight Dollars For One," *Colorado Transcript* (Golden), May 22, 1913, p. 1.

Mesas Region Management Plan, Jefferson County Open Space (JCOS), 2013, p. 20.

Nelson, Charles. *Southwestern Lore*, 33(1):1-13. 1967, p. 3.

Stephanie Velasquez, "Class III Cultural Resource Inventory of the Proposed Clear Creek Canyon Open Space Park, Jefferson County, Colorado," September 22, 1998.

Red Rock Canyon

Obee, Ruth. *History in Stone: The Story of Red Rock Canyon* (Boulder: Johnson Books, 2012).

Milito, Sharon. "A Survey of Fossils and Geology of Red Rock Canyon Open Space, Colorado Springs, Colorado," *The Mountain Geologist*, January, 2010, pp. 1-14.

Palmer Trail - Section 16

Athearn, Robert. "The Denver and Rio Grande Railroad," in Carl Ubbelohde, ed., *A Colorado Reader* (Boulder, Colorado: Pruett Press, 1962).

Sprague, Marshall. *Newport in the Rockies* (University of Ohio Press, 1987)

Captain Jack's

Jack, Ellen. *Fate of a Fairy.*

Cheyenne Mountain State Park

Cheyenne Mountain State Park Management Plan, Colorado Department of Parks and Wildlife, 2013.

D'Agostino, Davi. "Defense Infrastructure: Full Costs and Security Implications of Cheyenne Mountain Realignment Have Not Been Determined," United States Government Accountability Office memorandum, May 21, 2007. www.gao.gov/assets/100/94893.pdf.

Penitente Canyon

Carroll, Michael. *The Pentitente Brotherhood: Patriarchy and Hispano-Catholicism in New Mexico* (Baltimore: The Johns Hopkins University Press, 2002).

Horka-Follick, Lorayne. *Los Hermanos Penitentes: A Vestige of Medievalism in Southwestern United States* (Los Angeles: Westernlore Books, 1969).

Woodward, Dorothy. *The Penitentes of New Mexico* (Yale University Press, 1967)

Great Sand Dunes

Crofutt, George. *Crofutt's Grip-Sack Guide to Colorado*, 1880.

Zebulon Pike's Journal

Petroglyph Point Trail

Cole, Sally J. "Imagery and Tradition: Murals of the Mesa Verde Region," in David Grant Noble, ed., *The Mesa Verde World: Explorations in Ancestral Pueblo Archaeology* (Santa Fe: School of American Research Press, 2006), p. 98.

Petroglyph Trail Guide, National Park Service.

Overlooks Trail

Janssen, Marco, Timothy Kohler and Marten Scheffer. "Sunk-Cost Effects Made Ancient Societies Vulnerable to Collapse," 2002. www.researchgate.net/profile/Marco_Janssen/publication/23740106_Sunk-Cost_Effects_Made_Ancient_Societies_Vulnerable_to_Collapse/links/0912f5141efb4e2866000000.pdf.

Wright, Kenneth. "Water for the Mesa Verdeans," in David Grant Noble, ed., *The Mesa Verde World* (Santa Fe, New Mexico: School of American Research Press, 2006), p. 124.

McElmo Canyon Loop

Geological and Geographical Survey of the Territories (U.S. Government Printing Office, 1876), p. 380.

Kuckelman, Kristin. "Ancient Violence in the Mesa Verde Region," in David Grant Noble, ed., *The Mesa Verde World: Explorations in Ancestral Pueblo Archaeology* (Santa Fe: School of American Research Press, 2006), p. 134.

Hovenweep

Fewkes, Jesse Walter. *Prehistoric Villages, Castles, and Towers of Southwestern Colorado* (Washington D.C.: U.S. Government Printing Office, 1919), p. 49.

Hurst, William, and Jonathan Till. "Mesa Verdean Sacred Landscapes," in David Grant Noble, ed., *The Mesa Verde World: Explorations in Ancestral Pueblo Archaeology* (Santa Fe: School of American Research Press, 2006), p. 79.

Mt. Royal

"Colorado Place Names (F)," *Colorado Magazine*, January 1941, p. 35.

"Woman digs up the past in Frisco," *Vail Daily*, February 4, 2005. www.vaildaily.com/article/20050206/AE/102060010.

Iowa Hill

"Iowa Hill Hydraulic Mine," *Mining History News*, December 2004, p. 5.

Camp Hale

Williamson, Eileen. "Military Munitions Remediation at Camp Hale: the project, the history, the public," US Army Corps of Engineers Omaha District, August 18, 2014. www.nwo.usace.army.mil/Media/NewsStories/tabid/1834/Article/494372/military-mu.

Official U.S. Army reports.

Mayflower Gulch

Bergendahl, M. H. and A. H. Koschmann. "Ore Deposits of the Kokomo-Tenmile District, Colorado," United States Geological Survey Professional Paper 652 (Washington, D.C.: U. S. Government Printing Office, 1971), p. 16.

Doc Holliday Trail

Roberts, Gary. *Doc Holliday: The Life and Legend* (New York: Wiley, 2007).

Government Trail

Johnson, Kirk. Ian Miller, Jeffrey Pigati, et al., "Introduction to the Snowmastodon Project Special Volume," Quarternary Research, Volume 82, 2014, p. 473.

Holzwarth Ranch

"Grand Ditch Breach Restoration Draft Environmental Impact Statement Released for Rocky Mountain National Park." National Park Service, March 21, 2012. www.nps.gov/romo/learn/news/pr_grand_ditch_draft_environmental_impact_statement.htm.

"Grand Ditch Breach Restoration Plan." National Park Service, March, 2010. http://www.nps.gov/romo/learn/management/grand_ditch_breach_rest_eis.htm.

Grand Ditch: National Register of Historic Places Inventory—Nomination Form, 1976. http://pdfhost.focus.nps.gov/docs/NRHP/Text/76000218.pdf.

National Register of Historic Places Inventory—Nomination Form, Multiple Resource Nomination for Rocky Mountain National Park, June 1987. www.historycolorado.org/sites/default/files/files/OAHP/crforms_edumat/pdfs/642.pdf.

Moraine Park

Buchholz, C. W. *Rocky Mountain National Park: A History* (Boulder: Colorado Associated University Press), 1983, p. 68.

Sprague, Abner. *My Pioneer Life: The Memoirs of Abner E. Sprague* (Estes Park: Rocky Mountain Nature Association, 1999).

Sprague Lake

Sprague, Abner. *My Pioneer Life: The Memoirs of Abner E. Sprague* (Estes Park: Rocky Mountain Nature Association, 1999).

About the Author

Robert Hurst is a Colorado native who writes frequently about history and the outdoors. He is the author of several books about bicycling, including *The Art of Cycling, The Art of Mountain Biking: Singletrack Skills for All Riders, The Cyclist's Manifesto, Road Biking Colorado, Best Bike Rides Denver and Boulder, Road Biking Colorado's Front Range, Mountain Biking Colorado's San Juan Mountains: Durango and Telluride,* and more. This is his first hiking guide.

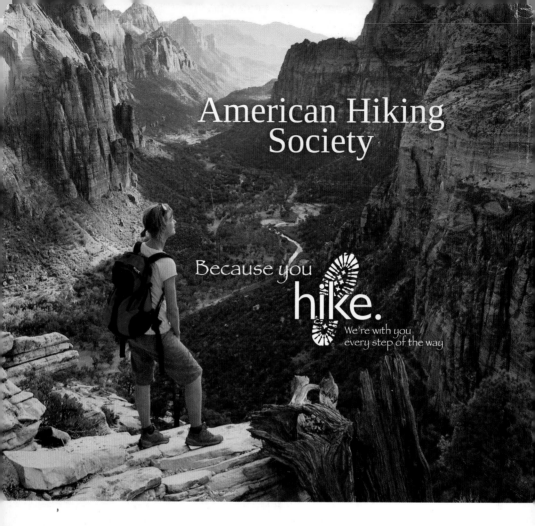

American Hiking Society

Because you
hike.
We're with you
every step of the way

As a national voice for hikers, **American Hiking Society** works every day:

- Building and maintaining hiking trails
- Educating and supporting hikers by providing information and resources
- Supporting hiking and trail organizations nationwide
- Speaking for hikers in the halls of Congress and with federal land managers

Whether you're a casual hiker or a seasoned backpacker, become a member of American Hiking Society and join the national hiking community! You'll enjoy great member benefits and help preserve the nation's hiking trails, so tomorrow's hike is even better than today's. We invite you to join us now!

American Hiking Society